INSIDE GITMO

COLLINS
An Imprint of HarperCollins *Publishers*
www.harpercollins.com

THE TRUE STORY BEHIND
THE MYTHS OF GUANTÁNAMO BAY

INSIDE GITMO

LIEUTENANT COLONEL GORDON CUCULLU

HarperCollins books may be purchased for educational, business, or sales promotional use. For information, please write: Special Markets Department, HarperCollins Publishers, 10 East 53rd Street, New York, NY 10022.

FIRST EDITION

Designed by William Ruoto

Library of Congress Cataloging-in-Publication Data is available upon request.

ISBN: 978-0-06-176230-7

09 10 11 12 13 WBG/RRD   10 9 8 7 6 5 4 3 2 1

TO THOSE MEN AND WOMEN SERVING IN TODAY'S
MILITARY—THE "ROUGH MEN" WHOSE DEDICATION
AND VIGILANCE ALLOW US TO SLEEP PEACEABLY
AT NIGHT—AND TO THE LONG LINE OF VETERANS
WHO PRECEDE THEM. MY DEEPEST THANKS
FOR YOUR SERVICE AND SACRIFICE.

TO MY MOTHER, ELIZABETH CUCULLU—WISH YOU
WERE HERE TO SEE THIS, MOM.

Contents

————

CAMP V

CAMP VI

CAMP IV

HOSPITAL

CAMP ECHO

CARIBBEAN

SEA

TAMPA
FLORIDA
ATLANTIC
OCEAN

GULF OF
MEXICO
MIAMI

NASSAU

KEY WEST
THE BAHAMAS

HAVANA

CUBA

GUANTÁNAMO
NAVAL BASE

HAITI

GEORGE TOWN ★ GRAND CAYMAN
PORT-AU-PRINCE

CARIBBEAN
SEA
JAMAICA ★ KINGSTON

CLOSE GITMO?

O N NOVEMBER 4, 2008, BARACK Obama was elected president of the United States. Almost immediately, his camp of advisors and specialists issued comments focusing on the closure of the U.S. military detention center at Guantánamo Bay, Cuba as a top administration priority.

During the campaign, Senator Obama had referred to the facility as "a sad chapter in American history." In an August 1, 2007 speech, he clearly spelled out his intentions: "As President, I will close Guantánamo, reject the Military Commissions Act, and adhere to the Geneva Conventions."[1]

The senator proffered few details on how he would deal with the many difficult legal and administrative issues involved. Nor was it clear that he had been fully briefed on the kind of men that are held at Guantánamo. Nevertheless, once elected, he appeared determined to act rapidly to satisfy the demands of his anti-war base.[2]

In tackling this issue, the new president is embarking on a path that winds and twists through the jungles of the U.S. judiciary system, the intelligence community, and—if detainees are to be moved to the continental United States—local politics. He is likely to encounter unexpected friends and opponents along the way.

Among his strongest support groups, for example, have been the American Trial Lawyers Association, the ACLU, the Center for Constitutional Rights, and legions of academics who champion full constitutional rights for Guantánamo detainees and other enemy combatants. Yet a newly formed Obama Department of Justice with access to the highly classified biographies of most of the remaining detainees may be less enamored of the concept of quick release or perfunctory trial. Merely attempting to determine how, where, and by what process detainees will be tried is going to be an enormous—and surprisingly contentious—issue.

Harvard professor (and Obama advisor) Laurence Tribe breezily dismisses such concerns as "theoretical." Tribe is confident that "bringing the detainees to the United States will be controversial, but could be accomplished." He is offhanded about the question of location, for example: "I think the answer is going to be, they can be as securely guarded on U.S. soil as anywhere else."[3] Others, as we shall see, are far less sanguine about the possibility of detainees being imprisoned—let alone released—in their neighborhoods.

Nor are all the president's supporters comfortable with the prospect of having to construct an entirely new legal system in order to deal with the detainees. Representative Adam Schiff (D-CA) has said that "there would be concern about establishing a completely new system . . . that includes American citizens and foreign nationals, that takes place on U.S. soil and departs from the criminal justice system."[4]

Such comments suggest that whatever new approach is eventually proposed may be difficult to pass, even through a compliant Congress, and is certain to be challenged by all sides, leading to potentially crippling legal delays.

If detainees are indeed prosecuted in U.S. courts, the issue of evidentiary standards looms large, as does the handling of classified intelligence data. The battlefield is a poor environment for forensic criminal investigations, which may result in some detainees being summarily discharged. In addition, many of these detainees hold information that, if publicly released during a trial, would be considered a national security breach by intelligence services.

Moreover, if detainees are acquitted, will they then be released into the U.S. population? Moves toward that end are already in process within the legal system. Considering that in summer 2007 a sense-of-the-Senate resolution passed 94–3 to forbid bringing Guantánamo detainees to American soil, pressing this issue too hard might generate push-back from Capitol Hill. Careless handling of the matter could give the administration's opponents a hot-button political issue to exploit in 2010.

These and other problems remain to be resolved and are certain to be the focus of intense debate. In the meantime, it behooves us not to lose sight of the actual object being debated—the nature, history, and functioning of the detention center itself. This book is intended to give readers a clearer perspective on the camp, whose image has been clouded and concealed by misinformation and myth.

GUANTÁNAMO: MYTH AND REALITY

T HE TROOPS WILL TELL YOU that good days are rare inside the wire. But by 0730, 18 May 2006, everyone in Joint Task Force Guantánamo, especially Joint Detention Group (JDG) commander Colonel Michael Bumgarner, knew that this day was going to be one of the really bad ones.[1] Just about the time of shift change—when guards who have pulled a 12-hour stint on the floor are relieved—three detainees were discovered in near-death condition. One was found in the modern Camp V maximum-security facility. Two others were in maximum-security, highly compliant Camp I. They were ISN 114, Muhammad al Shihri, and Murtadha al Said Makram, ISN 187, both Saudis. Both detainees were unconscious. White foam oozed around their lips. Their eyes were glassy, rolled back into their heads. Their breathing was shallow; their pulses were weak. Medics quickly suspected some sort of poisoning—probably a drug overdose. The unidentified detainee in Camp V was conscious, exhibiting seizures, and frothing at the mouth.

The three detainees were taken to the dispensary inside the wire and immediately evaluated by on-duty physicians. After consultation with the command, doctors recommended that the detainees be evacuated to the full-service hospital on Guantánamo Base a few miles distant, where specialists could treat them. Blood samples were analyzed, stomachs pumped and contents evaluated, and conclusions drawn. First estimates—which later held—were that the two Camp I detainees had swallowed a random mixture of prescription pills, primarily antidepressants and pain pills, in an overdose quantity. Since neither Shihri nor Makram had been prescribed any medications, it was assumed that they had been given the pills by other detainees. The conclusion was inescapable: They intended to kill themselves.

Later investigation would disclose that many other detainees had secretly hidden and accumulated medications "around the toilet area" and "inside the bindings of the Holy Koran"[2] in order to give sufficient pills to these men to accomplish their mission: to commit suicide and achieve martyrdom. Medical personnel concluded that the Camp V detainee may have had an adverse reaction to medication. Both Bumgarner and then facility commander Admiral Harry B. Harris argued that the timing was too coincidental and that the Camp V detainee was also a suicide attempt. "In all my time at Guantánamo," Bumgarner would write, "We never had a case of 'adverse reaction to medication.'"

But these findings would come later. At the moment, the command worried that they had a crisis of major proportion on their hands.

In his cramped modular office inside the Camp II/III wire, Bumgarner was fully aware of the long-standing threat of detainees to commit suicide. In 2003, 23 detainees had attempted to hang or strangle themselves, and a Bahraini, Muhammad al Dossary, had repeatedly attempted suicide. Armed with this knowledge, Bumgarner scanned the printed pages listing detainees spread on his desk. After more than a year into his tour of duty as JDG commander, no one knew the detainees better than Mike Bumgarner. Furthermore, he was aware that because of the hunger strikes that had begun in large numbers the previous fall, many Americans had a skewed perspective of Guantánamo. Detainee suicides would only exacerbate an already unpleasant image.

Clustered around his desk were his deputy, Navy captain Catie Hanft, and Brigadier General Edward Leacock, deputy to Admiral

Harry Harris, commander of Joint Task Force Guantánamo. Leacock, on active duty deployment from the Maryland-headquartered 29th Infantry Division, was new to the position and still learning the ropes. Nevertheless, Ed Leacock is a solid officer, sufficiently savvy to stand aside and let Bumgarner run his own show. Scanning the pages, Bumgarner would spot a detainee on the list that he regarded as especially conniving or dangerous. An individual who might be one of the natural leaders; one who would be capable of hoarding drugs in order to pass them on to a younger detainee who would then follow orders to commit suicide.

Bumgarner swiftly identified those he considered the greatest threat either as suicides themselves or as collectors of hidden drugs. Barking orders, he dispatched forced cell extraction teams (FCET) to locations throughout the camp. He had plenty of manpower at his disposal. The entire guard force—all shifts, including those who would normally have rotated off duty—had been mobilized to deal with the potential suicide crisis.

A five-to-eight-person team of Army military policemen or Navy masters-at-arms made up an FCET. They had donned special gear—body armor, helmet with clear face protector, gloves, batons, and pepper spray—but no firearms—and were ordered to stand by. "Detainee 123, November Block, cell 17. Go!" As each team received its assignment, it raced away to the cell.

Every moment was essential if the detainees were to be prevented from more suicide attempts. The three discovered so far were in the hands of the doctors. There was nothing more the guard force could do for them. But there were almost 400 more in possible danger. The assigned mission was "safe, humane care and treatment," and that meant protecting detainees from harm, including injury they might inflict on each other or themselves.

At the targeted cells, detainees were instructed to place their hands through the waist-level "bean hole," a 24-by-6-inch opening in the cell door through which food and other items are passed. They were handcuffed, and after having leg restraints secured through a lower access panel, led out of their cells. Cells were searched thoroughly, including each detainee's "comfort items" and religious paraphernalia. Each Koran was searched—many contained messages, plans, and hidden weapons and drugs—but only by Muslim guards or civilians specially trained in handling the book.[3] As the teams raided individual cells and "tossed" the contents, a veritable pharmaceutical cornucopia was uncovered. Those found with contraband were promptly transferred to one of the segregation-discipline blocks in Oscar-Romeo-November sections of Camp II/III. Those whose cells were clean were placed back inside.

In the corridors, howls and protests from the cells mounted into a cacophony of angry sound. Detainees were enraged. Many pelted the guards with feces, urine, semen, and spit "cocktails" along with the standard invective, much of it—to the surprise of outsiders—in perfect English. Racial epithets, sexual slurs, and general cursing are the norm when the detainees "act up," as the camp euphemism goes. Being called names like "fucking niggers," "lousy spics," "dirty whores," "queers," and "bitches" is daily fare for the soldiers guarding these detainees.[4]

By late afternoon all of the detainees in the maximum-security camps—I, II/III, and V—had been searched. As the brutal tropical sun and outrageous humidity beat down on the assembled troops, many of whom were passing the 24-hour mark without sleep or rest, focus at last shifted to the medium-security facility of Camp IV. After a day of yelling from camp to camp and observing their "brothers" being led away, the inhabitants of Camp IV had grown restless. Unlike the other camps, IV permits more communal living and free time. Detainees live in blocks of approximately 40 men, divided into four 10-man groups. Each group occupies one of four bays. A central fifth bay is a shared latrine-shower facility.

On orders from Colonel Bumgarner, Navy ensign Ramen Santos,[5] Officer-in-Charge of Camp IV, brought in his guards and instructed the detainees that their bays would have to be searched. Santos, of Southern California Hispanic origin, is medium height, and conveys more confidence in his abilities than most junior officers. He brings a matter-of-fact approach to the job, saying, "If I'm designated officer-in-charge, then I'll make my decisions accordingly." In Camp IV the relationship between guards and detainees tends to be more of a persuasive nature than authoritarian, so Ensign Santos tried quiet negotiations first. He was stonewalled by the detainees in Zulu Block, who adamantly refused to allow guards to search their areas. An Afghani detainee named Hafizullah, ISN 965, the self-designated leader of Bay 1, verbally confronted the officer-in-charge.

Santos suspected that this was turning into a power struggle. He contacted Bumgarner and requested that the Quick Reaction Force—a platoon-sized element specially trained and equipped to deal with unruly detainees—be positioned outside the Camp IV gates, out of sight of the detainees but available if needed. Within minutes, the QRF assembled near the gates. Bumgarner additionally began to move guards in two-person escort teams alongside the wire behind the QRF.

By now the afternoon heat exceeded 100 degrees and the humidity had crept near 98 percent. Guards standing in broiling sun in heavy protective gear flirted with heat injury. Support staff brought cases of water bottles up and passed them among the teams. "Hydrate" was the word passed down the ranks. Troops began to chug water, tossing the empty plastic containers pell-mell on the gravel laneway.

Inside Camp IV, detainees in the other blocks were cautiously watching Zulu Block. It was clear to Santos, who had served many months at the facility and knew the detainees well, that Zulu Block was taking the lead for the camp. He knew who the leaders were and attempted to reason with them. He used interpreters who had worked with the detainees and had good rapport with them. Santos even went to the adjacent Whiskey Block and asked that one of the elders—the oldest detainee there— speak to Hafizullah and other Zulu Block leaders. "There is no reason for this to be a fight," Santos pleaded. All to no avail.

"If you don't allow us to come inside then I'm going to have to send a team in forcibly," Santos said. The leader of the Zulu Block detainees spun on his heel and went inside to Bay 1. "In effect he was saying to me 'do what you have to do,'" Santos later reported. Over his handheld radio, Santos asked for clearance to deploy the QRF.

"I'm going to send the QRF into Bay 1 Zulu Block," he said.

"Affirmative, execute your operation," Bumgarner replied. The experienced Military Police officer had learned to trust the judgment of his junior leaders. "I try never to override the call made from the people on the ground," he said. Bumgarner immediately left his office and jogged the short distance to Camp IV.

Camp IV was designed so that within each of the four blocks— Yankee, Whiskey, Victor, and Zulu—any two of the 10-man bays would be able to mix during daylight hours. Usually they have the opportunity to pray and eat together. Typically during the day detainees will be washing clothes, conversing, playing sports or board games, or writing. Usually 20 men were able to gather at any given time.[6]

Ensign Santos ordered Zulu Block detainees to return to their bays. Within the long, single-story concrete-block structures of Zulu, the detainees slammed the doors behind them. The bays were locked down. Doors lock electronically and can only be unlocked from a central control station. In a practical but seemingly odd architectural arrangement, on the reverse side of the block American guards sit in two small areas inside the bays. The position is a triangular "V-bay" that pokes into each of the two bays and is screened from the detainees by strong wire mesh. From that semiprotected position each guard can watch everything that happens in the two bays under his scrutiny. One V-bay protrudes into bays 1 and 2, the other into bays 4 and 5. Bay 3 is the latrine. Both guard positions are occupied around the clock. Cameras in the ceiling provide the guards with additional observation.

Suddenly, within Bay 1, Zulu Block, at approximately 1730 hours a major disturbance erupted. Detainees pelted the observation guard with everything they could throw that would pass through the mesh, primarily human excrement. The guard backed out but was able to crouch behind a nearby wall and maintain observation. He relayed the situation to Ensign Santos on his radio.

Within the bay detainees went on a wild rampage, smashing the large, metal electric floor fan on the concrete floor and ripping it into pieces with their hands. The blades and sharp pieces of metal became weapons. "We provide fans in order to keep them cool," Army Lieutenant Colonel Michael J. Nicolucci, the JDG executive officer, said. "They were using the basket, or the grate of the fan as a shield, the blades as machetes, and the pole as a battering ram."[7] Bunks were ripped apart, the camera in the ceiling was smashed, and fluorescent lightbulbs were pulled from fixtures, broken, and turned into jagged weapons.

Alarms sounded throughout Camp IV. On orders, the QRF entered the Zulu Block gate, turned hard left, and filed down the length of the chain-link wire preparing to conduct a forced entry of Bay 1 if ordered. Meanwhile in nearby Whiskey, Uniform, and Victor Blocks the detainees began to shout and throw things, acting up in sympathy with the Zulu Block rioters. Oddly, Yankee Block detainees, who had acted up just the week prior, meekly withdrew into their respective bays and sat quietly.[8]

Ensign Santos directed that oleoresin capsicum spray or pepper gas be employed by the observation guard behind Bay 1 to quell the riot.[9] After a few sprays, the guard (who did not have a gas mask and was enduring the effects himself) observed a detainee standing on a bunk trying to secure a noose made of sheets to a ceiling fixture. When he saw the detainee place the noose around his head, the guard called a "Snowflake!" alarm over his handheld. In the internal code system used by the staff at JTF Guantánamo, a Snowflake alarm is a possible detainee suicide attempt. On that alert, standard operational procedures call for all personnel to focus on doing everything possible to intercept and deter the detainee.

At this point Ensign Santos had no choice. He ordered the QRF to make a forced entry into Bay 1. On command, the electronic door was unlocked and the first two members of the QRF—a lieutenant and a sergeant—entered. Because of the narrow doorway, they could enter only single file. As they ran into the room they found the floor covered with human excrement, urine, and soapsuds, a noxious mess designed to make them lose footing. Almost immediately they slipped and fell to the stinking floor. Unmasked, they also felt the effects of the OC spray. In a coordinated move, several detainees of Bay 1 pounced upon the two QRF guards and tried to stab them with broken glass and metal fragments torn from the fan. Other detainees mobbed the doorway to prevent the rest of the QRF from entering. It was a coldly calculated ambush.

Ensign Santos was faced with a difficult decision. He saw that his

QRF members were in danger. He also knew that nonlethal munitions—available to him in the hands of soldiers standing nearby—had never been used at Guantánamo. In some instances the overall commander might decide—long after the heat of the moment—that use of the munitions was unwarranted and relieve the officer in charge. Second-guessing from on high, particularly under intense media or political criticism, has a way of descending downhill onto the men in the fray.

Santos ordered the team to fire nonlethal munitions. In seconds, well-aimed rubber bullets from shotguns smacked into the bodies of detainees trying to cut the throats of American servicemen. A 40-millimeter "beanbag" round hit one of the rioters in the chest and knocked him to the ground. A few seconds later the rest of the QRF was inside the building, flex-cuffing the now quiescent detainees and leading them into the yard for escort to discipline blocks.

Swiftly, the now-reinforced QRF moved from bay to bay, leading out the subdued detainees. Long lines of escort teams, who had spent hours sweating in the heat, moved smartly into the yard, picked up their flex-cuffed detainee, and took him where instructed. Those detainees who had been hit by the nonlethal rounds were escorted to the dispensary for possible medical treatment. They were fine, although days later one of the officers observed that the leader in Zulu Block had a "grapefruit-sized" bruise on his butt. "Maybe next time he'll think twice about attacking our guards," the officer said.

As this orderly process was under way, a harried sergeant looked around at all of the discarded water bottles. "Pick these up," he ordered one of the female guards standing in protective gear in the long line of escorts. "Now?" she said, stunned at the inane order. Swiftly, she kicked the plastic bottles into a pile. Running back to the line, she saw that a larger sailor had moved up to the position she'd occupied. Without missing a beat she pushed back into the line. "That's *my* place!" she said. Within minutes her team had its detainee and was marching him to November Block.

Bumgarner was proud of his troops. He said, "They did a hell of a job under very difficult conditions. Most importantly we were able to prevent a suicide. That was our best accomplishment." When asked about first-time use of nonlethal munitions, he shook his head. "Admiral Harris backed me totally on its use. I'm not certain any other commander—under the scrutiny of this position—would have had the courage to support me in that decision. When I told him that I had to fire rubber bullets he said, 'That's what we issue them for.' "[10]

But Bumgarner as well as the commanders and other staff of the Joint Task Force knew the quiet aftermath of the May 18 riot was simply an interlude in an ongoing conflict between the detainees and the guards. "It's exactly the same in any detention center, civilian or military," one of the Army professional guards, Sergeant First Class Allen Rich, said. "In a short time they know the system. They learn how to communicate with each other, how to play the personalities of the individual guards, how to manipulate, and how to get what they want. These guys have been here way long enough to learn the system better than us."[11]

Bumgarner recognized the contribution of the troops. "They performed beautifully," he said. "Very professional, very dedicated. I'm proud of them." What about the detainees? Did he think they would continue to try to commit suicide?

"Shakir Ami [ISN 239] told me that he had a dream, a vision," Bumgarner said. "He based it on the ancient battle of Badr in which Muhammad won a great victory. First though, the Muslim side had to have three martyrs.[12] Shakir figures that if we can get three martyrs here then they will win. They will be released. We won this one but we know that they are going to keep trying."[13]

Less than a month later, Bumgarner's worst fears were to be realized.

AMERICANS AND THE WORLD AT large have been treated to some rather outrageous claims concerning the Guantánamo facility, including allegations of torture, abuse, human rights violations, religious intolerance, sexual misconduct, and desperate hunger strikes. Over the course of multiple visits to Guantánamo, backed by extensive research, I have determined that in fact some detainees were subjected to extremely harsh interrogation methods that are no longer allowed. These cases have been thoroughly documented not only by the military itself but by outside agencies including the FBI and U.S. Department of Justice. These cases are reviewed in this book.

That said, vigorous and prolonged investigations covering more than 24,000 interrogation sessions inside Guantánamo over a three-year period revealed a total of three violations, an amazingly low number considering the pressure-cooker atmosphere faced by detainees and military personnel alike, as well as the early inexperience of military interrogators operating under incomplete and unclear rules.

Unfortunately, because of these few unacceptable early cases, we have been bombarded with even more outrageous stories and some outright myths and falsehoods concerning the Guantánamo facility. Amnesty International, for example, actually referred to Guantánamo as "the gulag of our time" in its May 2005, 308-page report.[14]

Often we read that the detainees at Guantánamo are not "real terrorists" but innocents—goatherds, farmers, or Afghani peasants—who were arbitrarily picked up and brought to Guantánamo in a random or haphazard manner. Many, we have been told, were actually sold to American forces by unscrupulous men in order to make money or settle a personal score.

I had read of gratuitous abuse that was heaped upon these detainees from the moment of capture throughout their transportation to Guantánamo. I had heard stories of torture, abuse, and maltreatment directed from above as an integral part of U.S. policy. Further, I had been led to believe that such abusive treatment is routine—and indeed condoned and encouraged—at the facility to this day. The notion that torture of detainees is policy has become accepted as common knowledge among many in the world, including a former American president.[15]

Detainees are held incommunicado, I read. They are kept in tiny cells, isolated and solitary, and are denied communication with families, friends, each other, and the outside world.

Nor, according to many in the media, are they given legal process. They are being "confined without trial" and denied other judicial proceedings. And, they say, detainees have been forced to spend an extraordinarily long time in hopeless detention with no possibility of release or of even being charged with a crime.

Further, according to many commentators, confinement of these men has yielded little or no positive results as far as prosecuting the global war on terror is concerned. In fact, the entire affair has been a huge bust, with nothing more accomplished than to give an international black eye to America and exacerbate latent anti-American sentiment throughout the world.

Reports emerging from Guantánamo in the early days were worse than grim; they were appalling. Leaked FBI e-mails portrayed a military camp run amok with the worst kinds of behavior—perhaps not torture, but definitely abuse—being applied to the enemy combatants detained there. An FBI agent spoke of detainees short-shackled to the floor, soiled by their own excreta, hungry and thirsty, pulling their hair out in agony, and kept isolated for who knew how long.[16]

Other FBI-attributed reports spoke of civilian contractor interrogators who duct-taped a detainee's head because he "would not stop quoting the Koran."[17] Later investigation determined that the detainee "spit at" interrogators. According to the FBI agent, there was no plan evident to remove the tape painlessly.[18]

As a retired Army officer with 20 years of active service, I read such reports with alarm. For example, I had seen allegations from released detainees (repeated by their attorneys) that military police dogs were used to intimidate and frighten them. Because of the peculiar Muslim hatred of dogs, the charge was that loud, barking, growling dogs would terrify a detainee and soften him up for interrogation. (Investigation disclosed that in at least one instance dogs were brought into the interrogation room to intimidate a detainee.[19]) Though an infamous *Newsweek* report of a "flushed Koran" proved false upon investigation and was retracted, there were many others that described the book being kicked, urinated on, or otherwise mishandled in front of detainees. An FBI report told of a Marine Corps captain squatting over a Koran during an interrogation. It appeared as if Muslim sensitivities were being deliberately provoked.

I heard stories of a woman interrogator who feigned menstruation and placed what was later identified as red ink on a detainee in order to make him feel unclean. Released detainees told horror stories of women squatting over them and "spraying" menstrual fluid into their faces. Other female soldiers were said to perform "lap dances" on the detainees, to undress in front of them, and to otherwise use salacious or perverse sexual activity to confuse and upset them.

Investigation determined that some of these stories were not entirely correct. One female interrogator "straddled a detainee without putting weight on him," and this became the "lap dance" story. Many of these techniques were determined to be part of an approved interrogation plan designed to be "ego diminishing," intended to disorient a subject and induce him to talk.[20] Reputable reporters such as the *New York Times*' Neil Lewis told lurid tales of detainees being sleep deprived while forced to listen to ultra-loud recordings, "including songs by Lil' Kim and Rage Against the Machine and rap performances by Eminem." Others, according to Lewis, spoke of the annoying Meow Mix cat food commercial being played over and over at top volume.

One particular detainee, Muhammad al Qahtani, was said to have been flown around in a sealed aircraft for a long time and landed back at Guantánamo, but kept hooded the entire time so that he would believe he had been transported to an Egyptian prison. Lewis said that in order to make this charade believable, Qahtani was denied International Red Cross visits for months. He further asserted that prisoners were given forcible enemas as a means to degrade and break them down.[21]

A former enlisted soldier, Erik Saar, who was stationed there for six months and described himself as part of an interrogation team, published a book in 2005 co-authored by a *Washington Post* reporter in which he alleged that brutality, abuse, and maltreatment of enemy detainees were not only ongoing, but were official policy at Guantánamo. Saar said new interrogators were told they had great flexibility in extracting information from detainees because the Geneva Conventions did not apply to them. Saar's book, *Inside the Wire*, was widely cited as a whistle-blowing exposé from a conscientious soldier who could not remain silent in the face of the terrible things he had witnessed at Guantánamo.

Respected members of the U.S. Senate and House of Representatives could not resist piling on. In public hearings on June 15, 2005, Senator Ted Kennedy (D-MA) accused the military of making Guantánamo into "a symbol of U.S. hypocrisy on human rights," adding that it "embarrasses the U.S. in world opinion and makes some Muslims hate us."[22] At those same hearings, Senator Patrick Leahy (D-VT) declared that "Guantánamo is an international embarrassment to our nation, and remains a festering threat to our security." Senator Richard Durbin (D-IL) hyperbolically compared American soldiers in Guantánamo to "Nazis, Soviets in their gulags, or some mad regime—Pol Pot or others—that had no concern for human beings."[23]

In light of this adverse publicity, many have called for the Guantánamo facility to be shut down. Senator Mel Martinez (R-FL) thought that Guantánamo gave America a "black eye" in the world. "How much do you get out of having that facility there?" he asked.[24] Bowing to public pressure, then-president Bush himself said that he would like to close it down. It was the stated position of both nominees in the 2008 presidential election that they would do so upon taking office.

Along with the scandals of Abu Ghraib prison in Iraq, and with alleged military atrocities in the war, the facility at Guantánamo has assumed iconic status among disparate anti-American groups and individuals. The UN Committee Against Torture said "the United States should cease to detain any person at Guantánamo Bay and close this detention facility."[25] Colum Lynch of the *Washington Post* agreed, calling the report "a rebuke for the Bush administration."[26] The BBC's Imogen Foulkes said "the committee's conclusions will not make comfortable reading for the US."[27] Human Rights Watch's Jennifer Daskal said that she hopes "the United States will take heed of this report and really begin to rethink and change its policies."[28]

Much has been said and written about the facility, some of it intentionally slanted or untrue. Because of ceaseless media attention and political maneuvering, Gitmo has been raised to the Big Story level and is continually thrown in the faces of Americans as a place of shame.

But is that the truth? Is Gitmo really the vile, oppressive prison camp that some claim it to be? Or is there more to the story?

As an officer I had sworn an oath to defend the Constitution and the nation. When one devotes more than 20 years to service, one does not easily slough off the obligations such an oath demands. Reports of rampant prisoner abuse at Gitmo filled me with alarm. The stories I read threatened the core integrity and honor of the American military to which I had devoted much of my life. I therefore determined to find out for myself what really was happening at Guantánamo. Better, if the system was broken, to bring it to light and help fix it than to ignore what had become a terrible international liability for this country.

In order to learn the facts for myself, I made numerous visits to the detention facility at Guantánamo and interviewed scores of military and civilians serving there, men and women of all specialties, ranging in rank from flag officer to private first class. Over the course of several years I toured every camp and facility associated with detainee support, walked almost every square yard of the blocks, ate the same food that was served to detainees, observed interrogations, and walked through Camp IV the day after the May 2006 riots.

I intend to show you the real Guantánamo. You will see who is held there and form your own judgment as to whether continued detention of these men is legal, moral, and necessary. Further, you will be introduced to the brave men and women who serve at this remote, forgotten outpost of freedom in conditions that most of us would find repugnant and appalling. You will learn how the interrogation procedures work and why these dedicated specialists are still producing a wealth of actionable strategic intelligence.[29]

To understand the facility at Guantánamo is to comprehend that it is the sum of many disparate but related parts: legal, detention, interrogation, medical, food service, public affairs, and more. Few people are able to see the bigger picture—even those who serve there, because they are busy performing the tasks that brought them to Gitmo in the first instance. In order to try to understand this macro view, I conducted extensive interviews of current and former civilians, military, and other governmental officials in Washington, DC, New York City, California, and Connecticut, and, of course, at Guantánamo.

I visited Guantánamo on five separate occasions, was allowed access to the grounds of the facility, and walked the floor of every camp and block. I was able to speak freely with anyone on the staff and to hold rare interviews with interrogators. I spoke privately to officers, noncommissioned officers, soldiers and sailors, and civilians. In no way was access conditioned on a favorable outcome. The Department of Defense did not sponsor my trips—they were paid for by my own resources—and has not requested that I submit my findings for official vetting or approval.

More important, with more than two decades of military experience, I know how to talk to people in uniform. I gave every interviewee the opportunity to say whether they saw anything out of the ordinary or heard of actions that would cause them ethical or moral concern. None reported anything but the most professional activities and conduct. All interviewees adamantly denied that torture or abuse occurred in the camps. I even tracked down and interviewed officers, troopers, and former government officials no longer on active duty or associated with the facility in order to get their observations. I made certain that I had private time with them, won their confidence, and became a willing listener to their comments, complaints, and observations. The vast majority of this book is based on firsthand interviews with military service members, civilian employees, contractors, and public officials in and out of service.

Universally, they told me to report on what I saw without prejudice and to tell the true story of Guantánamo and of the men and women on duty there. I have attempted to tell their stories and to give readers a glimpse of what life is really like inside Gitmo wire.

INSIDE GITMO

CHAPTER I

WHY GUANTÁNAMO?

"Long-term detention was definitely not a sought-after mission."
DEPUTY ASSISTANT SECRETARY OF DEFENSE
MATTHEW WAXMAN, 2005

WHEN YOU FLY INTO GUANTÁNAMO, your pilot has to give Cuban airspace a wide berth. It is necessary to track south through the Windward Passage, skirting Cuba lying to your west with the deep green mountains of the Sierra Maestra Range, hideout for the young rebel Fidel Castro and his band, cloaked in semipermanent clouds. Off to the east it is easy to see the island of Hispaniola. The proximity of the country of Haiti makes clear why Guantánamo is a desirable haven for refugees from that dismal place.

At a predetermined waypoint called East Point on the Global Positioning Satellite system, the pilot banks into a 270-degree track. At South Point the pilot executes a sharp turn to the north, approaching Guantánamo's airport on a 360-degree course. The east-west–running airstrip is on the western or leeward portion of the U.S. military base. It is the smaller, 14-square-mile area of the facility. From your window you look across a mile-wide bay into the larger portion.

A white strobe light on a tower indicates that the boundary fence is nerve-wrackingly close to the airstrip. Without much room to maneuver, the pilot brings it in tight to the fence line, flips the aircraft over on its right wing, then quickly levels out and drops the nose. The aircraft bangs down on the asphalt.

Just adjacent to the landing strip at Guantánamo Bay Naval Facility, Cuba—Gitmo to those who live there—is a four-foot-high cairn made of mortared round stones. As its brass plaque proclaims, it is a monument commemorating Christopher Columbus's landing on this very spot in his 1496 expedition to the New World.

Columbus, the legend goes, stepped ashore, took a good look around, and having found neither gold nor gems, nor fresh water, nor a particularly appealing landscape, mumbled the equivalent of "this place sucks" in Italian and departed the very next day to find a more hospitable spot.[1] Every soldier, sailor, airman, marine, and coastguardsman who serves at Gitmo understands Columbus's reaction.

Here are not the legendary white sand beaches of northern Cuba. Nor will the visitor experience the mystery of the Sierra Maestra Mountains. The exotic hot spots of Havana are a long way distant. At Guantánamo Bay, on the extreme southeastern, leeward side of the island of Cuba, the terrain is arid, the vegetation an off-putting mix of desert-tropical, and the Caribbean laps against ancient, brown, eroded coral formations. Odd wildlife abounds. Banana rats, *hutia*, harmless vegetarian rodents the size of a toy poodle, are everywhere. Their carcasses, paws up on the roadway, feed the local bird, the turkey vulture. Iguanas are ubiquitous—though oddly, the iguana is considered endangered. Run over one and you can be facing a $500 fine. In the western part of the base the Guantánamo River empties into muddy, unattractive, rock-strewn beaches. Upriver, once weekly on Thursday, a Cuban abattoir dumps offal into the river. The bloody mass floats downriver to the bay, where it provides scores of sharks with a happy hour. The Coast Guardsman on the Viper boat, a 23-foot Boston Whaler configuration with twin 150-horsepower outboards, tells me that he has seen sharks so long that their bodies extend beyond his bow and past his stern. Nobody books a vacation here.

Guantánamo Bay Naval Station sits on the extreme southeastern tip of Cuba at the mouth of Guantánamo Bay, roughly at 75 degrees 9 minutes west longitude and 19 degrees 4 minutes north latitude. It is a 45-square-mile, semi-arid coastal leasehold that results from America's seizure of Cuba in the 1898 Spanish-American War.

In 1901 the United States, through passage of the Platt Amendment, granted Cuba independence with some provisos. Article I warned Cuba against "entering into any treaty . . . which would enable a foreign power . . . lodgment in or control over . . . the island." Article VII speaks to a continued U.S. presence. It says, *inter alia*, that to enable the United States to maintain the independence of Cuba, and to protect the people thereof, as well as for its defense, the government of Cuba will sell or lease to the United States lands necessary for coaling or naval stations at certain specified points, to be agreed upon with the president of the United States.[2]

By December 1903, the United States leased the land and water for use as a coaling station. In 1934, a treaty solidified the relationship. It granted Cuba free access through the bay (which it maintains today) and an annual payment in gold then valued at $2,000. Though the gold payment is valued at about $4,000 or more today, and checks for that amount are sent to Castro's government on a timely basis, Cuban authorities have yet to deposit one. Why? Because to cash the check would validate the legitimacy of the lease.

Straddling the mouth of the bay, the Guantánamo base itself is divided into two land parts separated by a wide, island-plentiful bay. Oddly, it seems to the visitor, the airstrip is on the smaller, approximately 14-square-mile leeward side to the west. After arrival visitors must transit the bay by launch, fast boat, or ferry to get to the larger, windward portion. Here is where things are happening.

Offices, housing, and—since 2002—detention facilities are all located on the 31-square-mile windward (eastern) side. Because relations with the Castro government are strained to say the least, you can't simply drive across the perimeter of the bay, enter into Cuban territory, then come back to the U.S. base. Barbed-wire fences, a cleared zone with mines, and Cuban guards on the far side prevent that. U.S. Marines man the gates on the friendly side. So transit to and from the air terminal is by boat.

Unable to depend on the Cuban "hosts," the Guantánamo facility has to be completely self-contained. It has its own desalinization plant, which produces 3.4 million gallons of fresh water daily. It generates more than 800,000 kilowatt-hours of electricity (a quarter of which is from wind power) and has two hospitals, extensive communications equipment, schools for dependent children, family and singles housing, administrative offices, maintenance sheds, ammunition storage depots, POL (petroleum, oil, and lubricants) tanks, and even a bit of retail shopping at the Navy Exchange. At one point in history it was a bustling, major Caribbean base, but as recently as eight years ago it seemed as though history had marched past. Guantánamo was recalled—if at all—by rare films such as the Jack Nicholson classic *A Few Good Men*.

But Guantánamo has changed dramatically since the waning days of the Cold War. On this base, which in fall of 2001 was teetering on the edge of oblivion with a caretaker cadre of fewer than 2,000, there now resides a contingent of 10,000 plus.[3] There are several reasons for the base's growth: upgrade to a strategic Atlantic Fleet base, to support counter-drug operations, and as a key point for migrant surge operations in the region. But most important was the need for secure confinement facilities to house a collection of enemy combatants snatched from the battlefields of Afghanistan in early 2002.

The U.S. government asserts that while a small number of detainees may have been brought to Guantánamo in error, most of the detainees are not confused goatherds or opium farmers drafted into service by angry Taliban imams. Nor are they innocent travelers cynically captured and sold to Coalition forces by bounty-hungry locals. They are hard men who are rabid fundamentalist radicals (they call themselves "jihadists" and "mujahedin"); men who have dedicated their lives to the destruction of America and Western civilization.

Some are astoundingly intelligent. Among the detainee population are al Qaeda financial specialists, organizational experts, bombmakers, and recruiters. Others are from the muscle side of the organization—alleged or self-confessed killers, many of whom have spoken of meeting frequently with Osama bin Laden and of being recruited, trained, and indoctrinated by al Qaeda hierarchy.

In these pages you will meet men who come from more than 25 countries and speak more than 17 languages. You will meet hardened, well-educated radical Islamic Saudis; barely literate Afghanis; Pakistani graduates of top schools in the United Kingdom; men who learned to fly aircraft at training facilities in the United States; others who taught bomb-making after graduating from prestigious American universities; toughs who matriculated at rugged al Qaeda training camps in Afghanistan; computer and financial specialists who moved millions of dollars in illegal funds; and thugs who trained to murder civilians in hijacked airliners by cutting the throats of camels and goats. Most of these men were transported to Guantánamo in 2002–2003, although seven were reported to be "renditioned" out of Bosnia in 2004.[4]

In September 2006, 14 new detainees, including al Qaeda VIPs Khalid Sheikh Muhammad and Abu Zubaydah, were transferred into Guantánamo from "secret" CIA camps. You'll meet them later, along with some of their infamous colleagues.

In the opening salvos of the war, Afghan forces, led and advised by American special operational forces and CIA operators, and later joined by American Marines and elite Army units, took thousands of prisoners from the battlefield.[5] Estimates are that as many as 70,000 Taliban and al Qaeda fighters were captured. More than 10,000 were vetted by American forces in Afghanistan and released, while less than 10 percent of those screened were moved to Guantánamo.[6] Most Americans are completely unaware of the sheer magnitude of the number of enemy combatants screened and tactically interrogated. Of that rather vast number, a tiny one-tenth of 1 percent—fewer than 800 captured fighters[7]—were deemed of such high intelligence value or posed such severe threat potential that they needed to be securely confined and thoroughly interrogated.

These men were considered to be the worst of the worst; they included some who were believed to have plotted the death and destruction of innocents. They had to be held somewhere that was isolated and secure, a locale from which they could not easily escape or be rescued. The decision was determined through a process of evaluation, comparison, and elimination conducted by the Office of the Joint Chiefs of Staff in the Pentagon and coordinated thoroughly among a number of other services and agencies, including the Department of Justice.

Army Brigadier General Vincent Brooks recalls that he headed the Joint Chiefs of Staff Western Hemisphere Division at the time of the staffing. "The action [setting up Guantánamo as a holding facility for enemy combatants] preceded the policy," he said, indicating that much of the selection of Guantánamo and its immediate use was done in crisis response to an unforeseen contingency. The entire facility and policy, as Brooks noted, are "an evolutionary work in progress."[8]

Guantánamo was by no means entirely—or, according to USAF Brigadier General Thomas Hemingway, principally—a Department of Defense selection. "Picking Guantánamo was a Department of Justice idea," Hemingway said, though he thought there were "compelling reasons" for the selection: "First was security. Camp X-Ray had been used in the past as a holding compound for dangerous prisoners from Haiti. Second, was the Eisentrager Opinion."[9] The latter was a Supreme Court opinion rendered in 1950 about a German who had committed war crimes in China during World War II, then was moved to Allied-occupied Germany to serve his sentence. This opinion gave legal basis for, among other things, the United States to remove enemy combatants from one overseas locale to another for legal processing. Because of this precedent, the attorneys at Justice thought an off-shore location like Guantánamo would best fit the needs of the U.S. government in what was already being called the Global War on Terror.[10] Hence, after extensive interagency staffing, the U.S. Naval Base at Guantánamo Bay was ultimately selected as a holding site for captured enemy combatants. As then–Defense Secretary Donald Rumsfeld put it, "Guantánamo is the least bad option."[11]

Rumsfeld "hated the very idea of being a jailer," according to Douglas J. Feith, one of the top Pentagon policymakers, who was close enough to the Secretary of Defense to know his mind on the subject.[12] According to several who worked with him during this period, Rumsfeld looked at the entire idea of running a detention center with revulsion. But America was at war. The country had been attacked, had retaliated against a vicious enemy, and had won stunningly rapid victories that netted a large number of detainees.

It is important at the outset to note the difference between a detention facility and a prison. Confusion between the two often skews understanding of Guantánamo's mission. Admiral Harris said it best: "Prisons are about rehabilitation and punishment. What we are about is keeping enemy combatants off the battlefield . . . because we know that many of them would go back to the fight." Harris went on to elaborate that many of them have kept fighting even while in captivity. "They are carrying out coordinated actions with the apparent goals of disrupting the camp's operations, furthering anti-American propaganda, and wounding and intimidating the servicemen who guard them."[13]

A Department of Defense release reinforces the point: "Detention of enemy combatants in wartime is not an act of punishment. It is a matter of security and military necessity. It prevents enemy combatants from continuing to fight against the U.S. and its partners in the war on terror. Releasing enemy combatants before the end of the hostilities and allowing them to rejoin the fight would only prolong the conflict and endanger coalition forces and innocent civilians."[14]

Initially it made sense to place the surprisingly large numbers of Taliban and al Qaeda fighters who surrendered in jury-rigged compounds for questioning and sorting. Language-trained CIA teams, part of the paramilitary operations directorate, backed up by Special Forces teams that were area specialists, began an initial screening process. Most of the detainees were rounded up by Afghani forces, and in the confusion of the battlefield it was difficult to determine the precise circumstances of their capture. It would have been foolhardy to release them without at least preliminary screening. With only small numbers of American teams dealing with extraordinarily large numbers of Taliban and al Qaeda fighters, the latter from more than a dozen countries, the focus was on finding anyone of high rank, obtaining critical operational intelligence, and removing dangerous fighters from the battlefield.

First, it was urgent that we learn whether the September 11 attack was a stand-alone event or part of a planned series of attacks. There were news reports that day of up to eight other aircraft that had been abruptly grounded along with the entire civil fleet after the initial four hijackings were discovered. All aircraft were searched and on those particular planes, knives and box cutters were found hidden underneath seats or in seat-back storage pockets.[15]

Authorities were properly concerned. Were follow-up attacks in the works, perhaps launched against America even as the war in Afghanistan was initiated? It is the nature of terrorist activities that once activated, these operations can continue independently of their leaders' oversight. We needed to know what kind of information these detainees held. And we needed to know it fast.

The possibility of a follow-on attack was universally considered highly likely if not inevitable. Moreover, concerns were very grave that the next wave of attacks would use dirty bombs, atomic weapons, poison gases, or biological agents. Recall, in the days following 9/11, the series of letters to political figures containing weaponized anthrax. Across America, five deaths were confirmed as caused by either inhalation or subcutaneous anthrax exposure. Another 11 deaths were suspicious, but insufficient evidence was present to link them directly to anthrax exposure.[16] This minor biological attack paralyzed and preoccupied much of America. Had another attack occurred killing hundreds or thousands, and it was later learned that one of the detainees confined at Guantánamo possessed prior knowledge of the attack, the outcry would be deafening.

Moreover, many of these captured detainees were not disposed to give up the fight. We could not afford to risk American lives interacting casually with these potentially dangerous individuals. Few soldiers relish the prospect of fighting the same enemy twice. In order to guarantee the security of our interrogators, and ultimately of the country, it was essential that they be confined in a place where escape or breakout opportunities were slim. They had to be taken completely out of circulation.

Another critical issue was identity: Who were these guys? They did not wear uniforms, had no distinguishable insignia or badges of rank, hid their weapons on many occasions, and tried to blend in with civilian bystanders to escape detection. It was vital that al Qaeda members be identified and removed from the general detainee population.

Osama bin Laden and his cohorts were well aware of the prisoner revolt on Koje-do during the Korean War. In this camp on a remote island off the South Korean coast, thousands of mostly Chinese communist prisoners were held in mass compounds. Later investigation showed that Chinese *agents provocateurs* deliberately allowed themselves to be captured in order to infiltrate and organize the camps for revolt. In September 1951 the prisoners rose, dragged the commanding general and his deputy into their camp, and demanded terms. Brigadier General Haydon Boatner led a full-scale attack against the prisoners who had armed themselves and fought a pitched battle.[17] Vince Brooks confirms that his people in the Joint Chiefs of Staff "remembered Koje-do" and that al Qaeda did also. "They probably used it as a model for training their high-level operatives," he said. "They certainly studied it."[18]

In hours of personal interviews with key Defense officials—several no longer serving actively—never did I hear an eagerness for the detention mission. Universally it is the kind of job that military people find distasteful. It is a dirty, messy, tension-ridden task. It comes with more oversight and outside "adult leadership" than any commander wants or needs. And it is the quintessential "aw shit" job in which praise is scarce and criticism abounds. In the vernacular of the Pentagon action officer: "One 'aw shit' wipes out all your 'attaboys'!" Such jobs rarely make but often break careers.

According to Deputy Assistant Secretary Matt Waxman, "No one in DOD" was interested in "becoming the world's jailer." "Long-term detention was definitely not a sought-after mission," Waxman said. But some of the detainees were thought to be major war criminals and top al Qaeda and Taliban leaders. "We had custody of some extremely dangerous personnel. We needed a place to hold them, and we also needed a secure place to interrogate them."[19]

Welcome to present-day Gitmo.

CHAPTER 2

MUHAMMAD AL QAHTANI

A TERRORIST CASE STUDY

*"I would really very much like to greet the 450
inmates, who are being held and tortured at
Guantánamo in opposition to human rights of
any kind, on the red carpet."*

DIETER KOSSLICK, DIRECTOR OF THE INTERNATIONAL
BERLIN FILM FESTIVAL[1]

THE POPULATION OF DETAINEES AT Guantánamo
was never high considering the numbers captured in Afghanistan and elsewhere. Fewer than 800 have been evacuated to the detention facility, and that number has steadily diminished over time. A score or more have been released outright. More than 300 have been transferred to the custody of their countries of origin, including Russia, the United Kingdom, Spain, Germany, Pakistan, and others. Moreover, let me clear away some prevalent myths. There are no women confined at Guantánamo and there never have been. All of the detainees are men. Nor are there minors, although a few who were minors when picked up on the battlefield have become adults here or have been released. However, it is important to note that in the terrorist world of al Qaeda and the Taliban, recruitment of minors is common practice.[2]

It is also important to recognize the boundaryless nature of radical Islamic terrorism. Among the men confined at Guantánamo are terrorists who have conducted operations in Eritrea, Somalia, Sudan, Chechnya, Afghanistan, the Philippines, Indonesia, the United States, Great Britain, Kosovo, Jordan, Israel, Lebanon, Turkey, Spain, France, Holland, Nigeria, Uganda, Tanzania, Kenya, Germany, and other countries. In addition to international recruiting, al Qaeda transfers funds seamlessly across national boundaries, has aggressively manipulated media, and is adroit at using the Internet as a weapon to train, recruit, fundraise, and proselytize. Radical Islamic terrorism has achieved a physical and ideological globalization that would impress a modern multinational corporation. Consequently, combating it requires a global outlook and strategy.

There are as many stories inside the Guantánamo wire as there are detainees. Some are more dramatic than others, but one of the most important detainees, ISN 063, Muhammad al Qahtani, has become a figure of note and is someone worth meeting.

O N AUGUST 4, 2001, AT 4:18 p.m.[3] on a hot and muggy central Florida afternoon, Muhammad Atta—a key al Qaeda terrorist who later crashed American Airlines Flight 11 into the North Tower of the World Trade Center on September 11—accompanied, some sources say, by Marwan al Shehhi, entered the parking garage of Orlando International Airport in a rented car.[4]

Qahtani arrived at this same Orlando airport on Virgin Atlantic Flight 15 from London at approximately 5:35 p.m.[5] (his flight had been scheduled to land at 4:40 p.m. but apparently was delayed). On his travel itinerary Qahtani had listed the telephone number of Mustafa Ahmed Adam al Hawsawi, the al Qaeda financial facilitator coordinating 9/11 preparations overseas. When immigration officials became suspicious of Qahtani, he told authorities that someone was picking him up but he didn't know who. He was moved to a private office for further questioning.[6]

Between 4:30 and 8:30 p.m., a total of five phone calls were placed using a calling card associated with Muhammad Atta from an airport pay phone to the same number Qahtani had provided on his travel itinerary—the number of Mustafa al Hawsawi. Frustrated by the problems with immigration authorities, Qahtani withdrew his application to enter the United States and flew back to Dubai, United Arab Emirates.[7]

Qahtani's flight left Orlando at 8:25 p.m. Muhammad Atta returned to the parking garage and left in the rented car at approximately 9:04 p.m.[8]

These facts were documented through a combination of airline, telephone, and bank transaction records, and apparently Orlando Airport parking-garage surveillance cameras. These facts are not dependent on later confessions or hearsay.

Unfortunately, the case against Muhammad al Qahtani has gone dreadfully wrong. There is much more to Qahtani and his history than the hard evidence summarized above, including his own admissions of meeting with Osama bin Laden at bin Laden's home in Afghanistan on multiple occasions,[9] and formal testimony by 9/11 mastermind Khalid Sheikh Muhammad describing how bin Laden personally selected Qahtani for a suicide mission in the United States.[10] Yet the controversies that arose from his confinement, including documented instances of abuse during his interrogations in the early days of the Guantánamo detention camp, have overshadowed efforts to bring him to justice.

While Qahtani's treatment ultimately led to implementation of protections and policies preventing abuse at military detainment facilities, his case has been portrayed by advocates in a manner that casts him as a victim while distracting attention away from the hard evidence.

Although Qahtani's case is unique, his background is quite typical of many of those confined at Guantánamo Bay. Here is part of his story.

TORA BORA, AFGHANISTAN, OCTOBER 22, 2001

From the distant desert valley of Bamo Khel, U.S. Special Forces soldiers hunkered down near the Pashtun village of Melawa were afforded a splendid view of the Spin Ghar. This range, translated as White Mountains in English, rises majestically in increasingly high waves until it blends into the Hindu Kush and reaches altitudes in excess of 21,000 feet.

It also borders what American Special Forces operators call "Indian Country," the al Qaeda–sympathizing province of Waziristan in neighboring Pakistan. For years the province has supported the Taliban and al Qaeda,[11] and it continues to offer refuge for what Special Forces, Delta, SEAL, and CIA strike teams term "high-value targets."

American forces advised and fought alongside native Afghan fighters—sometimes called "warlords" in the Western press—in a major successful campaign to rid the country of Taliban and al Qaeda control. The focus of the operation was a classic infantry mission: attack vigorously to take the high ground from the enemy.

It was a time of confusion and reaction for the al Qaeda and Taliban leadership, who were desperately attempting to regroup and, if necessary, escape. However, bin Laden's mind was still on more strikes against the United States. Perhaps he hoped that he could force America out of the war by inflicting unacceptably high casualty levels.

In any event, during the battle, bin Laden gave his satellite phone to one of his bodyguards, Abdallah Tabarak, with instructions to travel toward the Pakistani border, essentially serving as a decoy while bin Laden escaped in the opposite direction.[12] Qahtani also headed for the border, accompanied by approximately 28 al Qaeda fighters,[13] where Pakistani forces captured and detained him.

Qahtani claimed that his passport had been lost during detention in Afghanistan.[14] Less than two weeks later he was turned over to U.S. forces. After additional interrogation in the field, Qahtani was deemed of sufficient value as a possible intelligence source—as well as a high threat for more violence against America—that he was given the prisoner number ISN 063 and designated for evacuation to a secure facility. He was transported to Guantánamo Bay, Cuba, on February 13, 2002.[15]

Qahtani was born to a modestly wealthy family in Riyadh, Saudi Arabia, in 1975. He was a religious young man, praying five times daily as required by the Koran, observing fast days and the holy month of Ramadan, and becoming infused with the radical form of Islam preached at many Saudi mosques.[16]

The U.S. government has released background on Qahtani in various documents alleging that he began a basic terrorist training program in late 2000 through early 2001 at a camp known as al Farouk (sometimes spelled "Farooq" or "Faruq"), a site near Kandahar, "in order to participate in jihad, which he deemed a religious obligation."[17] Perhaps 20 or more other Guantánamo detainees as well as at least seven of the September 11, 2001 hijackers trained at al Farouk.[18] It was a major site for training Arab and other "foreign" fighters and was frequented by bin Laden and his top leaders.[19]

His trainee group would have been standard for the program and would have included 12 to 16 other jihadists like himself within a typical camp population of 150 to 200 trainees.[20] Many were from Saudi Arabia; others included Chechens, Yemenis, Iranians, and North Africans. The Australian jihadist David Hicks, a.k.a. Dawood al Australi, is thought to have trained there around the same time,[21] but that is still unverified. Later that year, starting on June 1, the American al Qaeda John Walker Lindh also trained at the camp and later described courses in weapons, orienteering, navigation, explosives, and battlefield combat.[22]

Training included introduction to small arms, typically the ubiquitous AK-47 assault rifle. The AK-47 is a sufficiently simple weapon that the fundamentals of sighting, firing, cleaning, and immediate action can be taught to illiterates with a high percentage of success. It is standard issue among the Khmer Rouge in Cambodia, the Pathet Lao in Laos, FARC (Fuerzas Armadas Revolucionarias de Colombia) narco-terrorist guerrillas in Colombia, revolutionaries in every African country, and across the Middle East. It is an amazingly rugged piece, a bit heavy but firing high-impact 7.62-millimeter military-standard small arms ammunition. It usually comes with a bayonet attached. Pack it with dirt and it blows the stuff away with the first round.

Along with training in the AK assault rifle, Qahtani would have learned how to aim and fire the RPG-7 rocket launcher (John Walker

Lindh described firing RPGs as part of his training at the camp[23]). This is another simple but amazingly effective weapon from the Soviet arsenal. Essentially a tube that sits on a fighter's shoulder with a simple aiming stake and a shaped charge that zips out to 300 meters, it is effective against vehicles, tanks, and personnel.

The al Qaeda recruits were also introduced to the RPK/RPD light machine guns. The guns fire a 7.62-millimeter round (the same as the AK, expediting logistics) and use a round magazine with nondisintegrating linked belts. They are simple, reliable, and tough to jam.

According to various sources, most notably including Muhammad Rashed Daoud al 'Owhali, who trained at al Farouk and other al Qaeda camps before participating in the twin August 7, 1998 U.S. embassy bombings in Kenya and Tanzania that killed 224 people and injured 4,500,[24] Farouk trainees received instruction in such skills as kidnapping and hijacking aircraft. Bomb-making is a signature al Qaeda specialty. The large, ammonium nitrate-base, plastic explosive-triggered truck bomb has been a favorite since the days of bombing sprees in Beirut.

We saw this kind of bomb in America at the 1993 World Trade Center bombing and the bombing of the Murrah Federal Office Building in Oklahoma City in 1995.[25] The technique surfaced again in the attack in Saudi Arabia against the U.S. billets in Khobar Towers and in attacks against the East African embassies.[26]

The mental indoctrination that accompanied physical and military training was the most important part of the curriculum. Many of the young men who came to Afghanistan were at the first stage of their commitment to jihad. They had all undergone some form of the *Iltizam* experience, as had Qahtani, but they were new to the intensity of extreme Wahabbist faith.

Imams in the camps, often the terror training leaders themselves, were a constant source of fundamentalist indoctrination. Prayer and study were constants. The history of Islam and the Arabs was repeated endlessly, with emphasis on the ancient glory days of the Caliphate and the ignominious defeats that the Faithful had suffered at the hands of the infidels and Crusaders.[27]

In addition to learning hatred for Christians and Jews, the youths were told of the treachery of false Muslims—those with weak faith who collaborated with the Crusaders to the detriment of the True Believers. "These false Muslims are a greater Satan than the Crusaders," the local imam intoned from his makeshift pulpit. "They must be destroyed as mercilessly as you would kill any other infidel. All must be destroyed: men, women, and even the children who bear the false seeds. Kill them all in the name of the Prophet."[28]

In late July 2001, Qahtani left Afghanistan, honed and ready, a human weapon. He was under orders to make his way to America for a crushing operation against the Great Satan. He would shortly board a commercial aircraft that would take him to Orlando, Florida.[29]

The young terrorist was coming to Disney World.

In April 2001, fully a year before the battle of Tora Bora, Qahtani had visited Osama bin Laden at his home in Kandahar to receive orders. By this time Qahtani had graduated from the terrorist training course at al Farouk, where he had met bin Laden for the first time and pledged his *bayat*, or lifetime allegiance. By late April, having completed his small-arms training, Qahtani went to Kandahar in southeastern Afghanistan.[30]

Kandahar was a short distance south of Darwana, the closest town to the al Farouk camp. By his own admission (later recanted[31]), Qahtani was informed by bin Laden personally that he had been selected for a special al Qaeda martyrdom mission that would take place outside of Afghanistan.[32] Qahtani was to visit the home of al Qaeda's number two, Khalid Sheikh Muhammad (KSM), alias Mukhtar, who also lived in Kandahar.

KSM would eventually provide key evidence during the 2006 sentencing trial of Zacarias Moussaoui in the United States. Moussaoui's 58-page deposition included KSM's personal recollections of Qahtani:

> Sheikh Muhammad said this was another operative who came into the operation very late, commenting that Al-Qahtani is an extremely simple man. Zubayr Al-Ha'ili had originally told Sheikh Muhammad that Al-Qahtani was suitable for a martyr-

dom operation, and Zubayr went directly to bin Laden about Al-Qahtani. Bin Laden, acting on Zubayr's recommendation, presented Al-Qahtani to Sheikh Muhammad as a candidate for the 9/11 operation . . .[33]

Qahtani was summoned back to Khalid Sheikh Muhammad's Kandahar home in late June. At that time he received the specific instructions that bin Laden had alluded to in previous conversation. On or about July 14, 2001, Qahtani went to Riyadh, Saudi Arabia, where he obtained a new passport.[34] Thanks to a U.S. State Department program designed to ease Saudi visits to America, he was able to "fast track" U.S. and U.K. entry visas. Two weeks later, Qahtani went to Dubai, United Arab Emirates, and contacted Mustafa al Hawsawi. He stayed in Dubai almost three weeks.

KSM—hardly a Qahtani admirer—recalled that when he told Qahtani to obtain a U.S., Swiss, French, Italian, or Australian visa, he needed to explain to him the existence of visa regimes. He confirmed that Hawsawi provided money to Qahtani in Dubai for his travel to the United States. "Al-Qahtani did not know the specifics of the operation, but did understand it to be a suicide operation," KSM's deposition notes, and it also states, "Al-Qahtani was first aware that the operation would take place in the U.S. in the summer of 2001," when KSM met with him again in Karachi, Pakistan.[35]

On August 4, 2001, Hawsawi drove Qahtani to the airport and gave him more than $3,000 in cash, mostly in U.S. currency, and a one-way airline ticket through London to Orlando, Florida. He was told that he would be met in the airport. KSM later stated that Qahtani did not know exactly who would meet him, and that he did not have contacts of his own in the United States.

While Qahtani was sufficiently motivated to carry out an attack on the Great Satan, he was poorly coached on how to deal with Satanic officialdom. Qahtani tried to enter the United States at Orlando International Airport on August 4, disembarking from the Virgin Atlantic flight from London. Not a bad choice of point of entry, as tens of thousands of international visitors—some businessmen but most families on vacation—transit the airport annually. Qahtani ought to have been passed through casually. But his training failed.

He was interviewed by Immigration and Naturalization official José E. Melendez-Perez. "He gave me the creeps," the INS agent later testified to the 9/11 Commission. Because of Qahtani's hostile and arrogant attitude, along with his refusal to disclose his plans within the United States, Melendez-Perez grew increasingly uncomfortable with the Arab man standing before him. Qahtani, he thought, acted like a hired killer.[36]

"My wife said I was watching too many movies," Melendez-Perez later said, but to him Qahtani acted like a "hit man." He had no return ticket, no hotel reservations, and refused to identify a friend who he said was to meet him at the airport and provide him with assistance.[37]

Melendez-Perez questioned the large amount of cash he carried—$2,800 in U.S. dollars—and his lack of credit cards, unusual for international travelers and Middle Easterners in particular. Qahtani stated he would be "vacationing and traveling through the United States for six days" (he would later insist to military interrogators at Guantánamo Bay that he came to the United States to buy a used car,[38] although according to Melendez-Perez's detailed statement Qahtani did not make this claim when questioned at the airport). But he would only say that someone was waiting for him and would take him "somewhere."[39]

Qahtani refused to explain who this person was or give contact information. Nor could he answer such elementary questions as "where will you be staying in the U.S.?" Growing suspicious, immigration officials took him to a private interview room and asked him to make a sworn statement of intent. Oddly, in retrospect, Qahtani refused to do so and abruptly withdrew his application for entry into the United States. On his way out the door, back to the international transit lounge to wait for a flight bound for Dubai via London, Qahtani faced the INS agent. "I'll be back," he said in English.[40]

Apparently, Qahtani had been tagged to join the September 11 terrorist attack, which he knew to be a suicide mission. But in what role? KSM made it clear in his deposition that "there was no reason for Al-Qahtani's late arrival in the U.S. aside from the fact that Sheikh Muhammad [KSM] wanted as many hijackers in the U.S. as possible." KSM also stated that "Al-Qahtani was a late addition to the operation, and, therefore, Al-Qahtani was not trained very well in dealing with Customs officials or the English language."[41]

There was clearly insufficient time to train him adequately in even rudimentary aircraft flight procedures. Qahtani certainly would not have had a primary role in the mission, such as piloting the aircraft. But just coming out of hard training in the Afghan terror camps, he would have been useful muscle in the hijacking itself, part of the gang that overcame and murdered several passengers and crew. Qahtani would have had no hesitation when called upon to cut the throats of helpless individuals—particularly those of American infidels.[42]

Much of the training had taken place at al Farouk, where the *9/11 Commission Report* notes "a dozen of them heard bin Laden's speeches, volunteered to become suicide operatives, and eventually were selected as muscle hijackers for the planes operation."[43] As time drew closer for the attack, specialty training conducted by the Jordanian terrorist Abu Turab at the al Matar complex focused on "how to conduct hijackings, disarm air marshals, and handle explosives. He trained them in body-building and provided them with a few English words and phrases."[44]

There is strong suspicion that Qahtani had been designated to be the fifth terrorist to fill out the attackers of Flight 93, which was over-taken by passengers and crashed into a Pennsylvania field. His presence on the plane might have tipped the balance in the terrorists' favor and allowed them to carry out their destructive mission.

A quick examination of Zacarias Moussaoui's role in these events leads to a fuller understanding of Qahtani's place in the 9/11 plot.

Sometimes referred to as "the 20th hijacker," Moussaoui pled guilty to conspiring to (1) commit acts of terrorism; (2) use weapons of mass destruction; (3) destroy aircraft; (4) commit aircraft piracy; (5) murder U.S. employees; and (6) destroy property.[45] The charges were filed in June 2002, and after years of legal wrangling, Moussaoui (who routinely referred to his case as "Zacarias Moussaoui, Muslim vs. U.S., Godless Government") eventually pled guilty to these charges in April 2005. While some federal investigators theorized that there was supposed to be a 20th hijacker and believed that Moussaoui had been picked for the 9/11 hijackings, Moussaoui himself testified in court that he was trained to fly a plane into the White House during a later attack.

KSM also stated that Moussaoui was intended for use during a "second wave" attack after 9/11, with his disposition noting:

> Moussaoui had been recruited to participate in a "second wave" of attacks that was originally planned to follow the September 11, 2001 attacks. This second wave of attacks was intended to utilize operatives with European and East Asian backgrounds whom Sheikh Mohammed believed would operate more easily in what he expected to be a more stringent security environment following the 9/11 attacks, especially as it related to Middle Easterners. Sheikh Mohammed used only Middle Easterners in the first wave for this reason and that Moussaoui was chosen for the second wave because of his French citizenship. Sheikh Mohammed stated that the second wave was not completely planned or ready for execution, but was on the "back burner." Sheikh Mohammed had no idea that the damage of the first attack would be as catastrophic as it was, and he did not plan on the U.S. responding to the attacks as fiercely as they did, which led to the next phase being postponed.
>
> Sheikh Mohammed immediately said that Moussaoui was never slated to be a 9/11 operative, reiterating previous comments that he had anticipated a need for non-Arab passport holders to conduct the second wave of airplane operations after 9/11. Despite Moussaoui's admittedly problematic personality, Sheikh Mohammed tasked Moussaoui to take flight lessons in preparation for the second wave attacks. Sheikh Mohammed reiterated earlier claims that the second wave was only in its most preliminary stages, noting that Moussaoui was one of the few potential pilots identified for the operation, along with Mussa and Abu Faruq al-Tunisi. Sheikh Mohammed also reiter-

ated that he had not identified any targets for the second wave operation . . .[46]

For what it's worth, in May 2006, Osama bin Laden himself apparently weighed in on the matter by releasing an audiotape translated by IntelCenter, a private company that does contracting work for U.S. intelligence. The translation included the following statement:

> I begin by talking about the honorable brother Zacarias Moussaoui. The truth is that he has no connection whatsoever with the events of September 11th, and I am certain of what I say, because I was responsible for entrusting the 19 brothers—Allah have mercy upon them—with those raids, and I did not assign brother Zacarias to be with them on that mission . . .

In other words, while Moussaoui was sentenced to life in prison for conspiring with al Qaeda to commit future attacks, he was almost certainly not the 20th hijacker of the 9/11 attacks in New York and Washington, DC.

It appears from investigation and documents cited that Qahtani, not Moussaoui, was intended to join the 9/11 attack. Further, evidence suggests two additional possibilities: that the 9/11 attack involved more than the four hijacked aircraft, or that a second, follow-on attack was in the advanced stages of planning. Interviews in Guantánamo never previously reported, as will be shown, support these hypotheses.

Frustrated in his attempts to enter America, Muhammad al Qahtani returned to Afghanistan via London, Dubai, and Karachi. He arrived back in Kandahar less than a month before the 9/11 operation in which he had been destined to achieve martyrdom.[47]

Shortly after the September 11, 2001 attack, bin Laden and his coterie must have realized that it had not had its desired effect. Rather than collapse into itself, America rebounded with unmatched fury. The United States and a coalition of international forces rapidly mounted a counteroffensive into the very belly of the beast: Taliban-controlled Afghanistan.

President George W. Bush vowed to hunt the terrorists down wherever they were and to "bring them to justice."[48]

Within weeks Afghanistan was overrun, the Taliban government had fallen, and al Qaeda's base of operations in the country was disrupted. Numbers of battlefield captures soared into the tens of thousands. Obviously not everyone captured on the battlefield was a hard-core Taliban or al Qaeda operative, but it was critical to identify and separate the hapless draftees from the committed terrorists. The Taliban, in its rigid control of Afghanistan, impressed soldiers into ranks as needed. Many of those captured were simply peasants or laborers who had the good fortune to be captured alive or were able to surrender before their leaders could murder them.

These men were gleaned for what is called tactical intelligence, that is, information of immediate value on the battlefield. Eventually most were disarmed and released. But mixed with these simple Afghan peasants were al Qaeda and Taliban hard men. They refused to capitulate and continued the fight even after pretending to surrender.

An illustrative incident took place on Sunday, November 25, 2001, at the 19th-century mud fortress of Qala-i-Jangi, five miles west of the village of Mazar-e-Sharif. The day prior, the Taliban town of Kundzu had fallen to Northern Alliance forces. By most estimates, upward of 800 prisoners—mixed Taliban and al Qaeda—were put on trucks and herded to the Qala-i-Jangi fortress.

There, under admittedly loose Northern Alliance guard, they were confined. But many had smuggled weapons into Qala-i-Jangi under their loose robes. The prisoners tied these weapons—hand grenades, pistols, knives, and even AKs—to their legs and genitals. Northern Alliance Afghans hated to touch the foreign fighters, because they considered them unclean. In any case their search methods were primitive at best, resulting in many weapons remaining in the hands of the prisoners.[49]

That Saturday afternoon, Northern Alliance general Nadir Ali was assaulted and killed by a suicide-bomber prisoner who had smuggled grenades into the prison. Another prisoner killed himself and senior

Hazara commander Saeed Asad that same night. Despite the grenade attacks, Alliance guards were not reinforced.[50]

The following day, two American CIA field operators, Johnny "Mike" Spann, 32, a northern Virginia father of three and former Marine captain, and his partner, "Dave," were walking alone through the compound interrogating large numbers of prisoners, conducting initial screening and trying to extract tactical intelligence.

In retrospect, it is easy to see that Mike and Dave made a huge mistake when they permitted the prisoners to crowd around them. Mike was trying to learn the motivating factor that brought the foreigners to fight in Afghanistan. "Why did you come here?" he asked one prisoner.

"To kill you!" shouted another captive, who leapt at Mike and began to beat him. Between them, Dave and Mike killed several of their attackers. But the tide of fanatic captives was unstoppable. Mike disappeared under a pile of crazed fighters who tore at him with fingernails, bit, punched, and kicked him. Mike Spann became the first American killed in Afghanistan.

The Qala-i-Jangi riot quickly turned into a desperate firefight in which more than 150 Northern Alliance force soldiers were killed, along with several hundred Taliban and al Qaeda prisoners. As one of the American Special Forces who led Northern Alliance forces back into the prison later said, "This was no riot suppression, this was a pitched battle."[51]

There is no unclassified indication that Muhammad al Qahtani was present at Qala-i-Jangi. But the point is that Qahtani and his fellow "Arab" fighters all came to Afghanistan with the same purpose: to kill Americans.

Pakistani forces intercepted a fleeing band of al Qaeda fighters and captured them on December 16, 2001. Muhammad al Qahtani had a weak cover story for the Pakistani authorities: He told them that his passport had been lost during detention. They didn't buy his story.[52]

Pakistani officials turned Qahtani over to American authorities—probably covert CIA Special Activities Division operators—who recognized both the real threat he posed and his potential intelligence value as a suspected al Qaeda member.

Qahtani was stripped, searched thoroughly, and clad in a bright orange jumpsuit. He was secured with handcuffs and leg irons, his head was covered with a hood, and he was then loaded into a USAF C-17 cargo aircraft along with scores of other captured fighters. Armed military policemen accompanied the flight. Qahtani was evacuated to Guantánamo Bay Naval Base, Cuba, on February 13, 2002.

CHAPTER 3

IN THE BEGINNING

CAMP X-RAY

THE HORRIFIC EPISODE AT THE battle of Qala-i-Jangi near the northern city of Mazir-e-Sharif on November 25, 2001 told planners that more focus had to be given to prisoner handling. "It is difficult to say how much Qala-i-Jangi actually affected selection of Guantánamo," one high-ranking Pentagon official stated. "We were aware of it certainly in our planning. The incident was a factor we considered, but may not have been the dominant reason for picking Gitmo."[1]

Other officials acknowledge that the vulnerability and inadequacy of interrogation in conditions such as the makeshift confinement area at Qala-i-Jangi spurred action to develop a safer, more permanent facility. If prisoners could not be adequately held for interrogation, nor for that matter, properly protected by the ad hoc mass detention centers characteristic of the Afghan battlefield, then other alternatives needed to be considered. As is usual in evaluating any need, the planners laid out the aspects of detainee handling that most concerned them. Foremost was safety of the prisoners and the guards. Any permanent or semipermanent arrangement had to accommodate those basic needs. Second was a facility in which the detainees could be removed from the battlefield and adequately held without undue risk of escape or of an outside attack to break them out. Third was the need to extract any relevant information these men held.

There was frenzied staff activity within the Office of the Joint Chiefs of Staff to determine the exact location for handling and inter-rogation of the battlefield captures. Locations outside the United States were preferred for simplicity in handling, reduced possibility of escape, and overall security. From the outset it made sense to do two things, the first of which was to get the worst detainees out of the battle area where an al Qaeda rescue attempt would be feasible or where local guards could be bribed or intimidated; hence the idea of an island made good sense. The second thing needed was to take advantage of an established American military presence so that new construction and infrastructure requirements could be kept to a minimum. Various pos-sibilities, including Guam, Hawaii, and Diego Garcia, were considered and rejected for one reason or another.

The selection process was elevated quickly to the interagency arena, with vigorous participation from the CIA, the State Department, and especially the Department of Justice. The DOJ was particularly enthu-siastic about Guantánamo as a location. The proximity of Cuba to the United States would expedite travel arrangements, and this was one of several important considerations. Ultimately, the staff recommended Guantánamo, a facility close enough to the U.S. mainland for easy lo-gistical support but secured and closed to outside access.[2]

Military engineers—primarily Navy Construction Battalion (Seabees)—began to fabricate a camp that could hold incoming de-tainees securely. Camp X-Ray, as it is known, was put together in a practical, albeit rudimentary fashion. Camp X-Ray occupied a site of approximately five acres, away from the main activity on Naval Base Guantánamo. It was rather primitive. Two high chain-link fences topped by coils of razor wire outlined the camp. Inside were some crude wooden plywood structures made for administrative use. Other visible structures included a hastily made dispensary (marked by a large red cross), and off to the side were several individual huts that were used for interroga-tion. Inside the double-camp wire were hygienic measures—latrines and showers made of concrete block—and rows of chain-link cages for handling individual detainees.

Each double row of cages was set on a concrete pad to keep detainees out of the mud and rain, and covered by a tin roof. All sides were open for ventilation. There were urinal tubes inside each individual cell so that detainees had to be taken out only for bowel movements, showers, interrogation, exercise, or medical treatment. At that time, all detainees were clothed in bright orange jumpsuits similar to the standard wear in most U.S. prison systems. Many were still malnourished and exhausted from recent combat. Quite a few were recovering from wounds or injuries incurred in the fighting, making it clear that they were in fact enemy combatants.

From the outset, it was the standard procedure to provide detainees three hot meals daily (it has sometimes been pointed out that detainees are fed better and at greater cost than American troops because of their Islamic halal dietary requirements[3]) and immediate medical attention (Brigadier General Jay Hood, commander of Joint Task Force Guantánamo, testified before the House Armed Services Committee in June 2005 that "the average detainee visits Guantánamo's modern hospital facilities four times a month. In comparison, the average American male only visits the doctor 3.7 times each year"[4]). Also from the beginning, detainees were given religious rights and allowed to pray daily, oriented in the direction of Mecca, and were soon given a Koran and prayer accoutrements.

Several hundred meters distant, General Purpose tents were erected for use by U.S. Army guards and military interrogators. These tents had dirt floors and no fans, and the troops ate Meals Ready to Eat (MRE) rather than hot chow.[5]

The pattern at Guantánamo has remained constant since: Any improvements in living conditions go first to the detainees, then to the American troops.

These days Camp X-Ray, which hasn't been in full use since April 2002, is a standard part of the VIP and media tours. Visitors find a forlorn, painfully neglected site as overgrown by tropical vegetation as an Angkor Wat temple. Tall, double chain-link fences serve to support local vines, and the view from the old wooden guard tower that my military escort, overly solicitous of my safety, implored me not to climb, looks down upon hastily constructed plywood buildings and tin roofs.

From the tower the original medical facility, marked by a faded red-cross insignia, supports a sagging roof that seems one hurricane away from total capitulation. If you follow remnants of a stony yellow dirt path angling away from a near corner you encounter a step-stone series of cobbled-up plywood huts that once served as interrogation booths. Everything inside is built-in, dimension lumber construction crafted with garage woodworker's skills into benches, tables, and chairs. A large eyebolt drilled into the floor near one bench marks the spot where detainees were shackled during interrogation.

Off on the adjacent high ground, debris from the abandoned American military camp affords future archeologists a kitchen midden of discarded MRE containers and disconnected pieces of jagged metal and wood.

Inside the wire of X-Ray, determined native plants have overcome the herbicide and plastic ground cover diligently applied by Seabees to penetrate gravel walkways. I pause for a moment, looking down the length of a chain-link corridor, and recall the famous photograph—shot from this precise vantage point—of hooded detainees in orange jumpsuits kneeling back-to-back while American guards watched.

Poking around the interior of one of the interrogation huts, I find scraps of silver duct tape. Could this have been the infamous hut inside which Muhammad al Qahtani was kept and that provoked a flaming e-mail from shocked FBI agents? They reported that the hut had been duct-taped shut so that anyone in the interior would have no sense of day or night—a scenario designed to impart confusion and dislocation. Now rodent droppings stain the rotted flooring that cracks ominously beneath one's feet, and the pervasive tropical rot portends a nasty fall for inquisitive visitors.

Camp X-Ray had become iconic in the world's mind, the very epitome of detention at Guantánamo. Now, as it rusts into oblivion, only banana rats and large fruit bats find comfort in its continued presence.

Qahtani was indeed subjected to degrading and abusive treatment in Camp X-Ray during the first year of his confinement. This was a very upsetting revelation to those of us who hold the American military in high regard. While subsequent investigations have determined that his treatment did not constitute actual torture, it was judged sufficiently abusive that government prosecutors have since dropped several of the charges against him on grounds that his self-incriminating testimony would likely be disallowed.

Because the case against Qahtani is significant and since his treatment, while unique, has been raised as a cause célèbre by Guantánamo opponents, it is useful to recount the known facts relevant to his interrogation.

When the first detainees were evacuated to Guantánamo Bay in January 2002, military intelligence and personnel there operated under procedures detailed in Army Field Manual 34-52 (FM 34-52). This 177-page document allowed for the following techniques during detainee interrogations:

Direct questioning;
Incentives: use of luxury items to reward cooperation;
Emotional Love: playing on a detainee's emotional attachments;
Emotional Hate: playing on a detainee's hates, such as desire for revenge;
Fear Up / Harsh: exploiting pre-existing fears with the use of a loud and threatening voice;
Fear Up / Mild: using a calm, rational approach while exploiting the detainee's fears;
Fear Down: soothing and calming the detainee to build rapport;
Pride and Ego-Up: use of flattery to prompt cooperation;
Pride and Ego Down: goading the detainee by challenging his loyalty, intelligence, etc., to induce the detainee to provide information disproving the interrogator;
Futility: rationally persuading the detainee that it is futile to resist questioning;
We Know All: to further convince the detainee that resistance during questioning is pointless;

File and Dossier: preparing a decoy dossier that everything is already known;

Establish Your Identity: insist the detainee is someone else to induce him to identify himself;

Repetition: to induce the detainee to break the monotony by answering questions;

Rapid Fire: questioning in rapid succession, without permitting the detainee to answer;

Silent: staring at the detainee for extended periods to induce nervousness;

Change of Scene: engaging the detainee in a different environment to ease his apprehension or catch him with his guard down.

These were approved techniques to be used during interrogations with Qahtani and others. Unfortunately for those involved and hampering efforts to bring him to justice, Qahtani would be subjected to much more strenuous interrogation processes than these approved techniques. There were many factors leading to the inexcusable circumstances of his abuse.

From the outset, military interrogators quickly concluded that the approved FM 34-52 techniques "were ineffective against detainees who had received interrogation resistance training."[6] This is hardly surprising when one considers not only counter-interrogation training received in camps such as al Farouk and detailed instructions guiding detainee conduct through al Qaeda's so-called Manchester Manual, but the example of what al Qaeda and Taliban extremists chose to subject themselves to while fighting at Qala-i-Jangi.[7]

On that day, November 25, 2001, approximately 330 men holed themselves up in the basement inside the fortress. According to the recollections of the American Taliban John Walker Lindh, the Qala-i-Jangi prisoners—many of whom had undoubtedly been trained at al Farouk just as Walker Lindh had been—spent six days in the dark while Northern Alliance guards threw grenades down the air shafts, poured in diesel fuel that was lit on fire, and flooded the basement with freezing water pumped in from an irrigation ditch. Walker Lindh, who knew of the intent to launch a major attack against the United States before 9/11 but failed to alert anyone, had been shot in the leg and played dead in the yard surrounded by bodies as the shooting continued for 12 hours. A fellow fighter then dragged him into the basement.

As reported in an *Esquire* magazine article based on interviews with Walker Lindh, those in the basement:

> . . . were blown up and then burned and then drowned in the dark. Men were dying continually, men were howling in pain and hunger, men were going mad. John Walker had a bullet in his leg, and he was also wounded from shrapnel, and he was sick from drinking the water fouled with the excrement of several hundred men and the effluvia of the sick and the dying. Yaser Hamdi, like all the rest, couldn't sleep and had to keep standing because at the end, to sleep meant to slip away in the water. And still for six days they held out and only began to surrender because they faced the choice of surrendering to Dostum or surrendering to the water, and John Walker is said to have reminded the others that suicide was strictly prohibited by the Holy Koran.

While Walker Lindh's Koranic interpretations are considered by Islamic scholars the more classic reading, Wahabbist extremists believe that suicide attacks will result in holy martyrdom.

The Taliban and al Qaeda fighters trapped in the basement had the option to surrender at any time and survive. Walker Lindh was among those who finally elected to do so. In all, after six days of refusing to budge, on December 1 a total of 86 finally came out. The rest had chosen to die in a dark, flooded hell rather than surrender.

Many of them were ultimately sent to Camp X-Ray. One of them would later commit suicide along with two fellow detainees in what military authorities called an act of asymmetrical warfare.[8]

These were extremely tough, defiant men familiar with giving and taking cruelty. The challenge faced by the military was to save lives by finding out what these men knew about al Qaeda, the Taliban, and, most critically, any future plots to attack the West. Military interrogators at Guantánamo thought that the approved FM 34-52 techniques would be ineffective in achieving this goal because they were dealing with incredibly hard men who had been drilled and trained to resist normal interrogation.

Qahtani arrived at Camp X-Ray in February 2002, but neither the military interrogators nor the FBI agents working with them were aware at the time that he had attempted to enter the United States on August 4, or that 9/11 hijacker Muhammad Atta had been at the Orlando airport to pick him up. Nor were they aware of his relationship with KSM and Osama bin Laden.

Between February and June 2002, Qahtani was questioned during "four or five sessions." He did not provide any useful information and claimed he had been in Afghanistan to buy and sell falcons.[9] In April all the detainees, including Qahtani, were moved from temporary holding facilities at Camp X-Ray into newly opened Camp Delta. There is no evidence that he was separated from or treated differently than other detainees during this period.

But the situation changed dramatically in July 2002, when the FBI belatedly identified Qahtani from fingerprint records as the person who had been interrogated by INS agents at the Orlando airport in August 2001. They also determined that hijacker Muhammad Atta's calling card had been used at the airport to call "a September 11 financier" (al Qaeda financial coordinator Mustafa al Hawsawi). FBI agents in Guantánamo were informed of these facts and immediately shared them with military counterparts.[10]

The FBI quickly sought to take the lead in interviewing Qahtani, arguing that they had originally discovered his identity and were also lead agency for the entire investigation into the 9/11 attacks. Qahtani, now understood by everyone involved to be a red-hot property (Major General Michael E. Dunlavey, the commander of Joint Task Force 170 [Interrogation], reportedly called him "a national treasure"), was moved from the general detainee population into an isolation cell somewhere inside Camp Delta.[11]

The FBI recommended moving Qahtani to an even more secure and isolated facility. On the basis of that request, the military transported him on August 8, 2002 to the Guantánamo Navy Brig. The FBI interviewed Qahtani for approximately 30 days before the military—which had been pushing hard for results—told them to "step aside" and took over.[12] Despite FBI disclaimers, some chide the agency for inaction during the period that Qahtani was in the Navy brig. "They had him there the whole time and did nothing with him," commented Paul Rester. "They ignored him."[13]

The already strained relations between military and FBI personnel at Guantánamo—both sides the subjects of intense pressure from higher headquarters to provide actionable intelligence or make a case—quickly began to deteriorate. FBI agents reported to their superiors that after the military took over Qahtani's interrogations, he was subjected to aggressive questioning techniques that including yelling, screaming, and calling him names.[14] A barking, growling military working dog was brought into the interrogation room to scare Qahtani. The dog was restrained and not allowed to have contact with him, but FBI agents were so disturbed by the tactic that they left the room.[15]

Electronic mail messages flew from Guantánamo to FBI headquarters. One of these was used by Senator Dick Durbin three years later, in his well-publicized denouncement of Guantánamo on the Senate floor in June 2005 that vilified undertrained and unprepared military personnel by vicious comparisons to Nazi concentration camp guards or to Pol Pot.[16] On October 8, 2002, one of the FBI agents e-mailed the Guantánamo on-scene commander, stating that Qahtani was "down to 100 pounds" and the subject of sleep deprivation, loud music, bright lights, and "body placement discomfort." The agent stated his belief that these techniques were not working because Qahtani still refused to cooperate.[17]

On October 11, Major General Dunlavey requested that the SOUTHCOM commander, General James Hill, approve 19 counter-resistance techniques that were not included in FM 34-52.[18] The 19 requested techniques were broken down into three categories. Category I included yelling and deception. Category II allowed for stress positions for up to four hours, light deprivation, removal of clothing, and using individual phobias (such as fear of dogs). Category III included "use of scenarios designed to convince the detainee that death or severely painful consequences are imminent for him and/or his family" and "use of a wet towel and dripping water to induce the misperception of suffocation."[19] The latter is now commonly referred to as "waterboarding." The request was then forwarded up the chain of command to Secretary of Defense Rumsfeld, who approved some of the techniques (waterboarding was specifically disapproved) in a memorandum dated December 2, 2002.

Meanwhile, the already strained relationship between the military and FBI escalated into outright hostility when DOJ counsel David Nahmias and the FBI's Military Liaison and Detainee Unit (MLDU) chief arrived on October 15, 2002 at Guantánamo for a three-day visit to help formulate the interrogation plan for Qahtani.[20]

At one point during their stay, they participated in a video teleconference call with newly assigned JTF GTMO commander Major General Geoffrey Miller and others. Also taking part on that call were a lieutenant colonel in charge of GTMO interrogations, the chief psychologist, a representative of the CIA, and, it is thought, DOD personnel at the Pentagon.

An argument erupted when the lieutenant colonel presented a military plan to use aggressive techniques on Qahtani. Reportedly, he claimed that all of the information military interrogators had obtained on Qahtani came through the use of aggressive interrogation practices. The MLDU chief lashed back and said, "Look, everything you've gotten thus far is what the FBI gave you on al Qahtani from its paper investigation." The discussion became heated and the teleconference ended.[21]

A month later, on November 12, 2002, SOUTHCOM General Hill approved the use of Category I and II techniques on Qahtani, but not the Category III methods (which had included waterboarding).[22] Against the FBI's strong objections, he also approved a military interrogation plan that called for daily 20-hour-long interrogation sessions, shaving Qahtani's head and beard, and use of blindfolds and stress positions if he continued to be uncooperative. The plan, scheduled to begin on November 15, was presented in the form of four phases:[23]

- Phase I permitted the FBI access to Qahtani until November 22. He would then be prevented from speaking for a week, on the theory that he would then want to talk and tell his story.

- Phase II centered on placing an undercover government translator with Qahtani in the hope that he would talk to a fellow detainee.

- Phase III called for the use of Survival, Evasion, Resistance, and Escape (SERE)–styled techniques. These techniques are used on U.S. soldiers and airmen during training to teach them to resist interrogation, and include dietary manipulation, use of nudity, sleep deprivation, and waterboarding.

- Phase IV would send Qahtani "off island" either temporarily or permanently to Jordan, Egypt, or another country that would use their own interrogation techniques to extract information from him.

FBI agents stationed at Guantánamo were deeply disturbed by the plan and refused to sign off on it. Two of Qahtani's FBI interviewers also claimed there was a "circus-like atmosphere" and "utter lack of sophistication" displayed by military personnel during an interrogation-planning strategy session.[24]

Adding to the chaos and confusion, on December 2, 2002, Rumsfeld approved the request for use of special interrogation techniques—only to rescind that directive six weeks later, on January 15, 2003. Rumsfeld then established his own working group to assess interrogation techniques for use in the war on terror.[25]

So what really happened to Qahtani during this intense period?

Beginning on November 23, 2002 and ending on January 15, 2003,[26] Qahtani—who had since been moved out of the Navy brig into a plywood hut in the otherwise deserted Camp X-Ray[27]—was subjected to harsh interrogations by a military "special projects" team. His treatment, confirmed by the Department of Defense investigative Schmidt-Furlow[28] and Church reports,[29] included 20-hour interrogation sessions, tying him to a dog leash, leading him through dog tricks, repeatedly pouring water on his head, stress positions, forced shaving, stripping him naked in the presence of a female, calling his mother and sister whores, instructing him to pray to an idol shrine, and turning the air conditioner all the way up to produce an uncomfortably cold temperature.[30]

Women's underwear was placed on his head and a bra was strapped over his clothing. A male interrogator danced with him and a discussion of "his repressed homosexual tendencies" took place. He was told other detainees would hear that he got aroused when male guards searched him. A female interrogator massaged his back and neck, he was shown pictures of scantily clothed women, and one female interrogator straddled him while he was restrained in a seated position (albeit without placing weight on him). In early December, Qahtani was briefly hospitalized with brachycardia, a possible result of the harsh treatment.

Highly detailed military interrogation logs, later released to the public under a Freedom of Information Act request, reveal that on November 25, two days after this intensive program began, Qahtani was given three and a half bags of IV fluids and told that he would not be allowed to go to the bathroom and had to urinate in his pants (which he did).[31]

It was at that time that Qahtani broke down and started talking. He told interrogators that he worked for al Qaeda and his leader was Osama bin Laden. His revelations were startling and continued for several months. At one point, according to an interrogator, he was led into a room with walls plastered with photos of scores of Arab men. "He walked around the room," said the interrogator, "and one-by-one, with no hesitation, picked out all 19 of the 9/11 hijackers and called out their names."[32]

By that spring, well after the harsh interrogation process ended, Qahtani was providing significant amounts of intelligence.[33] He helped the United States understand the process by which terrorist operatives are recruited and logistics flow to support their operations. He elaborated on planning aspects of the 9/11 terrorist attack, and clarified convicted terrorists José Padilla's and Richard Reid's relationships with al Qaeda and their activities in Afghanistan. Qahtani outlined infiltration routes and explained methods used by al Qaeda to cross international borders undetected.[34]

He related techniques Osama bin Laden used to evade capture by U.S. forces, and provided important information on bin Laden's health (at the time, rumors flew that the terror mastermind was in kidney failure and required dialysis, or had other serious health issues). Qahtani clarified many of those rumors. He also provided detailed information about 30 of Osama bin Laden's personal bodyguards, also held at Guantánamo, many of whom had successfully maintained a cover story of their innocence until then.[35]

This was clearly extraordinarily valuable, actionable intelligence.

Primarily as a result of excesses done to Qahtani, in April 2003 Rumsfeld approved issuing new interrogation rules that closely followed and further amplified and clarified those detailed in FM 34-52. Helping to dispel confusion, in December 2005 the Detainee Treatment Act required a uniform standard of treatment for detainees held in military custody. This was formally implemented in September 2006 through publication of a new Army Field Manual, 2-22.3, that, among other constraints, specifically prohibits the use of military dogs, nudity, sexual acts or poses, beatings, and waterboarding during interrogation.

While that helped resolve one issue, the problems created by the military's early egregious handling of Qahtani continue unabated. In October 2005, the Center for Constitutional Rights (CCR), along with co-counsel from the law firm Gibbons, Del Deo, Dolan, Griffinger & Vecchione, filed a habeas corpus petition on behalf of Qahtani. That December, Qahtani was visited by a CCR attorney at Guantánamo.[36] He ceased talking to interrogators and ultimately changed his story.

By 2006, Qahtani had recanted previous confessions and testimony.

He claimed that the information he gave was extracted from him using torture. In a nine-page letter submitted to the Combat Status Review Board, neatly handwritten entirely in English, Qahtani claimed that he was simply a businessman "kidnapped as a civilian" and illegally brought to Guantánamo. He retracted all his prior statements regarding al Qaeda and bin Laden.

It is unknown whether he was ever informed of Khalid Sheikh Muhammad's 58-page deposition introduced at Zacarias Moussaoui's April 2006 sentencing, in which the senior 9/11 al Qaeda planner described Qahtani's role in the 9/11 plot and his relationship with bin Laden.

In 2008, Qahtani was among six Guantánamo detainees to be formally charged with 9/11 crimes, yet the government has since dropped the case (nonetheless reserving the right to refile at some later date).

ONE OF THE CHALLENGES FACED in those early days was lack of expertise. After years of cutting back on trained interrogators and exotic language specialists, the Department of Defense—particularly the Defense Intelligence Agency, which has responsibility in the field—was called upon to mount a major interrogation operation at Guantánamo. Concomitantly, Central Command was screaming for trained interrogator staff to work in the combat theater.

"It is naïve to think that the military has a 'stable' of trained interrogators available," said Paul Butler, former Deputy Assistant Secretary of Defense for Special Operations Low Intensity Conflict. "Prior to 9/11 there were only a handful of interrogators who could deal with al Qaeda–trained terrorists."[37]

In many cases the gaps were filled by reservists or National Guard assets from units that may have been trained for other parts of the world. Shortfalls were plugged by newly minted interrogators or cross-specialists in the intelligence field who were told simply to "get the job done."

Complicating an already tangled web were the demands, usually conflicting, of other government agencies. The 9/11 strike had cut across artificial bureaucratic boundaries. Every agency that thought it might have a dog in the fight was quick to descend on Guantánamo, demanding immediate answers to their questions and insisting that its requirements were at the top of the priority list.

Federal Bureau of Investigation officers were among the first to arrive. Many were pulled right out of the field. Some had language training; none were trained to deal with enemy combatants. Their primary intent—based on all previous training—was to build a criminal case against any of the detainees that they thought might have committed crimes, particularly while in the United States. These officers brought with them a locked-down, hardwired approach to case work that included Miranda rights, restricted access to a subject, severely limited questioning techniques, and tough evidentiary guidelines needed to make a case stick. The FBI was, of course, interested in what operational plans might be afoot for future attacks against America but was primarily focused on a retrospective approach: how to bring people to justice for crimes already committed.

Central Intelligence Agency officers, on the other hand, were almost strictly future focused. They wanted to know—and know quickly—what attacks were being mounted against the United States and all the information necessary to thwart them. In this they were joined by kindred spirits in Defense, with the added caveat that they also wanted to extract information of interest to battle planners in light of the ongoing combat operations in Afghanistan.

The Drug Enforcement Agency was involved because of myriad ties that some al Qaeda and Taliban operatives had to international drug traffic, particularly in opium and heroin.[38] Local authorities such as the New York, Washington, DC, and northern Virginia police departments were involved because terrorist attacks occurred in their backyards. It seemed to interrogators who looked back on it, everyone came to Gitmo except the Little Sisters of the Poor and the Salvation Army Band.

As a result of the confusion, the end product was for the most part—confusion. "We would encounter detainees who were genuinely pissed off," Paul Rester, director of the Joint Intelligence Group, said.

Rester, a small, compact man whose sardonic sense of humor punctuates his professorial manner, is almost an anachronism. He has been in the interrogation game since before many of the detainees were born. As a young enlisted man he served in Vietnam, then moved on to Europe and became a seasoned interrogator working with Soviet and Eastern Bloc defectors and agents. He is on his second tour in Guantánamo.

Rester honed his interrogation skills competing against oil-smooth double-agent graduates of KGB disinformation schools and combat-hardened Soviet generals. In the rare moment that he drops the lecture-room approach and assumes his interrogator role, his eyes penetrate like lasers and his crisp voice commands total attention. In one such session, I broke a sweat during the role-playing. I would not have liked to have met Paul Rester in SERE training.

"[Detainees] would be passed from different agency interrogation team to different agency interrogation team, sometimes a day or two apart," Rester said, commenting on his early days in the newly formed Guantánamo facility. "They would sneer at us and say 'What the hell's the matter with you guys? Don't you talk to each other? I just told the other guys all this information yesterday.' It was a real cluster-fuck operation in those days."[39]

When Rester arrived at Guantánamo in 2002, he thought that the "gloves would be off" in dealing with these captured enemy combatants. He was trying to prepare himself mentally and professionally for how far he was willing to go with these interrogations, orders or no. To his shock, he learned that the rules in Guantánamo were "tighter than what we were allowed to do with a defector or suspected Soviet agent in Germany."

He said that he expected things to be "more flexible" as far as techniques for interrogation were concerned. To his surprise, he recounts, "we were very strictly controlled, very tightly supervised. There were techniques that we used routinely in Europe for years that were even published in the Army field manual,[40] and they were prohibited for use at Guantánamo. It was a much more restrictive environment than anywhere else I've conducted interrogations."[41]

The interrogations performed on Qahtani and a fellow detainee, ISN 170, Sharaf Ahmad Muhammad Marud, have subsequently become a cause for concern among human rights organizations and opponents of the Guantánamo operation. The interrogations of these two men and the resultant FBI memoranda and e-mails sent back to the States were the catalysts that in 2005 brought Illinois senator Dick Durbin and some of his Senate colleagues to the floor decrying activities at the camp. Durbin, and other critics, used the isolated example of Qahtani's interrogation and extrapolated it to be approved U.S. policy. It ought to be noted that Senator Durbin had not then actually set foot in the facilities in Guantánamo.[42]

Qahtani's botched interrogation was primarily a result of what law enforcement officials—including some military officials such as Colonel Brittain P. Mallow, commander of the Defense Department's Criminal Investigation Task Force from 2002 to 2005—saw as immature and undisciplined behavior on the part of some very junior military interrogators. "We're not talking about grievous abuse," he said. "But frankly some of the things my agents saw were just plain silly and stupid. The isolation back at the old Camp X-Ray in fall 2002 was a desperate move to try to get information about the next attack out of Qahtani. Everybody was scared of another 9/11 so they hauled him over there, out of the Navy brig where the FBI had dumped him and ignored him. They duct-taped up the building, subjected him to stress like lack of sleep, loud music, and continual talk. When that didn't work they tried some contrived ego-diminishing actions by having a woman interrogate him. Some of the procedures were not in the book. They were obviously amateurish and not likely to produce good results."[43]

Rester is also angry at the behavior. "It was like a Fort Lewis field training exercise," he snapped. "Once the interrogators-in-training can't figure out what to do they revert to frat-night behavior. It was stupid and ineffective. But it wasn't torture or abuse."[44]

The inability—or unwillingness—of different agency representatives to coordinate or speak with each other contributed to the problems. Interagency Beltway rivalries transplanted and flourished in the tropical climate. Tempers flared, jealousies rose, and little irritations became big ones. There was an ongoing, fierce debate between "competing goals of justice and security in the war on terror." General Geoffrey Miller, commander of the Joint Task Force that brought together the two equal but competing task forces of TF 160 (Detention) and TF 170 (Intelligence), acknowledged that "we were trying to get the intelligence and law enforcement groups to work together, to repair a situation where they were barely speaking."[45]

But there were, as experienced investigator Mark Fallon acknowledged, "almost insurmountable challenges at Guantánamo. Instead of having a crime scene . . . we had suspects. It was very much different from the way you would traditionally work a criminal investigation."[46]

A S A RESULT OF BOTH the Qahtani interrogation and the scandals that erupted at Abu Ghraib, a policy of intense command oversight has been implemented at Guantánamo. A field-grade officer (major or higher) is present in the area at all times. There are no basements or hidden areas for troops to drag detainees into and abuse them. Junior officers and noncommissioned officers are present on the floor 24/7.

When several highly placed elected officials finally toured the Guantánamo facility in early 2003 and discussed the situation in detail with the soldiers, staff, and medical and interrogation personnel, they had to admit that they did not see any instances or indications of even simple abuse, much less torture. Admiral Harry Harris, one of the commanders of the Joint Task Force, later said that "Guantánamo is the most transparent detention facility in the world."[47]

CHAPTER 4

CAMP DELTA'S MISSION

A WORK IN PROGRESS

D ESPITE THE LEGENDS AND STORIES that have grown around Camp X-Ray (including numerous still photos and video that continue to be used by the media), its useful life was quite short. Erected in January 2002, it was closed in April of that year, at which time the detainees were moved to newly constructed Camp Delta.

Work on Camp Delta began almost as soon as the initial load of detainees was brought in from Afghanistan. With contracts let to Kellogg, Brown and Root, a Halliburton subsidiary,[1] construction proceeded quickly. Camp Delta was constructed quite a ways distant from X-Ray, primarily because of the ability to secure a larger area on the far windward side and keep it isolated. Within Camp Delta sub-camps, numbered I through IV in order of fabrication, were built.

Each camp improved on the previous one because of lessons learned and input from all command levels. Construction of the camps is, in a way, a metaphor for the entire facility in that it is a process rather than an event.[2] All along the way, those involved have continually discussed actions, plans, and results, and have been able to make constant improvements and upgrades. Outside consultants from U.S. prison systems were called on for advice along with cultural consultants who could advise on the proper handling of Muslim detainees as far as dietary, religious, linguistic, and cultural requirements were concerned.

Originally the Guantánamo facility was a divided command. For the first 11 months of operation, two special Task Forces, TF 160 and TF 170, each commanded first by a full colonel, then a general officer, were charged with the responsibility of detention and interrogation, respectively. As even armchair analysts will tell you, that is a command structure doomed to fail. Much of the confusion of the early months can be laid at the feet of this unwieldy command relationship compounded by a cat-and-dog group of agencies, all in competition with one another to decide how the installation ought to be run.

Before General Geoff Miller came aboard to unify the two disparate missions, there was a constant struggle between the commanders of the two task forces to determine whose mission took precedence. Partially because the detention mission is the more public and visible, the scales tended to lean that way. It has been so since 2002 and for the most part continues as such today. Because detention is by nature and intent transparent and interrogation the opposite—we don't want the enemy to know which of his secrets we have learned—the command almost reflexively leans toward giving higher priority to detention.

Miller was forced to clean up the detention side because of the hurricane of rumor that swept Guantánamo. He said that "detention sets the stage for interrogation," recognizing the duality of his mission. His point was that a well-run, organized, and humane detention operation facilitates the primary mission. Others, like Steve Rodriguez, former head of the Joint Interrogation Group, agree. "The primary mission ought to be interrogation and intelligence gathering," he said. "That's how it started out, but over the years emphasis has been drifting to the detention side."[3]

From the start of his tenure in November 2002, Geoff Miller tried to run a quiet, orderly camp while permitting interrogators to do their jobs. Unfortunately for Miller, he ran into the buzz saw of Abu Ghraib. Once the lurid Abu Ghraib photos hit the press, the assumption was that worse things were happening at Gitmo.[4] By that time, Miller had put order into the chaotic early days of the Guantánamo facility to the point that much of the internal, interagency conflict was markedly reduced and product began to flow more freely. He instituted "Tiger Teams" that were combinations of interrogators—usually from multiple agencies—cultural and linguistic experts, and analysts. Suddenly the installation began to function with a discipline and efficiency that had been missing earlier.[5]

Miller was dispatched to Iraq in August 2003 to coach the commanders of several prisons, including Abu Ghraib, on how to run such a place humanely, efficiently, and transparently. But others did not see it that way. "Critics allege he was sent to 'Gitmo-ize' the Iraqi prison," *Salon* writers said.[6] Seymour Hersh wrote in the *New Yorker* that Miller "had been summoned to Baghdad in late August [2003] to review prison interrogation procedures." Hersh recognized that Miller emphasized interrogation as the reason to hold detainees and quoted a later military report, written by Army Major General Antonio Taguba, that Miller "recommended that detention operations must act as an enabler for interrogation."[7] Hersh puts a negative spin on this, claiming that it dwelt primarily on "special interrogation methods" including sleep deprivation, "stress positions" (the scare quotes are Hersh's), and other approved methods certified by the Office of the Secretary of Defense that he and others consider torture and abuse, with the strong implication that these had been used as common practice at Guantánamo.[8]

Others closer to the facts dispute this interpretation of Miller's assignment to Iraq. "General Miller didn't go to Iraq to train them to torture anybody," Paul Rester said. "He went to try to straighten up what had turned into a huge mess."[9] Either he was too late or they didn't listen. Unfortunately for Geoff Miller's reputation, the political opponents of Guantánamo assumed—consciously or not—the polar opposite: that Miller had been dispatched to Iraq to teach torture and abuse. For example, the *Washington Post* reported that Miller "promoted the use of guard dogs" at Guantánamo to frighten detainees and "soften them up" for interrogation, and that he carried with him this and other "special" techniques as part of his mission in Iraq.[10]

Nonsense, Steve Rodriguez said: "The Abu Ghraib situation was about abuse not interrogation. That was impossible at Guantánamo. It was far too open; there were no hidden basements, no old, medieval prisons to hide in." Everything was new construction and the standard operating procedures were built upon solid checks and balances. "In Guantánamo everyone was on the alert and reported any possible infraction. The staff judge advocate constantly was on the lookout for torture or abuse. Every allegation of abuse—especially one from a detainee—was investigated and checked and then checked again. Even in the case of the Qahtani interrogation complaints were filed and investigations made." "This was the most inspected, investigated post in history," Jay Hood said, with a pride that might surprise an outsider.

"General Miller caught on quickly after he got to Guantánamo," Paul Rester said. "He systematized the process. He got the military police out of setting the conditions for interrogation, imposed discipline, had things under control. He required the equivalent of a major or above and senior non-commissioned officer on the floors of the blocks at all times, and restricted the use of military working dogs." Dogs were a big issue in the accusations against Miller. "Military working dogs were present on the airport tarmac when detainees arrived, but were not used in interrogations period. When Muhammad al Qahtani (ISN 063) was undergoing special interrogation there were dogs at the Camp X-Ray compound but they were used only for control and to prevent possible escape, not in interrogation."[11] Later investigations of alleged torture and abuse during this time bear out Rester's observations.

By the time General Hood came to take command from outgoing General Miller in March 2004, the international furor over U.S. detention facilities was beginning to break wide open. Congressional Democrats, European activists, human rights advocates, much of the media, and agenda-driven domestic groups were screaming for Miller's head. "It's just a steppingstone going up the chain of command," Center for Constitutional Rights president Michael Ratner claimed.[12] Miller accepted early retirement and is still facing threat of lawsuits, civil actions, and yet another military investigation even though he has been thoroughly cleared of all accusations of wrongdoing. It is unfortunate, for those who are aware of the work he did admire him greatly.

"General Miller came into a very difficult situation," commented Vincent Brooks, the Army brigadier general who headed the Joint Chiefs of Staff Western Hemisphere Division. "He was action-oriented, didn't brook fools, and pressed unity of command. Miller created a multidisciplinary team that focused on the interrogation mission. He made Guantánamo a world-class interrogation facility."[13]

While that may have been true, when Hood took over he certainly did not have to fight too many contenders for the job. Flying down to Guantánamo, he must have wondered if the Army had sent him to a career-killing position. But to Hood's credit, he never publicly showed any doubt.

Jay Hood was a one-star brigadier general officer in his early fifties (at the time of this writing, Hood has been promoted to major general). He began his career as a field artillery officer and came to the Joint Task Force–Guantánamo fresh from plum duty as assistant division commander of the 24th Infantry Division at Fort Stewart, Georgia. He knew full well that the career of his predecessor, General Miller, had been sacrificed on the altar of political correctness.[14] Pressuring Miller into early retirement may have been a move designed to appease anti-Guantánamo politicians and a hostile media (he nonetheless received the Distinguished Service Medal after more than 34 years of service[15]). If that was the purpose, it didn't work. He remains incommunicado today, on advice of counsel, waiting possible civil suit from activist groups.

Meanwhile, every time Hood returned to the States to testify or had to deal with congressional delegations and media at the naval base he was put under the microscope and subjected to a firestorm of media criticism. Sometimes congressional members treated him with open contempt and hostility. Through it all Hood retained a polite, cool demeanor. Everyone he speaks to, regardless of rank or position, is either "Sir" or "Ma'am." He keeps his face a mask of inscrutability.

Hood was positive, focused, committed to the mission, and determined that there would be absolutely no abuse or torture, or even an unpleasant episode that would mar his command. Just one week after he got to the island, "a huge spotlight swung" from Abu Ghraib to Guantánamo.[16] Hood knew that he was a target, and though he always acknowledged the need for and importance of interrogation, he understood that the way he ran detention would make or break his tenure. "No detainee will be permitted to die on my watch!" was his daily mantra.

When Jay Hood took over at JTF GTMO he had the benefit of a fairly-well-functioning detention/interrogation system already in place. Not that his job was a simple one by any means. Competing agencies still demanded interrogation booth time with detainees and continued to bite each others' ankles. Congressional and media visits were avalanching down upon him. All came with an agenda. Meanwhile, the national command authority kept pressure up for both humane treatment and actionable intelligence production.

By no means were the detainees complacent during this period. "If I ever get the opportunity I will capture several Americans. I will sever their heads off," an Afghani detainee told his interrogator. Guards on the blocks were under constant stress. "When I tell my brothers who you are they will find your family in America, rape and kill your mother and sisters, and kill your brothers and father," the same detainee threatened.[17]

These men were fairly typical. In Paul Rester's words, they were "hardened, non-responsive to interrogation, and extremely dangerous." The interrogation staff, Rester said, was "under increasing pressure from the FBI, the Department of Justice, and the various concerned city police forces—primarily in Washington, DC, Northern Virginia, and New York—to build criminal cases against particular detainees, while the Defense Intelligence Agency and CIA wanted something they could use against al Qaeda operators in the field."[18]

Nor were things calm and quiet even within Hood's JTF staff. In 2005, reports broke of a blistering sexual abuse scandal—primarily involving adultery charges against the military police colonel who was in charge of the detention facility, his deputy who was an Army lieutenant colonel, and another lieutenant colonel who was in command of the security force.[19] Also involved were several female contractors and a female Navy junior officer. The senior male officers were married, and the sexual conduct—whether consensual or not—was considered at best inappropriate and at worse a violation of the Uniform Code of Military Justice. The incident quickly resulted in relief from duty of all three senior officers in charge of the detention and security side of the organization.[20] Brought in to replace the fired colonel in April 2005 was MP Colonel Michael Bumgarner, and for his deputy, Navy Commander (later promoted to Captain) Catie Hanft.

Bumgarner was not a traditional commander. He is a large man in every regard. In his office, bronze busts of two presidents—Theodore Roosevelt and Ronald Reagan—sat on top of a crowded bookshelf. A career military policeman, Bumgarner looked like his mere presence would stop a bar fight in any GI gin mill. But after listening to him, one suspects that he would be able to talk the combatants out of the fight by mere force of personality. For starters, he relocated his headquarters *inside* the wire. He and his executive officer, operations officer, and intelligence analysts (the latter are part of the JDG staff and separate from the Joint Intelligence Group staff) were within 25 yards or less of the detainees they supervised and guarded.

"I'm closer to the action here," Bumgarner said. "Within minutes I can stroll out there and see for myself what is happening. And I do that frequently. My officers, NCOs, and troops know that me or one of my people will pop in on them unannounced. It makes for good discipline and morale. We're right here along with them."

It may have been possible to find people on Bumgarner's staff smarter than he, but it would be difficult to find any with more energy. He was on top of all situations, anticipating many, and pushed his people to meet the extraordinarily high standards that he set for them— and for himself. "I will take anyone anywhere in any of the camps, anytime, 24/7, with no notice," Bumgarner said with confidence. "There's nothing here that I'm not proud of."[21]

Bumgarner became the man on the ground who interpreted and implemented Hood's orders, directives, and suggestions. Both men wanted a peaceful, humane detention center with no detainee suicides, and no unpleasant incidents for media and other critics to pounce on. Hood told him to keep the detainees and guards safe, prevent escapes, and consider how Guantánamo could be moved more in line with the Geneva protocols.

Halfway through his one-year tour, Bumgarner himself was convinced. "These people are without a doubt the worst of the worst," he said, referring especially to about 10 percent of the detainee population. "These are the really, really bad guys. The ones who have killed Americans and non-Wahabbist Muslims before, the ones who stoned women to death who refused to wear the veil, the ones who plotted to use weapons of mass destruction on the West. Just overall bad actors."[22]

During its several years in operation, the Guantánamo staff has been forced to spend a lot of hours reinventing the wheel. Since a combination interrogation/detention facility of this nature had never been required, a lot of fresh ground had to be plowed. Bumgarner and his people profited from the lessons learned by their predecessors and continued the pioneering tradition. His successor, Army Colonel Wade Dennis, readily acknowledged the work Bumgarner did. "It was an extraordinarily difficult job that he handled professionally and to the best of his ability," Dennis said. "And we're building upon it."[23]

By 2005 it had become widely recognized that for Guantánamo, there was no obvious termination point. If these men were so dangerous that they couldn't be released outright, then what was going to happen to them? With long-term confinement seeming to be a certainty, Bumgarner, encouraged by Hood, embarked on a months-long project to try to involve some of the detainee leaders in the management of the camp. He established relationships with two self-styled camp leaders, Saudi-born, London-raised Shakir Abdurahim Muhammad Ami, ISN 239 (nicknamed The Professor), and Ghassan Abdallah Ghazi al Shirbi, ISN 682, another Saudi (nicknamed The General).

Both men spoke fluent English, had much experience with foreigners, and by intelligence accounts were serious al Qaeda players. There is speculation that Shakir Ami may have embellished his standing within the detainee community by virtue of his English language capability.

Americans are always suckers for any foreigner who speaks good English, often mistakenly using a linguistic-capability yardstick to measure trust and intelligence.[24] Soon Bumgarner was meeting frequently with both men and encouraging them to provide him with suggestions for improving life in the camps. Bumgarner said that he "tried to deal with the detainees on a man-to-man basis." He often said that if he could just talk with someone freely he could usually "arrive at an accommodation."[25]

"I worked real close with Ghassan," Bumgarner wrote. "He helped me a lot in keeping calm in the camps. But he always made it clear, if he had the chance he would kill me. He was the second most powerful fish in the camps."[26]

Along with Shakir Ami and Ghassan al Sharbi, Bumgarner brought a Moroccan, ISN 590, Ahmed Rashidi, into the mix. Rashidi complained about several things. He said the drinking water tasted bad, so Bumgarner convinced Hood to authorize the issuing of bottled water to the detainees at meals. (The bottles were produced by manufacturers who used red, white, and blue stars-and-stripes logos on their labels. In order not to "offend" the detainees, guards had to scrape the labels off before giving them the water.) Rashidi also wanted the guards to cease referring to detainees as "packages" when they moved them about. Troops would say, "We've got a package for the hospital," for example. "We are not 'packages,' we are human beings," Rashidi insisted. Bumgarner agreed and directed his troops to modify their language.

Meanwhile, over at the Joint Intelligence Group, tempers were rising in frustration. One interrogator recalls having "my entire dependency program tossed out," something he had been working on with a particularly recalcitrant detainee for months. Dependency is an approved interrogation method during which the interrogator makes himself the source of all good things that happen to the detainee. By looking to the interrogator to bring him additional goodies he then will talk more freely, correctly expecting a reward. But for this stratagem to be effective, everything good has to originate with the interrogator. Bumgarner's reforms knocked that approach off the rails.

"The detention people gave him stuff that I had been holding out," the interrogator said, "offering in exchange for information. He got it all and more from them just for not assaulting the guards. What did he need me for at that point?"[27]

Bumgarner dismissed such complaints, stating that he "ran the camp." But what deal did he make with the detainee leaders? "I was looking for a way, with what General Hood was wanting, just to have a peaceful camp," he told *The New York Times*' Tim Golden.[28] To Shakir he made major concessions, saying, "Just don't hurt my guards. I want you to tell your people to leave my people alone."[29]

The precedent of detention calling the shots for the camps and leaving interrogation out in the cold had been there since inception, but solidified into policy under Hood and Bumgarner. The detention side now determined how detainees would be handled and treated, what perquisites they would receive, and what limited freedoms they would enjoy. Such a policy seemed to be a good idea, but how would it stand up when organized cells of detainees decided to test it?

CHAPTER 5

MEET THE "FOREIGN FIGHTERS"

"I think it would be imprudent of us to let down our guard believing that if there's no credible threat that you know of today, there won't be something tomorrow."
U.S. AIR FORCE GENERAL GENE RENUART

E VERY DETAINEE SENT TO GUANTÁNAMO has undergone a thorough screening process. Each detainee continues to undergo what former Deputy Assistant Secretary of Defense Matthew Waxman called "the extraordinary step during an ongoing war of . . . individual review processes."[1] These occur annually at a minimum and provide the detainee the opportunity to discuss his particular situation with a reviewing authority.

As a consequence of these extensive review processes—despite the persistent myth that the detainees have no legal recourse—the U.S. government has identified approximately 450 detainees who were transferred out of Guantánamo. Some have been released outright; more have been turned over to the custody of their home governments. There also exists a small pool of detainees still held at Gitmo because their home countries may execute or torture them if they are transferred.[2]

Throughout the process, Secretary Rumsfeld adamantly insisted that only those who are believed to be the worst terrorists be evacuated to Gitmo. He ordered strict screening procedures put in place to make certain that any captured fighters meet the criteria warranting evacuation and confinement in a high-security facility. It is not a default process. That is, evacuation for a terrorist is not automatically assumed by American field force commanders; just the opposite. Evacuation is a needs-driven process.

It must be strongly demonstrated that a particular individual merits in-depth interrogation, extra-secure confinement, or both. Hard questions are asked: Is there good and sufficient reason to think that by his possible position, access, or relationships he has high-value intelligence information? Do we consider him a high-level security threat? Has he confessed to being a bomb-maker, financier, ideologue, or possible martyr? Any of these reasons could be sufficient to get him a ride to Guantánamo.

All levels of command become involved and the ultimate recommendation from the field has to be approved by the Central Command commander, a four-star general officer. Recommendations then percolate up through parallel chains of command and are reviewed through the Joint Chiefs of Staff process and ultimately at the policy level by the Deputy Secretary of Defense acting for the Secretary.[3]

Among the tens of thousands of fighters captured on the battlefield, undoubtedly a majority were pawns of the Taliban or al Qaeda. There are peasants or low-level workers who were forced to join the fight, or who may have been vulnerable to peer pressure or a bandwagon effect. That's precisely why so many of them have been screened and released. But the United States government believes that many of those men who made the flight to Cuba are a far cry from the innocent taxi drivers, farmers, and bystanders they often claim to be. Al Qaeda terrorists are taught to assume these innocuous professions as a cover during interrogation.[4]

Some of the detainees were good enough to have successfully fooled professional interrogators and have been released. How do we know? It's empirical: The same thugs turn up dead in combat against

American GIs, or Coalition forces recapture them on the battlefield, or intelligence analysts see them in homemade terror videos. Their stories constitute the best evidence that the military regime at Guantánamo is not nearly as harsh and impenetrable as is frequently alleged. If anything, they suggest that the interrogation and review process leans too far in the other direction.

Thus I learned from Paul Rester that one former detainee killed an Afghan judge coming out of a mosque. Another was recaptured in Afghanistan after he fired on U.S. troops. He carried a letter of introduction on his person—from the Taliban.[5] Two more were killed in the summer of 2004 in Afghanistan engaged in combat operations.[6] Another, Abdullah Muhammad, an Afghani, was fitted with a state-of-the-art prosthesis for his lost leg while at Guantánamo. He convinced the annual review board that he "wasn't a terrorist fanatic" and was sent back to Afghanistan. According to author Jeff Babbin, he's "sought for involvement in the kidnapping of Chinese engineers and a bombing of the Islamabad Marriott, [and] is walking around on the artificial leg we evil Americans paid for."[7]

Slimane Hadj Abderrahmane, released after signing an oath to renounce violence, later told Danish reporters that he was heading to the fight in Chechnya, and that he considered the oath "toilet paper."[8] Transferred to Kuwait in 2005, Abdallah Salih al Ajmi infiltrated into Iraq through Syria four years later and, with two accomplices, killed seven people in Mosul by suicide bombing.[9] Abdul Rahman Noor, released in July 2003, participated in fighting against U.S. forces near Kandahar[10] and was identified as the man described in an October 7, 2001 interview with Al Jazeera television network as the "deputy defense minister of the Taliban."[11] Two Moroccans, Ibrahim bin Shakaran and Muhammad bin Ahmad Mizouz, were convicted in local courts after their release for recruiting fighters to join Abu Musab al Zarqawi's al Qaeda in Iraq.[12]

The list continues. Two Russians, Ravil Shafeyavich Gumarov and Timur Ravilich Ishmurat, were convicted, post-release, of a gas pipeline bombing.[13] Maulvi Abdul Ghaffar became a top regional Taliban leader after his release. His forces killed a UN engineer and two Afghani soldiers.

He was later killed by Afghan security forces.[14] Muhammad Ismail Agha, one of the few teenagers ever detained at Guantánamo, told the media upon release that "they gave me a good time in Cuba. They were very nice to me, giving me English lessons." When he was recaptured by U.S. forces during an attack near Kandahar, he carried a letter confirming his good standing as a Taliban member.

On July 24, 2007, Al Jazeera reported that a "leading pro-Taliban tribesman" had killed himself by detonating a hand grenade when Pakistani forces closed in on him. It turned out that Abdullah Mahsud, who was referred to as a "Taliban commander" in the headline, was a former Guantánamo detainee. He had spent 25 months in the prison until being released as no longer a threat or not possessing sufficient intelligence information to warrant continued detention.[15]

Mahsud had been captured in Afghanistan fighting alongside the Taliban in 2002. He was carrying a false Afghan identity card, and later said that while in Guantánamo he insisted that he was an innocent Afghan tribesman, although in fact he was a Pakistani with deep ties to militants. "I managed to keep my Pakistani identity hidden all these years," he told *Gulf News*. In another interview he stated, "We would fight America and its allies, until the very end."[16]

Mahsud, who was released from Guantánamo in March 2004, went on to kidnap two Chinese engineers who were working on a hydroelectric project designed to improve Afghanistan's long-neglected infrastructure. One of the engineers was killed in a rescue attempt by the Pakistanis. Keeping things in the family, Mahsud's brother, Baitullah, is reported to be a Taliban commander in the Waziristan area of the Afghan–Pakistan border region who is linked to dispatch of suicide bombers.[17] Mahsud blew himself up in the spring of 2007 to avoid being captured by Pakistani authorities.[18]

Gitmo has also produced a few celebrity alumni. Perhaps most prominent is Moazzam Begg, formerly ISN 558, captured in Islamabad, Pakistan in February 2002. Begg was held first at a detention center in Kandahar, then at Bagram for more than a year before being evacuated to Guantánamo. While at Kandahar, Begg told ABC News that he had seen numerous cases of torture and said, "I think the reality is that it would have proved beyond doubt that they were involved in interrogation techniques that are far from just robust, but actually moved into the realms of torture."[19]

At Bagram, Begg reportedly signed a statement before FBI interrogators in which he admitted that among other actions he had trained at three al Qaeda camps, and "was armed and prepared to fight alongside the Taliban and al Qaeda against the US and others. He had retreated to Tora Bora with Osama bin Laden and other al Qaeda fighters, finally making his way back to Islamabad where his family lived in a rental house."[20]

Prior to relocating from the United Kingdom to Afghanistan in August 2001 (he said he saw it as a fine, inexpensive place to raise a family),[21] Begg had been arrested several times for suspicious activities linking him to radical Islam. He had traveled on at least six occasions to Bosnia and Herzegovina, ostensibly to deliver aid supplies. Begg told the FBI that he "felt that jihad was an appropriate way to deal with those who harmed Muslims."[22] Since his 2005 release, Begg has denied all statements made previously, claiming that they were coerced through torture, and that "torture only generates lies."[23] Since his return to the United Kingdom, Begg has become a popular lecturer and media figure. In 2006 he was named one of the Top 100 Males by *GQ* magazine. Along with activist attorney Clive Stafford Smith, Begg is one of the founders and fundraisers for the organization Cage Prisoners, a UK–registered nonprofit that has as its mission "solely to raise awareness of the plight of the prisoners at Guantánamo Bay and other detainees held as part of the War on Terror."[24]

Begg has written a book, *Enemy Combatant: My Imprisonment at Guantánamo,* in which he cloaks himself with innocence and makes the claim, among others, that the reason he moved his family to Kabul, Afghanistan was in order to open up a school. As a UK reviewer noted, "Mr. Begg insists he had no interest in Islamic terrorism, and that he went to Kabul merely because he wanted to do charitable work. He does not come across as either naive or a total idiot. But in that case: what the hell was he doing in Afghanistan in August 2001?"[25]

All major U.S. security organizations—the DOD, FBI, and

CIA—continue to say that Begg was a committed terrorist and active supporter of terrorist organizations. His release by the personal intervention of President Bush, a decision that overruled all three agency recommendations that he be detained, was done, many think, as a political palliative to his friend and war supporter British prime minister Tony Blair, who was under much criticism at the time for not demanding immediate release of all British citizens held at Guantánamo.[26]

Interrogators at Guantánamo told me that Begg in their opinion is a hardened terrorist who has used the opportunity of release to enter the public information forum in a big way. "He is doing more good for al Qaeda as a British poster boy than he would ever do carrying an AK-47," Paul Rester said.[27] Meanwhile in the United Kingdom, some of the more politically active crowd, such as actress Vanessa Redgrave, have vigorously supported the proposition that Begg stand for election to Parliament.[28]

These recidivist detainees were the ones screened and considered to fall in the "no threat" category. Obviously they had been trained well enough and were sufficiently disciplined to maintain their cover, or at worst, fall back on the "cover-within-the-cover" technique that is taught to al Qaeda fighters. Let's say you claim that you were a simple peasant, an opium farmer forced by the Taliban to bear arms against the American-supported Northern Alliance forces. Then suppose the interrogator discovers sufficient holes in your story—perhaps a conflict in names, places, or dates—that it raises suspicion. You can then fall back on the cover-within-the-cover technique.

"Okay," you might say, "I really am not a farmer. I was a student in Yemen (or Saudi Arabia, or Dubai) who was inflamed by the teachings of Osama bin Laden. But I have since recognized the error of my ways and am recanting." Sometimes these stories are sufficiently convincing to seem to warrant release. It has happened, and even the most skilled interrogators get fooled. Interrogation is an art, not a science.

That said, the growth of the facility at Guantánamo as a combination interrogation/detention facility unlike any ever constructed, has uncovered sufficiently chilling stories from the captured terrorist detainees to warrant serious concern for the consequences if they are released. Many of those stories are included here, most for the first time.

It should be noted, however, that the stories told here are drawn from U.S. government charge sheets and their particulars have not been verified in court proceedings. With the exception of David Hicks and Salim Ahmed Hamdan, none of these men has yet been found guilty of the crimes with which he is charged. Nevertheless, I think it is legitimate to report what the government alleges pending final resolution of their cases.

The Money Man

Many of the terrorists captured in Afghanistan were relative newcomers to al Qaeda. Others had long records of terrorist activity. The majority were probably in their mid-to-late twenties and had been recruited after the embarrassing American retreat from Somalia. After the firefight with "General" Muhammad Farrah Aidid's street thugs that resulted in 18 American Delta Force and Ranger deaths, bin Laden proclaimed that "the American soldier is a paper tiger" and could not stand a fight.[29]

According to the soldiers who captured him, one Sudanese fighter whose status grew after Mogadishu was Ibrahim Ahmed Mahmoud al Qosi. They believe Qosi joined bin Laden in June 1989 in Sudan and worked for al Qaeda there and in Ethiopia, Yemen, Pakistan, Afghanistan, and other countries. His initial charge sheet lists offenses such as "attacking civilians, . . . murder . . . , and terrorism."[30]

Qosi is alleged to have begun his terrorist career in a manner similar to that of most recruits, by carrying out prosaic support duties. His charge sheet states that he "passed information between members of terrorist cells . . . and provided logistical support such as food, shelter and clothing for members of the terrorist cells."[31] Sources show that he was sent the following year to Afghanistan for training, using funds provided by al Qaeda.[32] The Office for the Administrative Review of the Detention of Enemy Combatants noted that he admitted to traveling from Sudan to Afghanistan to train for and fight the jihad in 1990.[33] He then reportedly trained for several months in Afghanistan at al Qaeda's rugged al Farouk camp, receiving instruction on the use of the "Makarov 9mm pistol, Seminov, AK-47, AKSU-74, RPG-7, RGD-5 Offensive Hand Grenade, F-1 Antipersonnel Grenade, and M-43 120mm Mortar."[34] He was then deployed to the mujahedin front line in Afghanistan, according to the summary of evidence submitted during his combatant status review.[35]

By September 1991 his financial skills were recognized (Qosi was a trained accountant) and he moved to Peshawar, Pakistan to assume accounting duties in what is known as *Mdktabh al Muhassiba*, the al Qaeda accounting office. At that time, Sheik Sayeed al Masri was chief financial officer and headed al Qaeda's finance committee. Other al Qaeda committees, according to the U.S. government indictment, include political, military, security, media, and religious/legal.[36]

Charge sheets indicate that in his new Peshawar office, Qosi was appointed deputy chief financial officer to al Masri. Most interestingly, they go on to allege that Qosi was placed in charge of "managing *donated* money from *non-governmental and charitable organizations* and distributing it for salaries, travel, and support of al Qaeda members, training camps, operations, and other expenses."[37]

It seems reasonable to assume that in this position Qosi would have had access to the mysterious Money Camps, the super-luxurious, transitory camps that appear in one remote Central Asian/Middle Eastern location, then evaporate to crystallize somewhere else. At these camps, Gulf and Saudi sheiks indulged in traditional Arab sports such as falconry and shooting while al Qaeda representatives collected vast sums of cash and financial transfers to fund The Base's global operations.[38]

It is unusual to see a non-Arab admitted into this highly secretive society, and as such it would be a demonstrable act of trust. Further, anyone in this deputy CFO role would be intimately aware of the "charitable" contributions coming regularly from the Wahabbist mosques and radical Islamic organizations set up around the world, including inside America and the United Kingdom.

Bin Laden moved Qosi back to Sudan in 1992 to help establish and run a major al Qaeda front, known as Taba Investment Company. Taba was one of several businesses designed to provide income for al Qaeda training and operations. It provided a legitimate cover for procurement of otherwise illegal items: weapons, explosives, chemicals, and sensitive electronic devices. The government alleges that in addition to his normal duties at Taba, Qosi reportedly became a money courier and worked black market exchanges. They also believe he couriered weapons, ammunition, and explosives within Sudan and to other countries.[39]

In 1994, after a failed assassination attempt on the emir himself from unknown rivals, bin Laden personally selected Qosi to join his newly formed bodyguards. Though the time line gets a bit fuzzy, Qosi had asked bin Laden's permission to authorize and finance a trip for him to Chechnya to fight alongside the Islamic militant forces there. Following his Chechnya experience, in 1996 Qosi made his way to the Tora Bora mountains in Afghanistan to meet bin Laden.

For the next several years, I believe he worked closely with bin Laden and top al Qaeda leadership, assisting in successive headquarters moves first to the "Star of Jihad" compound in Jalalabad, then to the more permanent site in Kandahar. If these allegations are correct, it would seem that in this time Qosi became a bin Laden favorite, accompanying him as armed bodyguard and driver on the emir's many excursions to training camps and meetings. He also procured supplies and cooked for the bodyguard detachment.[40]

One of the favorite forms of assassination in Arab tradition is poison. Anyone who handles food has to be one of the most trusted members of the entourage, and Qosi clearly had achieved that status.

Allegedly, bin Laden alerted Qosi that the September 11 attacks were imminent. When war began, Qosi is thought to have moved several times with bin Laden until he was captured. Qosi is thus a huge catch and potentially a major source of information on al Qaeda's finances, tactics, operations, and, maybe more important, the thought processes and behavior of Osama bin Laden.

In February 2008, Qosi became one of two Guantánamo inmates

to face trial through the first U.S. military tribunals convened since World War II.[41] Defiant, he refused to meet with his attorney, said he didn't want a lawyer, and vowed to boycott the court proceedings.[42] Speaking in Arabic through a translator, Qosi praised the September 11 attacks as a success for bin Laden, saying the terrorist leader "succeeded again enormously in exposing your hypocrisy."[43]

Qosi, whose trial is continuing as of this writing, has nonetheless pled innocent. Another foreign fighter, David Hicks, instead chose to plead guilty to providing material support for terrorism and attempted murder in violation of the law of war.

The Road from Oz

Perhaps a good shrink can explain why the concept of a traitor or turncoat is so repugnant. All we know is that traitors seem to trigger deep antithetical emotions. Such was David Matthew Hicks: Australian by birth, originally Christian by religion, and Muslim terrorist by choice.

Hicks, like other turncoats such as John Walker Lindh, uses Arabic aliases. His primary *nom de guerre* is Abu Muslim al Austraili. He also is known among his al Qaeda colleagues as Muhammad Dawood.

David Hicks was born in 1975 in Adelaide,[44] a pleasant southern Australian city facing the Tasman Sea. His father, Terry Hicks, described young David as "adventurous," and said, "We call him Indiana Jones, that's his nickname . . . I've always said he should have been born a few centuries ago with a sword in his hand."[45] At age 24, Hicks headed for the Balkans, abandoning a girlfriend and two small children.[46] In or about May 1999, he joined the Kosovo Liberation Army and reportedly "engaged in hostile action" shortly after arrival in Tirana, Albania.[47] Terry Hicks later recalled that when his son called to say he was joining the KLA, "I thought it was an airline."[48]

In fact, the KLA was one of the horrid Balkan paramilitary organizations[49]—little more than a guise for banditry, rape, and kidnappings—and fought on the side of the Albanian Muslims against the Serbs. Hicks had basic military training and may have participated in combat operations while there, but the war was nearing a truce phase. After fighting less than a year he returned to Australia, publicly converted to Islam, and began to study Arabic.[50]

In November 1999 he went to Pakistan and became a member of a group known as the Army of the Righteous, or the Lashkar-e-Tayyiba (LET).[51] This was an armed part of a primarily anti-Indian terror group formed by Hafiz Muhammad Saeed, a former professor of engineering at the University of Punjab. Saeed is known regionally as "the uncrowned terror king" who claims that "killing is a pious man's obligation: it is his duty 'to destroy the forces of evil and disbelief.' "[52]

While the LET has as its primarily military objective a Muslim seizure of Indian-controlled Kashmir, it spreads a big tent when it comes to defining its enemies. As the government charge sheet explains, "LET's known goals include violent attacks against property and nationals (both military and civilian) of India . . . and violent opposition of Hindus, Jews, Americans and other Westerners."[53] A year prior to Hicks's joining LET, Professor Saeed called for a holy war against the United States. Supposedly he initiated this call for jihad after a 1998 U.S. Tomahawk missile strike killed some LET operatives who were training at the al Qaeda terrorist camp of Khowst in Afghanistan.[54]

Hicks's beliefs around this period were partially revealed in a letter he wrote to his mother, Sue King, in 2000: "The western society is controlled by the Jews . . . [it] keeps Islam weak and in the Third World."[55] After a two-month training period at the LET's Mosqua Aqsa training camp in Pakistan, Hicks left to participate in hostile anti-Indian actions for the LET in Kashmir.[56]

An older charge sheet on Hicks filed in 2004 provided the additional allegation that it was sometime in January 2001 when Hicks, carrying a letter of introduction to Ibn al Shayk al Libi, a senior al Qaeda leader, and with funds provided by the LET, headed to Afghanistan to attend al Qaeda training there.[57] For clarity, references to events and related information from the 2004 charge sheets that were not repeated in the 2007 charges that Hicks pled guilty to will be presented in italics.

Libi was a tough, experienced, longtime senior al Qaeda trainer who later admitted to the CIA that he ran the camp at al Khaldan[58] (he recanted this confession some years later, however[59]). This was the same facility where Zacarias Moussaoui,[60] Ahmed Ressam (who planned to bomb Los Angeles International Airport on New Year's Day 2000), Muhammad al 'Owhali (convicted of bombing the U.S. Embassy in Kenya in 1998),[61] and others of particular note were trained. Libi was close to Abu Zubaydah[62] and has ranked high on U.S. government terrorist lists post–9/11. He was captured by Pakistani authorities on November 11, 2001 and turned over to American CIA officials. When questioned, he affirmed a strong link between al Qaeda and Saddam Hussein, but later recanted his original testimony.[63]

Although the sets of charges Hicks pled guilty to in 2007 did not mention Libi, they did agree that he attended al Qaeda training camps in January 2001.[64]

U.S. authorities charged that at an al Qaeda safe house, Hicks met Libi and gave him his passport. He was then given the pseudonym "Muhammad Dawood."[65] Charges filed against him in 2007 allege that he also met Richard Reid, Feroz Abassi, and other members of al Qaeda at a guest house,[66] although references to Reid were ultimately withdrawn as part of Hicks's plea bargain.[67] Dawood/Hicks then traveled to the infamous al Farouk camp outside Kandahar. Although already fairly well trained, Hicks underwent the standard al Qaeda basic weapons, explosives, and terrorist tactics course for eight weeks,[68] honing and adding to his physical fitness and terrorist skills.

By spring of that year Hicks, having served in the field, returned for advanced seven-week training programs at al Farouk that included "marksmanship, small team tactics, ambush, camouflage, rendezvous techniques, and techniques to pass intelligence to al Qaeda operatives."[69] He met Osama bin Laden on several occasions, and discussed the lack of English-language training materials with him.[70] (*The 2004 charge sheets further noted that Hicks took on the assignment to translate much of the training material from Arabic to English.[71]* In addition, as a technical matter during his trial, Hicks had the record changed to state that he had only asked bin Laden about the lack of English materials, not expressed concern about it.[72]) Presumably al Qaeda was preparing a major recruiting campaign in America and the West.

Apparently, Hicks did well in training and impressed al Qaeda military commander Muhammad Atef and his deputy, Saif al Adel. After interviewing Dawood/Hicks in June 2001, they had him sent to Tarnak Farm to attend a special urban warfare training program.[73] This is the location that is often shown on B-roll file videotape, copied from al Qaeda training film captured during Operation Enduring Freedom, in which masked al Qaeda fighters storm buildings, fire AK-47s wildly, negotiate obstacles, rappel down walls, and otherwise prepare for urban combat. Here, Dawood/Hicks learned marksmanship, use of assault and sniper rifles, rappelling, and kidnapping and assassination techniques.[74]

In letters to his family, Hicks explained that training with terrorist organizations was designed to ensure "the Western-Jewish domination is finished" and warned his father to ignore "the Jews' propaganda war machine."[75]

Two months after finishing the course at Tarnak Farms, in August 2001, Hicks was sent to an intelligence collection and surveillance program in Kabul in which he and his fellows trained by spying on the British and American embassies, among other targets. The surveillance program has been described as including use of disguises, drawing diagrams depicting embassy windows and doors, covert photography, and "submitting reports to the al Qaeda instructor who cited the al Qaeda bombing of the *USS Cole* as a positive example of the uses for their training."[76] The government also claimed that Richard Reid visited the same surveillance course on two occasions; after Hicks completed the training, he apparently attended a class taught by Reid at the Kandahar airport on the meaning of jihad.[77] However, this specific charge was dropped when Hicks pled guilty in March 2007.[78]

On a trip to Pakistan to visit a friend in September 2001, Hicks expressed his approval after watching television reports of the attacks on America[79] (during his trial, Hicks asked for the formal record to be changed to read that "his friend interpreted his gestures to be approving" of the attacks; the charges were also revised to note that he did not have personal knowledge of the attacks in advance[80]). He quickly returned to Afghanistan the next day and heard reports that the attacks had been carried out by al Qaeda.[81]

Saif al Adel, then al Qaeda's deputy military commander and head of the security committee for al Qaeda's *shurt* council, gave Hicks the choice of fighting in one of three different locations: city, mountains, or airport.[82] Hicks volunteered to fight against American and Coalition forces with a group of al Qaeda fighters near the Kandahar airport. He was issued an Avtomat Kalashnikova 1947 (AK-47) automatic rifle.[83] Hicks also armed himself with 300 rounds of ammunition, six ammunition magazines, and three grenades.[84]

He had been at the Kandahar airport for two weeks when Coalition forces began bombing the complex on October 7.[85] After two nights of enduring the bombing attacks, Hicks was reassigned to guarding a tank with an armed group outside the airport. He received food and daily updates on what was happening from the al Qaeda leader in charge there.[86] The updates included news that there was heavy fighting at Mazar-e-Sharif, that Kabul would be next, and that the United States and other Western countries had joined with the Northern Alliance.[87]

Hicks was reportedly frustrated with the lack of enemy activity at Kandahar, and he therefore sought an opportunity to join the fighting in Kabul.[88] On October 17 he told the al Qaeda leader in charge about his intentions and then traveled to Kabul, still armed to the teeth.[89]

He linked up with a former friend from the LET, who asked Hicks to go with him to the front lines of the battle near Konduz.[90] They arrived there around November 9, the day before Mazar-e-Sharif was captured by the Northern Alliance and U.S. Special Forces. Hicks joined a group of al Qaeda and Taliban fighters there. The government alleged that John Walker Lindh was among this same group of fighters, although this specific allegation was removed from the final package of charges to which Hicks pled guilty.[91]

Hicks spent approximately two hours on the battlefield before the front line collapsed. With bullets flying and Northern Alliance tanks coming over the trenches, Hicks ran.[92] He was chased and fired upon by the Northern Alliance for two or three days before taking refuge in the city of Konduz. It was there that he asked some of the Arab fighters about their plans. They said they were going back to fight to the death. Hicks apparently didn't like this idea, since he then decided to flee to Pakistan using his Australian passport.[93]

He sneaked off to a *madafah*, an Arab safe house inside Konduz, where he wrote a letter to the Arabs stating that they should not go looking for him since he was okay. Still armed, Hicks then crept off to another safe house and holed up there for several weeks.[94] He was staying with a shopkeeper who helped him sell his AK-47.[95]

A week after the Northern Alliance grabbed control of Konduz from the Taliban, in December 2001, Hicks took a taxi and fled toward Pakistan. He was captured by the Northern Alliance in Baglan, Afghanistan.[96]

There is speculation that David Hicks participated in the fighting around the Mazir-e-Sharif sector and may have been brought to the camp at Qala-i-Jangi as a battlefield capture by Northern Alliance forces. In those chaotic days, the Northern Alliance fighters were bringing al Qaeda and Taliban to the makeshift camp in every bit of rolling stock they could find. Hicks could have been one of the several detainees there who were identified by "Mike" Spann and his partner "Dave" as "Irish" foreign fighters and singled out for special interrogation. If so, Hicks was quite probably a participant in the violent revolt that led to hundreds of deaths. We know that several others who were at Qala-i-Jangi were evacuated to Guantánamo and it is quite possible that Dawood/Hicks was among them. It is of note that Hicks was assigned ISN 002 and John Walker Lindh, the most infamous capture at Qala-i-Jangi, was assigned ISN 001.[97] Numbers that close together might indicate physical proximity at time of capture and interrogation.[98]

The capture and confinement of a terrorist like David Hicks is extremely important. Because of his foreign status, he had access in some cases to the very top of the organization, such as bin Laden, Muhammad Atef, and Saif al Adel. Also, because Hicks comes from another culture, one more identifiable to interrogators perhaps, it is possible to see and learn unique things about the al Qaeda organization's strengths and weaknesses that may not be observed by an indigenous fighter simply because to him it is all normal, not at all unique.

In 2005, an Australian Broadcasting Corporation program titled *Four Corners* broadcast for the first time transcripts of an interview that the Australian Federal Police conducted with Hicks in 2002.[99] In them, Hicks disclosed certain key facts: that he had trained with al Qaeda in Afghanistan on guerrilla tactics and urban warfare, and that he met Osama bin Laden. He denied fighting against American or Coalition forces.

The *Four Corners* journalist, Debbie Whitmont, confirmed that in Guantánamo, Hicks signed a statement saying that "I believe that al Qaeda camps provided a great opportunity for Muslims like myself from all over the world to train for military operations and jihad. I knew after six months that I was receiving training from al Qaeda, who had declared war on numerous countries and peoples." During the program discussion all of Hicks's attorneys, including U.S.–appointed military attorneys, defended his innocence and said basically that he was in the wrong place at the wrong time.

One of the British detainees who was released after review proceedings, Moazzam Begg, claims that Hicks told him, "Tell people my sanity is at risk here." In a letter to his family, Hicks said that he was "teetering on the edge of sanity after such a long ordeal." He added an odd comment: "They [U.S. authorities] also make sure that I'm disadvantaged as possible when it comes to defending myself." Considering that Hicks had two military lawyers, Navy lieutenant commander Charles Swift and Army major Michael Mori, had Josh Dratel as his civilian attorney and was represented by Stephen Kenny, and that he had further support from civil rights attorney Clive Stafford Smith, that complaint is puzzling. In consonance with published al Qaeda training instructions, seen in the Manchester Manual, Hicks made elaborate statements of abuse and torture that are backed up by Moazzam Begg and others who have been released.[100]

During most of 2005 through 2006, David Hicks, ISN 002, spent his time in Camp II/III, Tango Block. He is known among other detainees as the Australian Cowboy. Hicks was later relocated to the modern Camp V facility. His move was part of the overall consolidation of detainees into the modern facilities and also a protective measure. While confined, Hicks had a tendency to flip-flop ideologically. For a time he appeared to be an apostate, requesting that his interrogators provide him with a Bible (they did). He announced that he had quit Islam.[101] Later he claimed to have returned to being a practicing Muslim.[102]

Even after his ultimate release back to Australian authorities, David Hicks works to keep up his image as an innocent bystander caught up in out-of-control events. Public outcries in Australia for his release were met with disapproval by the government. Once the legal roadblocks were finally cleared, Hicks appeared before a Military Commission in March 2007 charged with conspiracy, attempted murder by an unprivileged belligerent, and aiding the enemy. The Military Commission accepted a guilty plea from Hicks on 35 counts of abetting and supporting terrorism, although charges that he specifically fought against American military forces were dropped. The court, which could have issued a life sentence, agreed to a plea bargain for a seven-year sentence. With credit for time held in Guantánamo, Hicks left Guantánamo looking at about nine months in an Australian prison.[103]

The Terror Master

Readers have already been introduced to Khalid Sheikh Muhammad through his lengthy deposition regarding, among other subjects, Muhammad al Qahtani and Zacarias Moussaoui. Without doubt, KSM has been the highest-value target captured alive that we know. Results of his interrogation have led directly to thwarting other al Qaeda operations and have pulled the curtain away from the super-secret methodology for recruiting, enabling, funding, and planning al Qaeda terror attacks.

After KSM and 13 other detainees were moved to the highly secret Camp 7 Guantánamo in September 2006, his case was deemed sufficiently strong that it was added to the list of those to be tried by the

Military Commission on February 11, 2008. The 9/11 Commission described him as "the principal architect of the 9/11 attacks," and he has openly taken credit for that operation and more. "I was responsible for the 9/11 operation, from A to Z," he affirmed before his Combat Status Review Tribunal.[104]

KSM has taken credit for a lengthy list of additional terrorist operations, such as the killing of *Wall Street Journal* reporter Daniel Pearl.[105] "I decapitated with my blessed right hand the head of the American Jew Daniel Pearl," KSM bragged.[106] "For those who would like to confirm, there are pictures of me on the Internet holding his head."[107]

There is controversy over KSM's statements, because his defenders allege that he spoke only while under torture. CIA officials have acknowledged that KSM was subject to waterboarding while in their custody.[108] As a result, attorneys in the American Civil Liberties Union and the Center for Constitutional Rights, and activists such as Clive Stafford Smith, have discounted all of KSM's statements. "As a result of torture, KSM himself falsely implicated various other people who he says are innocent," said Stafford Smith.[109]

On the other hand, his statements, according to forensic psychiatrists, "do not appear to be the result of torture but might be exaggerated for tactical reasons, as part of his continued fight against the United States." Other observers infer that while KSM may have had a tangential role in such operations as the Bali bombing, the 1993 attack on the World Trade Center, and others, by expanding his role in al Qaeda he was attempting to deceive authorities and cause them to expend resources on false leads. According to Dr. Michael Welner, "by offering legitimate information to interrogators, Muhammad had secured the leverage to provide disinformation as well."[110]

Even if one accepts the premise that KSM's lengthy, highly detailed confessions were originally extracted through use of aggressive techniques (the official U.S. policy is that waterboarding is authorized for use by intelligence agencies but not by the military and that the technique is not torture), that does not explain why he continues to stand by his story. Others in his position, such as Qahtani, have recanted and withdrawn statements during Annual Review Board or Military Commission proceedings. But KSM has not done so.

To the contrary, KSM has stood by his statements and has even insisted that he be put to death. "I have been looking to be a martyr for a long time," KSM, who has claimed to be al Qaeda's third highest leader, told a stunned military judge.[111]

In his comments to the tribunal, KSM, who insists on representing himself, went on to denounce (inaccurately) the U.S. Constitution. "I consider all American constitution evil because it permits same-sexual marriage and many other things that are very bad," he told the military judge, Colonel Ralph Kohlmann. "Do you understand?"[112]

Another on the docket with KSM, one of al Qaeda's admitted operators and a 9/11 facilitator, Ramzi bin al-Shibh, also begged to be killed quickly. "'I've been seeking martyrdom for five years,' the detainee said in Arabic. 'I tried to get a visa for 9/11, but I could not,'" a *Wall Street Journal* observer reported from the proceedings.[113]

Bin al-Shibh, a Yemeni, had been a roommate with Muhammad Atta in Hamburg. His visa application to the United States was turned down on four occasions, so by default he became a coordinator between Atta, who was in America planning the attacks, and KSM in Pakistan.[114] According to Al Jazeera reporter Yousri Fouda, who interviewed both KSM and bin al-Shibh not long after the attack, "Bin al-Shibh actually went to Osama bin Laden prior to September 11 to tell him that the date had been chosen."

When the attack occurred, Fouda said, "bin al-Shibh was watching TV. And they would say that they were very proud of it, praying for the rest of the flights to do what was planned for them to do. They would scream and chant and feel like they were part of the operation themselves."[115]

On December 9, 2008, while appearing before a military commission, KSM originally pled guilty, then asked to withdraw that plea temporarily. He learned that the death penalty would not be immediately forthcoming and wished to reconsider. The other four detainees at the proceedings followed his lead. Far from recanting previous confessions—although Gitmo opponents and defense attorneys made extravagant claims that statements were extracted by torture—KSM and his cohorts bragged about their terrorist activities and repeatedly stated that they were proud jihadists who sought martyrdom.

Especially chilling were Ramzi bin al-Shibh's comments at the conclusion of the hearing. "I want to send my greetings to Osama bin Laden and reaffirm my allegiance. I hope the jihad will continue and strike the heart of America with all kinds of weapons of mass destruction."

The presence, for the first time, of some 9/11 families at the Military Commission did nothing to dampen the spirits of the men in the dock. They laughed, joked among themselves, and appeared quite comfortable admitting to some of the most heinous terrorist acts in recent years. At the time of this writing, ultimate disposition of their cases is underway.[116]

The Dirty Bomber

According to his charge sheet, Benyam Ahmed Muhammad, a Nigerian by birth, was a fairly late convert to Islam. He was alleged to be a trained electrical engineer who journeyed to Afghanistan in May 2001 to participate in terrorist training at the infamous al Farouk camp. After completing Terrorism 101, which stresses weaponry and physical training, Benyam Muhammad was reportedly told by Osama bin Laden in early summer of 2001 to "get ready" because "something big is going to happen in the future."[117]

The U.S. government charges that after finishing al Farouk in August, Benyam Muhammad was sent to the al Qaeda urban warfare training program in Kabul. At this time training ammunition was short, for some reason, and he was sent to Bagram to get some combat experience fighting the Northern Alliance. By September 2001, Benyam Muhammad allegedly had expanded his military proficiency to include mortars: laying, map reading, targeting, and firing. He was pulled off the front and returned to the camp near Kabul, where he learned explosives, including improvised bomb-making. Apparently participating in the class with Benyam Muhammad was Richard Reid, the notorious British "Shoe Bomber" who later attempted to use a homicide bomb to destroy himself and an airliner filled with innocent passengers.

Benyam Muhammad must have impressed al Qaeda leadership with his proficiency, dedication, and ability to attack into the West. Reportedly he was ordered first to Kandahar, an al Qaeda stronghold, then to Zormat, where he met with Abd al Hadi al Iraqi. Hadi was a senior al Qaeda operator who by 2005 had been assigned to command al Qaeda forces remaining in the southwestern provinces of Afghanistan.[118]

At this time, authorities believe, Benyam Muhammad was told that al Qaeda had a special mission for him. He was dispatched to Birmel and there was introduced to Abu Zubaydah, who is viewed as "the" coordinator between al Qaeda and its affiliated cells.[119] (Zubaydah was captured in Pakistan in 2002 and after spending time in a "secret" CIA prison, evacuated to Guantánamo in September 2006, where he remains awaiting trial for war crimes.) Benyam Muhammad was promised advanced explosives training in Pakistan to build remote-control bombs (now called improvised explosive devices, or IEDs, by the American military). He became sufficiently proficient to return to Afghanistan to make the devices for use against Americans and teach other terrorists how to make them.

According to the charge sheet, Benyam Muhammad and Abu Zubaydah traveled together from Khowst, Afghanistan, making their way cautiously from safe house to safe house, using madrassas for cover. Along the way they first met José Padilla, along with Ghassan al Sharbi and Jarban Said Bin al Qahtani. They were all told to begin work quickly on the IEDs.

After leaving the Khost madrassa, Benyam Muhammad and Padilla reportedly made their way together to a safe house in the Pakistani capital of Lahore, where they learned how to make an improvised dirty bomb. Ghassan al Sharbi translated the instructions into Arabic and read them aloud to the group of prospective dirty bombers. Apparently they had learned about dirty-bomb manufacture from "computers," probably through surfing the Internet.[120]

A dirty bomb is not a fission weapon such as we are familiar with from film. It is not a Hiroshima-type weapon. Rather it is a conventional explosive—the bigger the better—that is tainted by highly poisonous radioactive material such as plutonium.[121] When the bomb explodes, it initially has the same profile as any similar explosive. It will cause concussion, blast, fire, shrapnel, and collateral damage. But after the initial explosion passes, it will have distributed a lethal substance, perhaps plutonium—the most toxic, poisonous substance in the world—perhaps highly enriched uranium, into the blast pattern. Many victims will die instantly of radiation poisoning, others more slowly from cancer. Ground in the vicinity of a dirty bomb may be uninhabitable for decades.[122]

At some point in this training, Abu Zubaydah apparently drew Benyam Muhammad and José Padilla into his confidence. He took them away from the group for private meetings in which he explained that he preferred that Benyam Muhammad conduct international operations rather than return to Afghanistan to fight the Americans and the Northern Alliance. At this time Benyam Muhammad reportedly agreed to carry out an attack against the United States, preferably based on use of a dirty bomb. At other meetings, Abu Zubaydah included Padilla in discussions of plans against the United States. Ideas discussed included blowing up gas tankers—this may have referred to liquid propane storage tanks, which could be devastatingly powerful if they exploded, akin in force to a small nuclear detonation.

One of the more bizarre possibilities the three terrorists apparently considered was spraying people in nightclubs with cyanide. Abu Zubaydah told Padilla and Benyam Muhammad that these attacks would help "free the prisoners in Cuba," referring to the facility at Guantánamo that was still in its early stages of construction and use.

The group reportedly continued to move among various safe houses, eventually making their way to Faisalabad. At this time, Padilla and Benyam Muhammad were sent on to Karachi to meet with high-ranking al Qaeda leaders. In Faisalabad, Khalid Sheikh Muhammad and Saif al Adel told Benyam Muhammad that his and Padilla's mission would include targeting high-rise apartment buildings that relied on natural gas. The plotters would rent an apartment in a targeted building and use the natural gas in that building to initiate an explosion.[123]

At a mission launch meeting with Khalid Sheikh Muhammad early in April 2002, they were given funding for the mission (roughly $6,000 for Benyam Muhammad and $10,000 for Padilla) and instructed to fly to Chicago, Illinois. Both men were detained at the Karachi airport, Padilla for visa issues, Benyam Muhammad for a forged passport. Inexplicably, both were released. After returning to Khalid Sheikh Muhammad for instructions, Benyam Muhammad was given a new forged passport and directed to depart immediately for Chicago. Benyam Muhammad was intercepted, questioned, and arrested in Karachi while attempting to fly to London. He was turned over to American authorities by the Pakistani authorities. Next stop: Gitmo.

The Second-Gen Jihadi

Omar Ahmed Khadr was born a Canadian, spending the first four years of his life in the Muslim section of Toronto. In 1990 the family moved back to Peshawar, Pakistan. According to official charges, Khadr came into terrorism naturally. His father, Ahmad Sa'id Khadr, was a co-founder and manager for a radical Islamic charity that used a humanitarian organization as a front. Called innocuously the Health and Education Project International–Canada (HEPIC), it was supposedly chartered to funnel relief funds to Afghani orphans. Secretly, however, Ahmad Khadr was a close associate of Osama bin Laden and the top al Qaeda hierarchy. The elder Khadr used HEPIC as a conduit to send money to bin Laden to fund the terrorist training camps in Afghanistan.[124]

For years the Pakistani authorities were passive about al Qaeda. Some in the Pakistani intelligence section, the ISI, were even supportive. But what eventually broke ISI and Pakistani leaders' patience were unrestricted terrorist operations within Pakistan, particularly assassination attempts against President Musharraf and other top leaders.

Ahmad Khadr was allegedly complicit in funding a bombing of the Egyptian Embassy in Pakistan. Omar would have been about eight years old then, and was sent with his siblings back to Toronto to live with grandparents. Omar attended school for his year in Canada, returning to join his father after his release in 1995. Apparently unwilling to trust the continued good will of the ISI, Ahmad Khadr moved his family to Jalalabad, Afghanistan after they were reunited.

Throughout these formative years, Omar Khadr reportedly came to know bin Laden, Ayman al Zawahiri, Muhammad Atef, and Saif al Adel. Omar spent time as a youth at al Qaeda safe houses, madrassas, and training camps.

After September 11, 2001, the family began to move repeatedly within Afghanistan. Meanwhile, just three months shy of his 16th birthday, in June 2002, Omar Khadr is thought to have received a private, one-on-one al Qaeda basic military training course. This training was apparently a favor done for his father. It was small repayment for the hard work the elder Khadr had done for al Qaeda over the decades.

The training was reportedly conducted by a mysterious al Qaeda operative with the *nom de guerre* of Abu Haddi. Omar learned how to use small arms, grenades, and explosives. Immediately following training, he was deployed to an airport near Khost. There he conducted reconnaissance and surveillance missions directed against the U.S. military and Northern Alliance forces. He was primarily observing U.S. supply convoys with an eye to interdicting them.

In July 2002, according to the U.S. government, he was pulled off the recon mission and given a month of intensive training in land mines. Later that month, Omar and fellow terror camp graduates worked frantically to convert land mines—of which Afghanistan had a surfeit as a result of the long, brutal Soviet occupation—into remotely controlled explosives. The group then deployed to the Khost airport area—the site that Omar had surveyed—and planted the mines on roads that American forces were expected to transit.

Meanwhile, things were heating up in Afghanistan for the elder Khadr. By July 2002, the Taliban and al Qaeda had collapsed in major urban areas around the country. Operations around the Tora Bora area and Operation Anaconda had been successfully completed to the point that al Qaeda leaders were fleeing to Pakistan and Iran. A Special Forces–based task force composed primarily of Delta Force operators,

CIA field operators, and the 160th Special Operations Aviation Regiment designated as Task Force 11 had been specifically tasked to track down high-level Taliban and al Qaeda leaders. One of the 10 most wanted men on the D-boys' list was Ahmad Sa'id Khadr.

Task Force 11 identified the village where the elder Khadr was hiding and hit it on July 27, 2002, with a snatch-and-grab operation. Although taken by surprise, the al Qaeda defenders—mostly Chechens and foreign "Arabs"—put up a vigorous defense. A five-hour firefight ensued before the compound fell.

In the course of the raging firefight a Delta Force medic, Special Forces Sergeant First Class Christopher J. Speer, was wounded by a hand grenade. He was evacuated with head wounds and died in a hospital in Germany on August 6. Robin Moore recounts that "two days before the firefight, Speer, a combat medic with SFOD-D [Delta Force], had gone straight into a minefield to save two injured Afghan children."[125]

Although the elder Khadr apparently escaped, Omar Khadr was captured and several others in his gang were killed or captured in their compound. It was determined that Omar Khadr tossed the grenade that mortally wounded Sergeant First Class Speer. It had been a bloody, intense firefight. In addition to the loss of SFC Speer, two Afghan Militia Force members were killed and five Delta Force soldiers wounded.

Omar Ahmed Khadr became a person of extreme interest—a high-value subject identified for extensive interrogation—because of his broad family ties to the al Qaeda organization and his VIP status within the organization through his father's links. He became a possible subject for war crimes because he took up arms against the U.S. government and, as an unlawful combatant, is alleged to have murdered an American serviceman. Omar Ahmed Khadr, ISN 766, was on the way to Gitmo.[126]

The Bodyguard

Only the most trusted al Qaeda operatives are selected to become drivers, bodyguards, or personal staff for Osama bin Laden. It is a mark of total *bayat*, or personal commitment to the emir, and recognition of that loyalty, that distinguishes a member of the elite personal entourage. Salim Ahmed Hamdan achieved that coveted status within al Qaeda by hard work and total dedication to the ideology and persona of bin Laden.

Hamdan was allegedly one of the operatives that frequently were dispatched on special missions. A good part of covert tradecraft is for clandestine operatives to use many different monikers, widely different cover trades and professions, and a myriad of forged papers. Hamdan apparently excelled in all of these methods.

It is quite likely that Salim Hamdan had been an al Qaeda foot soldier for several years. He surfaced in the spotlight in 1996 when he reportedly traveled to Kandahar and met bin Laden for the first time. He apparently made a positive impression on the emir, and was hired shortly thereafter as a personal driver and bodyguard. Hamdan was trusted with a series of missions that relied heavily on his loyalty and put him in close proximity to bin Laden and top al Qaeda leadership over the next five-year period.

While not driving the Toyota Hi Lux trucks that he had procured especially to drive bin Laden and the bodyguard unit, it was apparently common for Hamdan to be sent on courier-type missions. Messengers had become increasingly important ever since a Clinton Administration staffer, eager to court favor with the press, was said to have irresponsibly leaked that America was monitoring Osama bin Laden's satellite telephone system.[127]

Wise to America's listening capability, the al Qaeda leader had immediately introduced a higher degree of operational security. He relied far less frequently on telephone communications, used disposable cell phones, and put trust in messengers to convey the most important information or carry out critical tasks. That job description applied to Salim Hamdan.

During the time that Hamdan was courier and expediter for bin Laden he moved weapons, explosives, ammunition, supplies, and other items, often directly into the hands of major al Qaeda players like Saif al Adel, the head of al Qaeda's security committee in Kandahar. Hamdan listened to conversations and was fully aware of the impending attacks on the U.S. embassies in Tanzania and Kenya in August 1998. He knew of bin Laden's sponsorship of the attack on the USS *Cole* in October 2000, and of al Qaeda's responsibility for the September 11, 2001 attacks.

As Hamdan drove bin Laden and his entourage around Afghanistan in three to nine vehicle convoys in those days, he heard much that was intended only for the ears of bin Laden's innermost circle. He listened to many versions of bin Laden's encouragement to conduct a "martyrdom mission" in which the bomber died along with his infidel victims. Often bin Laden would talk about driving the infidels out of the Arabian Peninsula, away from the Holy Sites.[128]

During his five-year stint in Afghanistan, Hamdan often received training at the al Farouk camp. He was a principal aide to bin Laden and privy to knowledge of terror attacks that he did nothing to prevent. At the least, Hamdan, ISN 149, is charged with being complicit in and abetting acts of terrorism against civilians and as an unlawful enemy combatant.

As will be discussed below, Hamdan's name has also become synonymous with a landmark Supreme Court case (*Hamdan v. Rumsfeld*) that is part of the ongoing legal battle surrounding the very existence of Guantánamo.

The Bomb Squad

We do not know for certain that when Muhammad al Khazan graduated from London University with an engineering degree he envisioned a career in bomb-making.[129] However, it is likely, given his background, that heroic pictures of jihadist activity may have begun to consume his imagination. The son of Pakistani immigrants to the United Kingdom, Khazan had watched his parents labor in dead-end jobs all their lives. A product of British private schools (public schools in the U.S.), Khazan was bright enough to receive a scholarship to London University. He majored in electrical engineering, receiving his degree while in his early twenties.[130]

According to the government charge sheet, Khazan and his male friends attended a mosque in the mostly Pakistani area of Leeds near London, known for its hard-core fundamentalist view of Islam. The imam, a short, dark individual with a long, tangled beard, was himself trained in Saudi Arabia by some of the most virulent Wahabbist imams known, and dispatched back to the United Kingdom with instructions to proselytize his flock in the dangers of Christianity, Judaism, and assimilation by the West.

Under no circumstances, he was told repeatedly, must you even hint that friendship or accommodation with infidels is desirable or permissible. Like the other Saudi-trained Wahabbist imams, he took his instruction seriously. His mosque became legendary as the one with the most extreme, fire-breathing sermons. As with the al Aqasa mosque in Finsbury Park, in north London, his mosque became a magnet for disaffected youth and bitter immigrants.[131]

Outwardly, Khazan would not have caused you such fear as to chase you from a shared subway car in the London tube. He wore short-cropped hair, was beardless, and dressed in a preppie manner. He was clean, neat, and appeared somewhat shy and introverted around strangers. I now believe that this seemingly self-effacing demeanor reflected his total disgust with forced proximity to the *kafir* infidel and his loathing for any contact that might show friendliness or kindness. Such behavior, he apparently feared, might compromise the unadulterated hatred for these people that had been taught to him by his imam.

Khazan was an obvious and surprisingly easy target for the London-based al Qaeda recruiters. Ideologically he already belonged to the Movement; it was simply necessary to persuade him to commit his physical self in the direction that his faith had taken him. Shortly thereafter Khazan traveled to Afghanistan, where he trained at al Farouk. He completed his basic terrorist training successfully and even had the opportunity to hear a speech by Osama bin Laden, the emir himself, who visited the camp.

Because of his unusual education and his proclivity for things electrical and mechanical, Khazan was a natural for bomb training. By his own account, he went to two other camps, one in Afghanistan, the other in a still classified out-of-country location, possibly the Ansar al-Islam training camp that existed at the time in Saddam Hussein's Iraq near the Iranian border. He demonstrated extraordinary proficiency and imagination in bomb design and manufacture.

In summer 2001 Khazan returned to Afghanistan, where he participated in fighting against Northern Alliance forces. He was captured in November 2001 in the battle for Kandahar, where hundreds of Taliban and al Qaeda fighters were swept up in the battlefield. After extensive preliminary interrogation, he was considered a high-value prospect and recommended for evacuation.

When the detainees landed at the Leeward Field at Guantánamo Base they were taken off the U.S. Air Force C-17 transport aircraft shackled, hooded, and in orange jumpsuits. They were loaded on a special watercraft, always under constant guard, and ferried across the mile-plus of open water. At the Windward dock they were loaded into vehicles that took them to Camp X-Ray. There they would undergo preliminary interrogation, medical evaluation and treatment, and begin to receive proper nourishment and recover from their battlefield trauma.

While confined in Gitmo, Khazan has been remarkably open with interrogators. It is an odd trait that many of these highly committed terrorists once captured become voluble, almost bragging about their accomplishments. Former FBI special agent in charge I. C. Smith says that they "have a remarkable propensity to talk," and do so "at a much higher rate . . . than members of the Mafia."[132] Khazan fit the mold. He has been fully cooperative with interrogators to the point of drawing schematic diagrams of bombs that he designed and constructed in the past. Of course, it is always possible that at some point he will recant these admissions and claim that his cooperation was coerced.

Still, the intelligence acquired from Khazan has proved tremendously useful to ongoing operations in Iraq and Afghanistan against the dreaded IEDs, the improvised explosive devices that have accounted for so many U.S., Coalition, and Iraqi casualties. Khazan has gone so far as to provide the names of seven other explosives trainers still not captured.

Others in the Bomb Squad are from different countries. One is a veteran of the Chechen guerrilla war against Russian forces. He was captured on the Afghanistan battlefield, as were many other Chechen Islamic fundamentalists. He has been cooperative with interrogators, and has described a system that is being used against our forces in Iraq to command-detonate the IEDs. This is a complex system called a dual tone multifrequency (DTMF) encoding and decoding system. Members of the special IED Task Force have had this information shared with them and are exploiting it to assist with countering IED attacks in the field.

Many detainees were wearing a particular type of watch when captured. It turns out that the Casio F91W watch is especially useful as a timing device because it allows al Qaeda bomb-makers to set the alarm time more than 24 hours in advance. Astoundingly, according to retired FBI agent David Williams, who was an investigator in the 1993 World Trade Center bombing and now runs a counterterrorism consulting business, "you can set a time delay for up to *three years* [emphasis added] that's accurate to the second."[133] Two such watches were picked up on the Millennium Bomber, Ahmed Ressam, when he was apprehended crossing into the United States from Canada with the intention of detonating a device at Los Angeles International Airport. Ramsi Yousef, nephew of terrorist kingpin Khalid Sheikh Muhammad, said during his trial for the 1993 World Trade Center attacks that he had used the same watch as a detonating timer. The Casio F91W became a "calling card" of Yousef in multiple bomb attacks around the world, including a foiled plot called Operation Bojinka to detonate bombs in up to a dozen U.S.–bound civilian airliners out of the Philippines.[134]

While some dispute the evidentiary nature of merely wearing a watch "available to millions" (as Saudi Arabian detainee Mazin Saleh Musaid claims), there is also such a thing as too much coincidence.[135] Seldom reported is that this particular watch was "a graduation present at the al Qaeda Afghanistan camps like al Farouk and Tarnak Farms."[136] Being alerted to such peculiarities enables our forces to pick out potential al Qaeda operatives. Is everyone who wears this watch an al Qaeda member? Of course not. But if a Casio F91W watch is found among the possessions of a young foreign male captured on the battlefield in Afghanistan, it would be sufficient justification to probe deeper into his story.

Many of the detainees at Guantánamo have been trained in low-level bomb manufacture. Usually this means what are commonly called booby traps, simple devices such as soft-drink cans turned into grenades or small antipersonnel bombs, or grenades triggered by trip wires or movement. But in the camps those fighters with particular education or talent were selected, as was Khazan, for special advanced training. A lot of this training took place in Afghanistan, some in other, undisclosed places. We know, for example, that Ansar al Islam maintained a bomb-making and poison gas training facility in northeastern Iraq during Saddam's heyday that may have been used by al Qaeda operatives.

Documents discovered by special operations forces that attacked and overran the Ansar al Islam facility included sophisticated training manuals for bomb manufacture and the use of chemical poisons such as ricin. Could Khazan and his fellow Bomb Squad members have attended training sessions here or in other places such as Iran, Syria, the Bekka Valley, or Chechnya? It is entirely possible, even probable.[137]

Regardless of location, these technically inclined fighters learned to make what the Pentagon describes as "highly sophisticated, remotely triggered bombs made with explosives manufactured from household items." We have seen the effects of some of these products in the first attack on the World Trade Center, the Oklahoma City bombing, and the Millennium Plot, among others. Some of the Bomb Squad were "explosives trainers who passed their techniques on to others through structured courses."[138]

The importance of confining Bomb Squad members cannot be overstated: Not only are they providing information that assists American forces to defeat the insidious IEDs, but they are off the field and out of the training business. Who knows how many more trained IED makers would be out there if the Bomb Squad were free and on the loose?

The New Guy and the IED Gang

In the days post–9/11 it was common to see jihadists flock to the radical Islamic cause, drawn to Afghanistan to fight the infidel. One such jihadist recruit was Jarban Said Bin al Qahtani (no relation to the "Twentieth Hijacker" mentioned previously). An example of the value of martyrdom operations to recruiting was that Qahtani, an educated, reasonably-well-off young professional, got caught up in jihad fever and left his Saudi home shortly after September 11, 2001, headed for the training camps of Afghanistan to fight the infidel. Qahtani was an electrical engineer, a graduate of the prestigious King Saud University in Riyadh. As the government charge sheet alleges, he told his friends and the Wahabbist imam at his local mosque that he intended to fight against American and Northern Alliance forces in Afghanistan.

By October 2001, the level of al Qaeda training had intensified. Qahtani reportedly attended a newly opened terrorist training camp located north of Kabul and became familiar if not proficient with the standard AK-47 and the RPD/RPK machine guns. He showed promise and was told in December 2001 to head for Faisalabad, Pakistan, where he would obtain further training.

Waiting for al Qahtani at Faisalabad, authorities believe, were two fighters who had been with al Qaeda for several years, Ghassan Abdullah al Sharbi and an Algerian, Sufyian Barhoumi. One first hears of Barhoumi in 1998, when he allegedly attended an electronics and explosives course at al Qaeda's Khalden Camp, a facility that specialized in advanced demolitions study. Barhoumi became exceptionally proficient at constructing and dismantling explosive devices, particularly those that are triggered electronically. He was selected to be an explosives trainer and began a peripatetic lifestyle, traveling from camp to camp training recruits on improvised explosives.

Almost two years after Barhoumi first appeared in Afghanistan, a twenty-something Saudi, Ghassan Abdullah al Sharbi, left America on a quest for jihad. Sharbi was a graduate of Embry Riddle University in Prescott, Arizona. He had been an electrical engineering major, considered by many the most challenging of engineering specialties. Almost a year later, in July 2001, Sharbi is alleged to have matriculated from the al Farouk camp, where so many of the al Qaeda volunteers underwent basic weapons training. While there, he is thought to have met Osama bin Laden on several occasions.

As we have seen, bin Laden, knowing of the approaching attack on America, was making increasingly frequent appearances at the camps, especially al Farouk, encouraging the trainees to be pure jihadists, and to hold the vision of a martyrdom operation as their highest goal in life.

The government believes that over the next two months Sharbi, along with other English-speaking terrorists, provided translation services for the manuals, downloaded information from computers, and even translated the *bayat*, the required oath of allegiance, that each terrorist made personally to Osama bin Laden. Sharbi may also have worked with David Hicks during this period, as they were both in the same camp performing translation services.

Sometime around July 2001 the head of al Qaeda's military committee, Muhammad Atef, reportedly tasked the *emir* of the al Farouk camp, Abu Muhammad, with identifying two "brothers" to receive special electronics-based explosive training in Pakistan at the Faisalabad facility. His stated goal was to establish a new, independent section of the military committee based on this IED capability. At this time one can deduce that Sufyian Barhoumi and Ghassan al Sharbi were the two fighters selected for this mission.

Within two days of the 9/11 attack the al Farouk camp was hastily cleared. The al Qaeda leadership expected a reprise of the Tomahawk missile attacks that characterized the Clinton Administration's response to terrorism. Bin Laden was confident that once more the American paper tiger would shoot a few expensive cruise missiles at the desert camps, declare a victory, and withdraw.

By December 2001, in reaction to the intensity of the conflict growing daily in Afghanistan, Abu Zubaydah, a high-level al Qaeda recruiter and operational planner, was reportedly pressured to expedite formation of the special bomb unit. Authorities believe he made certain that the designated fighters—Sharbi, Qahtani, and Binyam Muhammad— were moved from Bimel, Afghanistan, down to Faisalabad, Pakistan, a location the leadership considered safer. Apparently Sufyian Barhoumi was already there.

By March 2002, it is believed, all players had closed into the safe house in Faisalabad. Barhoumi, being the most experienced and most proficient, was going to train Sharbi, Qahtani, and Binyam Muhammad in "building small, hand-held remote-detonation devices for explosives that would later be used in Afghanistan against United States forces."[139] Barhoumi was given approximately $1,000 to purchase necessary components to conduct the training.

Apparently, Barhoumi, Noor al Deen, and others went on a shopping spree. Given a five-page-long list of electrical components and devices including everything from flashlight bulbs to circuit boards and the soldering irons and tools to work on them, the group hit the Faisalabad electronics market. Along the way they appear to have purchased six cell phones—of a specific model that could be used to command-detonate an IED remotely. After they returned to the safe house, Qahtani and Sharbi received training from Barhoumi on bomb-making. He used an electronics manual picked up on the shopping trip to supplement his experience. (By this time Binyam Muhammad had been pulled from the group and, as we have seen from government charge sheets, along with José Padilla was being coached to conduct a dirty-bomb attack on America.)

March 2002, it is thought, was a frantic time for the group. Abu Zubaydah urged them to construct as many remote-controlled explosive devices as possible. At the end of the month they were to take the products they had built back to Afghanistan for use against the Americans. Once back in the fight they would use their newly acquired skills to train other al Qaeda fighters. But as has frequently happened with al Qaeda leadership, it failed to take into account changing political situations.

By March, Pakistan's president, Perez Musharraf, had been convinced by President Bush that Pakistan's best interests lay in fighting al Qaeda. It may have been that Musharraf had long awaited this tipping point, because he purged the ISI members who were sympathetic to al Qaeda and the Taliban and began to seek out and eliminate terrorists hiding inside Pakistan.

On March 28, 2002, in what could only have been a day or two before the group took off to return to Afghanistan and the fighting there, Pakistani forces busted into the safe house in Faisalabad and made a stunning high-value catch: Abu Zubaydah, Barhoumi, Sharbi, Qahtani, and several others were captured with all of their bombs and equipment. After tactical interrogation by Pakistani authorities they were turned over to the Americans, hooded, and chained by their hands and feet. Barhoumi, Sharbi, and Qahtani were loaded unceremoniously into the back of a C-17 transport aircraft under heavy guard.

Destination: Guantánamo Bay and Camp X-Ray.

The Filmmaker

Meet Ali Hamza Ahmad Sulaman al Bahlul, ISN 039, bearer of more AKAs than a Mafia hit man. Bahlul comes originally from Yemen, a hotbed of Wahabbist ideology and a fertile al Qaeda recruiting ground. He enjoyed a peripatetic career as he followed al Qaeda into Pakistan, Afghanistan, and East African countries. He is charged with conspiracy in that he was allegedly in league with Osama bin Laden and other al Qaeda bigs such as Ayman al Zawahiri and Muhammad Atef in "attacking civilians, attacking civilian objects, murder by an unprivileged belligerent, destruction of property . . . , and terrorism."[140]

Bahlul, a converted jihadist, is believed to have traveled to Afghanistan after bin Laden delivered his famous 1998 fatwa calling for the "killing of Americans and their allies, both military and civilian." Reportedly, Bahlul left Yemen in 1999, taking a well-trodden terrorist path through Pakistan across the border into the al Qaeda training camps of Afghanistan. Authorities believe that he met with Saif al Adel, head of security for al Qaeda, who then arranged for Bahlul to undergo military training at the Aynak camp. There he also pledged *bayat* to Osama bin Laden, affirming his "willingness to perform any act requested by bin Laden."[141]

Bahlul then apparently moved to al Qaeda–owned housing in the

Kandahar area and was personally assigned by bin Laden to duties in his media office. It is critical to realize that al Qaeda deliberately assumes the guise of a peasant movement, or a grass-roots organization, when it is in fact extremely sophisticated, especially in the use and exploitation of modern media and advertising techniques. Bahlul apparently created several videotapes used for recruiting new al Qaeda fighters and instructing those at the camps. Among his other projects, Bahlul was ordered by bin Laden to prepare a video "glorifying . . . the attack on the USS *Cole*." This video was intended to "recruit, motivate, and 'awake the Islamic Umma to revolt against America.'" The video inspired continuation of violent attacks against American life and property.

In response to American reaction post–September 11, 2001, Bahlul reportedly evacuated the Kandahar office and moved to the mountains near Tora Bora. Though tasked by bin Laden to set up satellite communications so that the hierarchy could watch world news reports, the mountainous terrain prevented his ability to make the downlink. Nevertheless, Bahlul continued to gather media reports and assess the economic damage inflicted on America by the attacks.

As the American and Northern Alliance noose began to tighten on the mountain redoubt, the government believes, Bahlul was "promoted" to serve as personal bodyguard for bin Laden. He was outfitted with an explosive-laden vest and pledged to defend bin Laden at the cost of his own life. When the wheels came off the Taliban and al Qaeda bandwagon in Afghanistan, probably when bin Laden and his entourage were split and on the run, Bahlul was captured and turned over to American authorities.

CHAPTER 6

MAXIMUM SECURITY

CAMPS I, II, AND III

---

*"The heroes are the soldiers and sailors who
work inside the wire."*
U.S. NAVY CAPTAIN PAT SALSMAN, OIC OARDEC

S UMMER OF 2006 WAS A difficult time. With both a new
commander and deputy in place, and the Joint Detention Group
commander due to rotate out within a month or so, the detainees were
aroused as never previously.

Until the uprisings and suicides of summer 2006 showed graphically
that the system in place was not working, detainees at Guantánamo had
been incentivized to behave properly. The most uncooperative—
those categorized as "noncompliant" because of their refusal to comply with routine and obey orders, their proclivity to attack guards
or other detainees, and their overall recalcitrance—continued to be
confined in a maximum-security facility clothed in highly visible
orange jumpsuits.

Other detainees have more privileges. Those who cooperate, obey
instructions, and do not attack guards are offered the opportunity to
move to more relaxed facilities. They trade their orange jumpsuit for

loose, tan or white cotton clothing and have more time for recreation and mixing with other detainees.

It is important to note that "compliance" refers strictly to behavior and does not imply cooperation with interrogators. Amazingly, many of the worst detainees who regularly assault guards with feces and urine, with fingernails and feet, with threats and insults, are very cooperative with interrogators. One high-level detainee even chides his fellows for *not* talking to interrogators, saying that they "must be proud of their jihadist activities."[1]

Conversely, a "compliant" detainee might never say a word to an interrogator. This gives us a clearer understanding of the complex balance between the dual mission of detention and interrogation at Guantánamo. Compliance is doing what the guards require of a detainee; cooperation with interrogators is an entirely different affair, and the two are not necessarily linked.

One notoriously noncompliant detainee is regularly provided with a box of a dozen doughnuts by his female interrogator. I observed him undergoing an interrogation while he cheerfully devoured doughnut after doughnut until the box was empty, chattering away the entire time. When I learned that he "really liked" the doughnuts and got them every time he was interrogated, I asked the obvious question: Why? "Because he typically throws his food trays at the guards, he eagerly looks forward to the doughnuts," General Hood explained.[2]

Major General Jay Hood, it must be noted, is the foremost proponent of absolute discipline among the American guard force and staff. He understands that while there are occasions where force is required, there are others where it is clearly not acceptable. He is tough on the troops but also on himself. At Guantánamo, Hood's soldiers considered him to be hard and respected that trait, but were often disconcerted when it appeared to them that he was erratic in his guidance and seemed at times to go to extraordinary lengths to micromanage details of detention operations.

Hood is a field artillery officer and paratrooper. Of medium height and with thinning brown hair, his face reflects the stress of difficult assignments successfully completed. He comes across as fully knowledge-able of his entire command, answers questions directly, and while unfail-ingly polite to visitors, was blunt about the challenges he faced. He had the reputation among his JTF GTMO subordinates of being extremely smart, detail-oriented, and involved with all aspects of the mission.

Some say too involved and call him a micromanager or nitpicker. Others recognize that Hood realized that at Guantánamo, "almost right" wasn't going to be good enough, and "perfect" might not have satisfied some critics either. As a realist he had to insure not only a smooth-running facility under the most difficult conditions imagin-able, but concomitantly safeguard his professional reputation.

Hood set high standards for the guard force and challenged his officers and noncommissioned officers to exceed them. He compiled an extraordinarily detailed series of standard operational procedures—the daily checklists essential to effective military operations—that lay out chapter and verse on how guards are expected to behave.

"We've got more SOPs in this command than any other in the military," Hood laughed. But he was not kidding. All eventualities are covered on paper, and the troops are trained to know how to act in every situation. Failure to meet these standing orders results in disci-plinary action.

On one occasion, a detainee who was being moved attacked a guard and bit his face. The guard struggled to get the man off him. Another nearby guard, a specialist, used a handheld radio to hit the detainee several times. It stopped the attack, but the specialist had violated the rules. He was disciplined, reduced a grade in rank, and underwent ad-ditional training.[3]

One of the SOPs that General Hood insisted upon was that an of-ficer in a military grade of O-4 or higher, that is, major or lieutenant commander or above, and a senior noncommissioned officer be present in every camp 24/7, 365 days a year. "We saw what happened at Abu Ghraib, primarily because of lack of supervisor presence," Hood said, "and we are determined that it won't happen here. I insist that my of-ficers and NCOs maintain constant supervision. They are not surprised to see me or General Gong [deputy commander under Hood] at any hour of the day or night conducting an unannounced inspection."

But the intensity of Hood's oversight also became off-putting. "He was a nightmare, especially for the younger troopers," said one of Bumgarner's subordinate officers, a major from the California National Guard's 40th Infantry division, then pulling its deployment in Guantánamo. Back home he was a practicing attorney, but on active duty his military specialty was as a field artillery officer, so he worked not in the Judge Advocate General's office but inside the wire. "General Hood wanted a 'happier, lovelier' camp. He was constantly imposing his orders on the most microscopic details of management, constantly changing the SOPs that we were trying to follow."[4]

Hood held to the conviction that if he relaxed the rules and permitted the most freedom possible to certain detainees, then they would respond with good behavior. It was the kind of thing that might work in an American prison. But he forgot one thing: "These guys are not like prisoners back in the States," said one of the more experienced sergeants. "On the blocks here, every one of these guys is waiting for the opportunity to kill us."

Nevertheless, Hood pressed for a way to distinguish those who worked with the command—who obeyed orders and didn't attack guards—from those who were continually violent and disobedient. At first the command attempted to use a system of number levels, 1 through 4, that equated to a detainee's behavior. The detainees resisted the system, however. Shakir Ami complained that the labeling was "impersonal" and "dehumanizing." The command accepted the criticism and came up with new designations. Major Timothy O'Reilly, Bumgarner's operations officer, claims credit for coming up with the new "compliant" designation: "We were stuck with the need to come up with some way to differentiate between those who obeyed and those who didn't. The detainees didn't like the labels—even though we got them from the U.S. Federal prison system—and we were told by General Hood to get rid of them. I wracked my brain and finally came up with level of compliancy."

O'Reilly laughed. "Looking back on it I'm not sure that's something I'm proud of or not."[5]

W HEN ONE WALKS THROUGH CAMPS I, II, and III today it is easy to see improvements from block to block. Much was learned from experience and from negative lessons imparted by the detainees themselves. A thorough cleanup of the workplace environment during construction, for example, became of paramount importance as detainees picked up every piece of wire, wood, pipe, or metal and made weapons from them.

The new camps were constructed on concrete piers and floors were raised about four feet off the ground, tropical style, with lots of open space for air circulation. The initial cells, each six by eight feet in width and length and eight feet high, were constructed of special wire mesh. A wire mesh bunk welded to corner posts was approximately 40 inches high. An Asian-style, squat toilet was in the back of each cell along with a sink and faucet. A black arrow painted upon the floor of each cell pointed toward Mecca. High roof space allowed for better air circulation, aided by large floor fans at the ends of the corridors and sometimes at the midpoint.

Off the ends of each block were fenced areas in which detainees took recreation or exercise. As each section was finished, stationary bicycles or other equipment was placed in the recreation areas. Arrows pointed toward Mecca in case a detainee might wish to pray while there. Two or more individual showers were located between the block and the rec area. As operational procedures for confinement were defined, duration and frequency of showers and rec access were established and posted for all detainees to understand. Even the most hostile and abusive of detainees is offered some recreation time and access to hygienic facilities each week.

Camps I, II, and III were intended to be maximum-security camps with no communal living. In some cases in Camp I, where detainees categorized as "compliant" were eventually held, they could take recreation in groups of two or three. As noted above, compliance refers to

EVALUATING A DETAINEE

	Cooperative	Uncooperative
Compliant	1	2
Noncompliant	3	4

1. *Compliant-Cooperative*: a detainee who obeys orders, does not threaten others or attack guards, and willingly shares information with interrogators.
2. *Compliant-Uncooperative*: a detainee who obeys orders, does not threaten others or attack guards, but refuses to share any information with interrogators.
3. *Noncompliant-Cooperative*: a detainee who regularly attacks guards either physically, verbally, or by throwing bodily fluids at them, who may attack other detainees, but who willingly discusses information with interrogators.
4. *Noncompliant-Uncooperative*: a detainee who regularly attacks guards either physically, verbally, or by throwing bodily fluids at them, who may attack other detainees, and who never shares information with interrogators.

the detainee's willingness to obey instructions, interact benignly with other detainees, and not harm himself or others. Someone who spits on guards, beats up other detainees, and does not follow directions would be considered noncompliant. A detainee who cooperates fully with interrogators, shares information, identifies photos, and is open about his personal history is considered cooperative. In the evaluation matrix above, these various combinations are made clear.

All of the Camp IV population is categorized as either group 1 or group 2. They are compliant but may or may not cooperate with interrogators. Their reward for good behavior is to wear white or beige clothing, live in 10-man communal facilities, and have a great deal of outside recreation time. (Camp I is also designated as a compliant holding area, but the detainees live in single cells there.) None of these categorizations is permanent. A formerly noncompliant detainee can through good behavior be moved to one of the communal living camps. This has happened over time for the vast majority of the populace. Almost 90 percent of the current population wears white or beige clothing and lives communally. The other 10 percent are bad guys who are identified by the orange jumpsuit, which they hate because they think it makes them look like common criminals instead of proud jihadists.

Even in the so-called compliant camps there were still attacks on guards and other detainees, and many weapons were discovered. At times detainees would pull the wire from their bunks and fashion shanks out of them. They learned that the metal "feet" that straddled the Asian-style toilet in each cell could be removed by working and bending them. Once out, the sharp edges were used to cut and gouge. Even treats that guards gave them—candy and extra food—were used. Wrappers were rolled, braided, linked, and made into garrotes. The ability of some of these detainees to fashion weapons almost from thin air was uncanny. They had learned their lessons well in the camps of Afghanistan.

Each block within Camps I, II, and III (later Camps II and III were integrated for administrative purposes) was given an alphabetical designation. Hence blocks ranged from Alpha to Tango in these camps. Camps II and III housed some of the very worst, most dangerous detainees. Within November, Oscar, and Tango blocks were the discipline and segregation cells. Here, detainees who assaulted guards or attacked other detainees were confined. They were not physically abused but were subject to a more rigorous form of discipline than that of Camp I, for example.

As Colonel Mike Bumgarner told it, "In Camp I, where we're dealing with supposedly compliant guys, a guard might try to reason with a detainee who didn't want to obey right away. Maybe the guy was having a bad day. So the guard would tell him to do something. Pass his empty food containers out, maybe. If the detainee wouldn't obey right away then the guard would give him some time, come back a few minutes later, try to reason with him. We'd work hard not to make something trivial into an issue. But in discipline block the word was passed out from the start: you get one opportunity and one only to obey the guards. If not then a forced cell extraction team is coming in."

How did they react? "Most of them learn their lessons well," Bumgarner said. "But a few just like to push the system. Some of them are fighters and just are aching for a fight. We don't go in there to rough them up. My people are very strict about that. But a guard's orders will be enforced immediately on discipline block. That's the price they pay for acting up. And most of them get that message right away and don't come back."

How long did detainees stay in discipline? "Usually not long," Bumgarner said. "But there are some, a very few, who like it there and don't want to stay anywhere else. Some of them are pretty hard cases and are ideologically committed to jihad, whether inside the cells or outside in the world." Yet most are there for a brief period of time and are anxious to get back to the relative comfort of the other blocks.

There were no solitary cells in Camps I, II, and III or anywhere else. "We don't do solitary," Bumgarner said. "That's against the rules. We can and do enforce segregation at times." What's the difference? "A lot. Solitary is total isolation, limited food, no outside time. Segregation is hard but it's not solitary. I take away all but the most basic issue comfort items and give them absolute minimum requirements of recreation and shower privileges weekly. But they still get their regular meals, do get outside a bit, and can communicate with other detainees by shouting from cell to cell." Bumgarner noted that he "discouraged" communications by running fans nearby, using white noise to mask conversation.[6]

A Navy senior chief in Camp II/III has spent the last six months of his 13-year career on the blocks. "It's not bad duty for me," he said, "but it's very tough on the junior enlisted. For some of them this may be their first real assignment out of basic training and specialty training. And this is what they end up dealing with? It ain't easy."

He told stories of Camp I and the constant badgering of the guards, the vile names: "They call us shitheads, niggers, fucking donkeys. They call us zeroes. Then they'll ask the guards to bring them something. They have our kids running up and down waiting on them hand and foot like flight attendants on an airplane. We spend 90 percent of our time bringing them food, taking them to rec, escorting them to a shower. And the guards take it all day long, day in day out.

"My troops get hit with shit, listen to the constant complaining, constant whining. They give more trouble to the blondes and the black females. I've gained a whole new respect for American troops watching these young people."

Does he feel more comfortable working in Camp I or in II/III? "I don't think this 'compliant' stuff works very well. They're supposed to be compliant at Camp I and we get the most trouble from them. We were taking one of the detainees to rec and a female guard, a blonde, turned her back on him. He didn't have his feet shackled. First he punched her in the back, knocked her down, then kicked her. She just got back up, and helped the others put him back in the cell. She showed no anger. But inside I was raging. Once I told a detainee that I had to take him to rec a bit early. They like a strict schedule and don't want any change, but we were trying to accommodate the ICRC's [International Red Cross] demand that they got more rec time. He called me over. I asked how I could help him. He threw feces in my mouth and nose.

"One of the games they like to play with the guards is to take the Styrofoam box their meal comes in, tear it into tiny pieces and throw it through the mesh or the bean hole onto the deck. They did this every day to one of my guys, a black sailor. 'Pick up the trash, nigger!' they'd yell after they threw it out. The place looked like a snowstorm. Day after day with this same guard. And he was great. He showed no emotion, just got the broom out and swept it up. I have a lot of admiration for him.

"It's not like that in Camp II/III. When they come here we give them the rules first thing. They are to listen to the guards and do exactly what they are told to do. Here we tell them once and they do it or we send a team in to enforce the rules. That's my definition of compliant. If it were my call, I'd make the entire camp like II/III."

Any particular stories from detainees? "A Saudi, Sa'ad al Bidna,

ISN 337 is the 'snowball' king. He repeatedly fakes trying to hang himself. He'll put soap in his mouth to create foam. Then we stop him. In a few minutes he complains 'cause his neck hurts. And, of course, that means we have to take him to the hospital for a check. It's a game with him. And we're the entertainment."

He was also annoyed at the news coverage given to the Camp IV incident. "They said it was a 'riot' and it never got to that proportion. It was a planned, well-conceived ambush of our guys. And I read afterwards that the 'detainees had control of the camp.' That's ridiculous. It never happened and we handled the incident exactly the way we were trained to do. It was picture-perfect response. We had a real team going there."

He talks about the brutal schedule the troops keep here. "They say it's a 12-hour shift but you know the military. Get here at least an hour early; stay at least an hour late. Then we've got training and PT because we still have annual requirements to meet. The stress is enormous but the bonding experience is the closest thing you can get short of combat."

As you shall see, much of the layout, usage, and operational procedures in Camps I and II/III changed after the disturbance and suicides that occurred in summer 2006 and with the opportunity presented by construction of modern facilities in Camps V and VI.

No one among the American guard force, past or present, doubts for a moment that if these "worst of the worst" were released they would go right back to the battlefield. Some would make the battlefield right in the United States. Many of them have American connections. There are among the detainee population graduates from the University of Arizona, Purdue, LSU, and Emory Riddle. Quite a few bad actors are scions of wealthy or middle-class Middle Eastern families and have spent time in America or Europe. Many are originally from Saudi Arabia, but other countries are well represented too.

"We get grief for being *too* nice to some of these guys," Bumgarner said, talking about the conditions in the facility. He noted that among other evidence of humane treatment they are fed up to 4,200-calorie meals daily. "A lot of them are getting fat."

Bumgarner himself had a lot to do with the food service because in his dealings with "the Council," as he began to refer to the collection of detainee leaders with whom he met frequently, food complaints were loud. In a meeting with Shakir Ami in midsummer of 2005, the detainee told Bumgarner that detainee meals were being poisoned. Bumgarner protested loudly but offered to work out a plan that would ameliorate detainee suspicions and improve the food. Ami a few days later was said to have offered up a list that included a two-week menu with suggestions for vegetarian meals, with fish, bland diets, and standard fare. Reportedly this became the core plan on which food service at Guantánamo is currently based.

A TOPIC ABOUT WHICH BUMGARNER was adamant was the attempt to establish a system of personal responsibility among the detainees. He said, "They need to know that they can be rewarded for good behavior and punished for breaking the rules."

Bumgarner and Hood, along with other staff members, had formulated some initiatives in 2004–2006 to accomplish that goal. Rewards were easy to comprehend: discarding the hated orange jumpsuit, moving to a facility with more recreational time, and being able to interact in a communal atmosphere. Punishment means segregation to an individual cell and highly restricted behavior, not "solitary" or "isolation" as some critics claim, for they see other detainees across the hall, at exercise period, and when showering.

The strictest area according to Bumgarner was November Block, a place where detainees arrived only by assaulting guards or other detainees. In November Block no detainee was isolated. They had scheduled recreation time; just not a lot of it. They were permitted to shower at least twice weekly. They received all the heavily laden meals that other detainees got, including any medically designated special diet meals if appropriate. They heard the five-times-daily call for prayer, and had the standard-issue prayer-packet of Koran, beads, oil, rug, and arrow pointing to Mecca. Even in discipline block, the command bent over backwards to try to accommodate detainee sensitivities. In response to a suggestion by his primary detainee contact, self-styled leader Shakir Ami, Bumgarner instructed his guards to place orange "prayer cones"—small rubber traffic cones—at the head of each block aisle during prayer time as a signal for the guards to be quiet and not talk too loudly so that detainees would not be disturbed.[7]

But in November Block detainees had no frills, no luxuries, and were permitted no deviation or delay in complying with a stated schedule or with guards' orders. Life for detainees in November Block was intense and was designed to be that way. If they began to shout and abuse guards or other detainees, they were not silenced, but simply made to compete with "white noise." Large rotating floor fans, for example, could be placed outside their cell so that their shouting was drowned out.

Rarely did detainees spend more than a few days in November Block before they cleaned up their act and asked to be moved to a more benign area. "Once they've spent a few days there nobody wants to go back," Bumgarner said. "It accomplishes its purpose."

Bumgarner's greatest concern was for the safety and welfare of his troops. His constant fear was that the "brotherhood mentality" that permeated the camps would drive detainees to do something that all concerned would later regret. He was aware that the "worst of the worst" have a stated goal to capture guards or interpreters and kill them or hold them for blackmail purposes; failing that, to torture, dismember, and behead any American they could catch.

"They want to kill as many of us as they can," Bumgarner stated. "And we're doing everything we can do to make that kind of action impossible for them to accomplish, while at the same time treating them humanely and with respect." Because of the constant threat, Bumgarner was convinced that "segregation works," and that the most dangerous outcome would be to allow these dangerous men to live communally.

Yet experimentation with communal life in 10-man groups such as in Camp IV had been attempted and to some extent continues, though I was told of repeated, low-level rumblings of several plots. In addition to the attempt to hijack a food truck, plans for a detainee revolt originated in Whiskey Block, as well as talk of an attempt to capture and kill a guard. This was the block that included Omar Khadr as well as some of the rougher, but fully compliant, al Qaeda types.

Despite these and other adverse indicators, General Hood was convinced that communal living was possible and that accommodations could be made with the detainees. Bumgarner, also a proponent of a positive, professional relationship between the two sides, also supported a reward–punishment program including the possibility of more communal activities. In fact, during early 2006 as ground was being broken for new construction, plans were in preparation for up to 20 or more detainees to live together. This was the original concept of Camp VI, where individual cells could be opened so that 20 detainees at a time could socialize and eat together. The setup was going to be extremely flexible, allowing detainees to mix and rewarding them by giving them more outside time and more communal time. The outdoor recreation area was going to be a large space surrounded by high walls but intended to be available to large groups at a time.

Even in the more "compliant" environments the guard force is repeatedly trained, cautioned, and retrained in how to handle themselves and safeguard themselves from violent detainees. The trick is constant vigilance, iron discipline, and rigorous adherence to standard operational procedures.

Meanwhile in Washington, DC, attorneys who had been filing habeas corpus suits in Federal District Court were given the green light to begin representing Guantánamo detainees. Almost immediately— and in contravention of voluntarily signed agreements—the attorneys apparently began to coach detainees in hunger strike techniques. Not that hunger striking was unknown. As early as 2002 there had been some sporadic attempts at this. Now it began to snowball, thanks, most JTF officials agreed, to coaching and suggestions from the habeas attorneys. By July of 2005, 68 detainees had stopped eating. By mid-September the number had grown to 128.[8] It would peak later in the fall at 131. Hood's orders were clear: "No detainee will die by hunger striking on my tour."

The detainees constantly push the envelope with the guards. Bumgarner remained convinced that the habeas lawyers—authorized to represent the detainees in various legal actions—were bringing outside world news to them. This is prohibited by the agreement the attorneys are required to sign with the U.S. government. "Seven days after you see it on the news," Bumgarner said disgustedly, "news will be all over the camps." The detainees use news, particularly bad news from Iraq or repeating something derogatory that an American politician has said about Guantánamo guards, as a prod to anger the guards and possibly get them to let down their vigilance.

Many of the guards were told by detainees that "if you were a real soldier you'd be in Iraq where the mujahedin would kill you." If they learn of anything done diplomatically they disparage it, referring to Secretary of State Condoleezza Rice as "that nigger bitch." They use any bad news of the war—"more Americans are dying in Iraq and you will lose!"—as a way to provoke the guards. So far they have been largely unsuccessful. Occasionally a guard, despite extensive training, will lose his cool and yell back at a detainee or exchange insults. Such behavior results in disciplinary action taken against the guard. Encouraged by the results, the detainees persist in taunting them.

After all, what else do they have to do with their time other than read the Koran (called the "jihad book" by several of the detainees) and hatch plots? This was especially true when they were permitted group activities like recreation and impromptu meetings at the hospital that facilitated plotting and coordinated actions. In camp inspections, it was discovered that detainees were being trained in bomb-making, weapons handling, and tactics, through use of handcrafted expedient materials. Many of the more serious plots to kill guards emerged from the communal, medium-security blocks of Camp IV.

But the rough summer of 2006 was just getting under way. After the incidents with "compliant" detainees in Camp IV had been subdued, within weeks three detainees in "compliant" Camp I hanged themselves in a successful suicide attempt.

IN SPRING 2006, BRIGADIER GENERAL Jay Hood completed his tour in Guantánamo and was replaced by Navy Rear Admiral Harry Harris. The admiral, a former P3C Orion pilot, was acutely aware of the growing tension among detainees. Harris is a brilliant officer, extraordinarily well read, whose mind is as quick as his smile. But he has little patience with fools, and his coal eyes narrow when he thinks that he is being patronized or toyed with by staff or outsiders. Generations of Japanese Bushido culture, inherited from his mother, lie just beneath the surface of a rock-calm exterior. "No one," an aide assured me, "ever screws with the admiral."

Harris came to the assignment fully aware of the adverse international reputation of the facility and of the potential crisis situation building there. Unlike his predecessor, Harris believed in delegating authority to subordinates and trusted their judgment until proven wrong. He was also fully informed of the value of intelligence emerging from Guantánamo and was highly supportive of the interrogation side of the mission. Morale improved, but no one inside the camp was happy.

By June 2006 there was little laughing inside the Guantánamo wire. On the heels of the attempted suicides by drug overdose in May and the uprising in Camp IV, a further shock awaited. Early in the morning of June 10, Camp I guards discovered three detainees hanging in their cells from nooses made from torn sheets, towels, and clothing. Among the others, Colonel Mike Bumgarner recoiled in horror: The "three martyrs" requirement that Shakir Ami had told Bumgarner had to be fulfilled prior to mass release had been engineered by the detainees. Bumgarner's first reaction was bitter disappointment. All the months and effort he had spent with Shakir Ami, Ghassan al Sharbi, Ahmed Rashidi, and the others trying to establish a smooth-running, humane camp based on mutual trust and respect had been destroyed. He told Tim Golden of the *New York Times*, "We tried to improve their lives to the extent that we can—to the point that we may have gone overboard, not recognizing the real nature of who we're dealing with." He had grown confident in the success of his and Hood's "kinder-gentler" management plans, and said, "I'm ashamed to admit it, but I did not think that they would kill themselves."[9]

To a reporter from a North Carolina newspaper doing a piece on a hometown boy he was more blunt: "The trust level is gone. They have shown time and time again that we can't trust them any farther than we can throw them. There is not a trustworthy son-of-a-bitch in the entire bunch."[10] That statement probably reflected a much more factual and realistic appraisal of the situation than his previous rose-tinted approach.

"My guys probably made some mistakes; I made some mistakes," Bumgarner said quietly several months later. What took place to set up the conditions for not one, but three successful suicides?

In his many conversations with Shakir Ami, Sharbi, and Rashidi, Bumgarner had worked hard to accommodate what seemed to be reasonable requests based on the premise that he was dealing with reasonable men. As we have seen, he was determined that neither guards nor detainees be injured on his watch and if a few seemingly minor concessions would help accomplish that, so much the better. The prayer cones placed in the hallways were one of the ideas that seemed to pacify detainees and cost relatively nothing. So, he thought, were requests to dim the lights in the compliant blocks in Camp I at night and to allow the detainees extra clothing and bedding in their cells.[11] As it turned out, all of these concessions were used against him.

Both Joint Detention Group and Joint Interrogation Group personnel are thoroughly convinced that this suicide was no accident, no "reflection of despair" that some claimed it was. CCR attorney Barbara Olshansky was not surprised when she learned of the suicides, and said, "I think people [at Guantánamo] have this incredible level of despair that they will never get justice."[12] William Goodman, legal director at CCR, lambasted Guantánamo: "These are the latest victims . . . in the ongoing effort of this administration to impose a lawless system that denies justice, fairness and due process . . . This is an act of desperation because they have no way to prove their innocence. . . . a system without hope."[13] Baloney, say the authorities at Guantánamo.

While it indeed may have induced, as *Time* magazine said, a "bitter taste" in all who are concerned with Guantánamo, those closer to the action recognize that the suicides were part of a larger, fully coordinated plan.[14] "They've been trying to pull off a suicide since they got here," Paul Rester said. "A lot of the self-styled imams inside of the wire coach the younger ones that while the Koran forbids suicide, taking your life inside makes you a *shaheed*, or martyr, so you get the entire martyrdom package: paradise, virgins, the whole bit."

From the start, Admiral Harris dismissed allegations of "desperation" as a motive for the suicides. "This was not an act of desperation, but an act of asymmetric warfare directed against us," he said. Harris confirmed the story that "three detainees must die" in order to secure their release.[15] The *Telegraph* quoted Harris as describing the detainees as "smart . . . creative . . . committed. They have no regard for life, neither ours nor their own."[16] General Bantz J. Craddock, head of Southern Command and Harris's boss, was also at Guantánamo speaking to the press. The detainees, he said, "are a determined, intelligent, committed element. They continue to do everything they can . . . to become martyrs."[17]

Over the years at Guantánamo there had been 40 or so suicide attempts from about 21 different detainees. Juma Dossari, ISN 261, alone had tried more than a dozen times to end his life. In conversations with Ghassan al Sharbi, Bumgarner and his staff had been alerted to the possibility. Following the narcotics overdose of May 18, they were even more alert, but they still had faith that the system of "trust" was actually holding.

For the suicides to succeed, certain criteria had to be met: Appropriate "martyrs" had to be selected and schooled in the efficacy of the action, an appropriate time had to be selected so that the attempt would have a good chance of success, and the nearby detainee population had to be convinced or coerced to remain silent. The last requirement was especially important, because in the past it was common for nearby detainees to summon a guard if they saw a suicide attempt. On the night of June 9–10 no alarm was raised, suggesting to Guantánamo officials that inhabitants of Alpha Block Camp I were suborned or threatened with retaliation if they did not cooperate. In a compliant camp like Camp I where detainees take recreation together during the week, it would be relatively easy to retaliate against someone who spoiled their plan.

The three men who killed themselves, Mani al Utaybi and Yasser al Zahrani, both Saudis, and Ali Abdullah Ahmed, from Yemen, were young, under 20, and had all been on hunger strike. They were vulnerable to preaching and coaching from the other detainees. During the night they hung up extra bedding that was authorized by the JDG as part of the relaxation program, to give them a privacy screen from the guards. They used the extra clothing, also provided by Bumgarner, to stuff under a sheet on their bunk to look like a sleeping man. With the lights turned down, as Sharbi had requested, it was difficult to see into the cells.

The men had torn bedding and clothing into strips that they made into crude ropes. Officials suspect that others in the block may have helped and passed the strips down through the mesh. Sheets of paper with knot-tying instructions were found in the cells also, indicating that some outside coaching occurred. Tim Golden reports that "there were also indications that Ghassan al-Sharbi . . . had helped plan the suicides."[18]

When it came time to act, the three men stuffed fluff from ripped pillows into their mouths. Was it to stifle moans or to aid in suffocation? We don't know. One of the men, standing on his sink, tied his legs together, presumably to prevent wild kicking. After they had placed their heads in the nooses—and on a signal from a leader on the block who was watching for signs of activity from the guards and timing their actions—the three men stepped off the sinks, fell approximately 18 inches, and strangled themselves.

It was not a sufficient distance to snap their necks, so death likely "took at least four or five minutes, maybe longer," according to a British doctor, David Nicholl, who has been "coordinating international opposition to Guantánamo."[19] Where were the guards during that time? It is difficult to say. In a conversation weeks later, Bumgarner hinted that the guards might have been slack about making their appointed rounds. Or it could have been that the detainees were keen to their routine and hit the timing perfectly. The answer to those and other questions emerged after the investigation.

When the men were discovered, they were, according to a later JTF release, "unresponsive and not breathing. Medical teams . . . provided immediate emergency medical treatment in attempts to revive them."[20] But it was for naught. The three men were dead.

While criticism mounted around the world, it was oddly muted considering the dire predictions that had been made. The president expressed his sorrow about the suicides, and told the world that he would like to close the facility but that it played a vital role in the war on terror.

Our "allies" the Saudis implied the men were murdered, stating, "Since suicide is a grave sin in Islam . . . some question whether Muslim men would kill themselves. . . . but defense lawyers and some former detainees said that many prisoners . . . are wasting away in deep despair."[21]

Mahvish Ruksan Khan, in her first-person account of visiting detainees held in Guantánamo Bay prisons, hypothesizes that one explanation for three simultaneous suicides is that "they were killed" by U.S. captors. She reinforces this alarming hypothesis by one family's quote that their son "would never have committed suicide."[22]

More than two years later, in August 2008, the Navy Criminal Investigative Service completed an exhaustive report on the suicides. Despite accusations by Gitmo opponents, the conclusions drawn by the NCIS were definitive. Notes found on the person and in the cells of the three men were worded in suspiciously similar language. Interviews from other detainees yielded a confirmed report that one of the detainees who did not commit suicide had walked through the block earlier saying "tonight's the night." There was a distinct possibility, NCIS investigators concluded, that "someone within the Camp Delta population was directing detainees to commit suicide."[23]

Hospital commander Captain John Edmunson told a press conference that the men had psychological tests shortly before they took their lives, which did not indicate depression. One of the detainees had told the doctor that he "felt great." "We have lowered the threshold to determine when a detainee is at risk of being suicidal," Edmunson said. "Any detainee thought to be a suicide risk is placed in a tear-proof anti-suicide smock. There are currently about 20 in such smocks."[24]

There was no precipitate closure of the facility. Indeed, by summer of 2006 it was brutally clear that many of the original definitions of "compliance" had to be changed because of atrocious detainee behavior. With Admiral Harris replacing General Hood and the JDG section also changing command, the transition to new SOPs was made somewhat easier. Mike Bumgarner's successor as commander of the Joint Detention Group, Colonel Wade Dennis, shared many of his values but has imposed his own leadership style on the camp.

Toward the end of Bumgarner's tour, there was an incident whereby persons who ought not to have overheard classified information were inadvertently (some say carelessly) allowed access to it. Michael Gordon of the *Charlotte Observer* and a colleague were seated in Bumgarner's office while discussion of material deemed classified was carried out openly. Someone reported the incident. Bumgarner was temporarily suspended from duties, then after some checking was absolved.[25] Reportedly, Admiral Harris had heated words with Bumgarner in which he said, "I could have been relieved for your carelessness." The affair turned into a non-event, and Bumgarner left an extraordinarily difficult tour with his head high and a recommendation for an award for a job well done. Still, it was an unsettling experience for all concerned.

Consequently, Wade Dennis took no chances on leaks; since his office is located smack in the midst of a staff humming with information ranging from unclassified to top secret, he hosted meetings with visitors in a conference room far removed. Dennis held information closer than his predecessor but enthusiastically shared his concept of the value of the detention center and of the need to keep these men confined. "If they tell me to ship them out, I will," he said, noting that a DMO—detainee movement order—was occurring that very day. "But until then my mission is safe, humane treatment and care of these detainees. I don't want them to escape, harm my guards or hurt themselves."

Dennis hit the ground when everything the previous command had attempted to do to establish a balanced, harmonious relationship in the camp between the American captors and the detainees seemed to have come crashing down. The collapse of the previous system was capped by three successful suicides less than a month before Dennis arrived. So does his mission now include new precautions to prevent suicide?

"Absolutely," he affirmed. Dennis leaned forward, his posture reflecting the intensity of his focus. "We have re-structured Camp VI from its original intent as being very open and communal to look more like Camp V. It is tightly structured and re-engineered to make it less accommodating to someone intent on hurting himself." He continued, "We are going to act completely professional, and keep a distance between ourselves and the detainees."

At that point, Dennis urged me to go on a tour of the camps.

CHAPTER 7

COMPLIANCE REWARDED

INSIDE THE CAMP IV WIRE

*"There is a danger that some of the guards
get 'reverse Stockholm syndrome' and begin to
sympathize with the detainees. It could
get them killed."*

JOINT TASK FORCE DETENTION OFFICER

CAMP IV IS A PARADOXICAL place. Opened on February 28, 2003, it is the only medium-security detention facility in the Camp Delta cluster and home of the detainees adjudged to be most compliant. *Mother Jones's* reporters described it as "a sort of honor society," but it is far from that idyllic picture. As far back as November 2004, Camp IV had bred conspiracies like a nasty-bacteria-infused petri dish. A detainee, not wishing to be part of an incident that could have gotten him killed, reported a plot that involved use of homemade weapons to hijack a meal delivery truck that entered the Camp IV compound three times a day. Though it was officially described as an escape plot, the detainees had no real desire to escape per se. Their plan called for them to kill guards, hijack the truck, use it to knock down fences to free more detainees, and stay in the area killing guards until they themselves were killed.

Several detainees later told interrogators that they intended to create an international incident, embarrass the United States, kill as many infidels as possible, and achieve martyrdom in the process. During the lead-up to the planned uprising, Camp IV residents constructed a variety of shanks, knives, garrotes, clubs, and other weapons. In fact, most of the weapons confiscated among the several camps originated from Camp IV. Former Camp IV officer-in-charge, then–Navy Lieutenant Donna Baptiste had the confiscated weapons mounted on boards for display. As is the case in most confinement situations, detainees made weapons from anything that could be used to strangle, puncture, cut, tear, or bludgeon. Pieces of discarded construction material were especially desirable. Despite efforts to police the area, many scraps of mesh, pipe, rod, wire, and glass were picked up by detainees during the initial, rapid construction period of Camp Delta.

Later, after the May 2006 uprising, it was learned that detainees in Camp IV had turned the place into a mini–al Farouk terror training camp. Leaders used makeshift, field-expedient training aids to instruct their fellow detainees on map-reading, bomb-making, weapons use, unarmed combat, and small-unit tactics. Rather than being an "honor society" or Boy Scout camp, Camp IV had—in a manner reminiscent of all U.S. prisons—morphed into a graduate school for violence. As Lieutenant Colonel Michael Nicolucci said with classic understatement, "We are in the process of re-thinking how Camp IV will be configured in the future."

Nicolucci is pulling a yearlong tour of active duty with the 29th Infantry Division, headquartered in Maryland. A senior corporate executive in civilian life, he brings exceptional organizational skills to the exec's job. At six feet four inches tall, Nicolucci towers over most of the detainees and guard force as well. In office conversation he slides his chair back to allow sufficient room to extend his desert boots to comfort level. He is fatalistic about the assignment to Guantánamo.

"At first I didn't like the idea," he said. "In a lot of ways—like a lot of the guys here—I would rather be deployed to a combat theater like Iraq or Afghanistan. But after I arrived I came to realize that in its own way Guantánamo is just another battlefield in the war. Maybe even tougher because we have to be under stricter self-discipline than even the guys who are fighting. This is a necessary mission and we're committed to its success. We are committed to keep these men confined safely and give them all humane treatment. If we can pull it off successfully, and I'm confident that we can, then we'll have made our contribution to the war effort."[1]

L IKE THE OTHER CAMPS, CAMP IV is surrounded by at least two tall chain-link fences topped with coils of razor wire. Guard towers are placed strategically. A sally port, a security arrangement that dates from ancient times, allows a visitor to enter the outer gate. Then that gate is secured before the inner gate is opened. Both gates are never opened at the same time. The process is reversed for exit.

The first thing facing you after entering through the sally port is a regulation-sized basketball goal at the edge of a concrete pad about 30 feet by 20 feet.

"The detainees are learning how to play basketball," the Navy master-at-arms guard in charge said. He noted that some of the Camp IV residents consider basketball a decadent, infidel game and boycott it in favor of soccer. They curse the basketball-playing detainees, usually Afghanis, who play the game with enthusiasm making up for lack of skill, as "traitors to Islam." Perhaps they ought to tell that to Houston Rockets player Hakeem Olajuwon. Nevertheless, the chief petty officer adds, "a lot of the detainees are beginning to enjoy basketball too."[2]

Just behind the basketball court sits a soccer field, with a waist-high fence designed more to keep the ball confined than to keep people inside. As long as they do not assault or threaten guards or other detainees, Camp IV residents have earned the right to wear white, loose-fitting cotton smocks and trousers rather than the hated orange jumpsuit. The chief petty officer pointed out that many "prefer to have the light brown clothing because it doesn't show dirt as much as the white."

So the groups of detainees engaged in communal activity present a mixed white-beige appearance. On outdoor clotheslines, various items are sun-drying. As I watch, pairs of detainees are wringing and tugging on their clothes to squeeze the water out of them prior to hanging them up.

At the midday mealtime the yard bustles with activity. Food is hot, fresh, varied, nutritious, and flavorful. I know, because I sampled some back at the kitchen. The food is brought to Camp IV—and the other camps—in sealed, insulated, thermos-like boxes. Meals are contained in individually marked Styrofoam shells. The detainees have the option of taking individual meals or mixing them and eating communally. Within the sally port the containers are opened and food is carefully inspected by medical personnel. These inspectors have already checked the temperature, packing, contents, and freshness back at the preparation facility. They accompany it to the distribution point for another, final check. Only after they approve is it distributed. Meals rejected for a variety of reasons—too cold is the primary fault—are taken back to the kitchen, discarded, and replaced with freshly cooked servings.

The food is distributed to the various blocks, each of which bears an alphabetic name, U through Z (though no X, because Camp X-Ray already used that letter), or Uniform, Victor, Whiskey, Yankee, and Zulu in the International Phonetic Alphabet. Each block has a covered shelter off the end with picnic-type tables. Food is delivered there and distributed among the detainees. Some sit and eat with their fellows; others take their portion back to the communal room—where there are 10 bunks to a room—to eat by themselves. The choice is theirs. This system is preferred by the detainees who make their desires known. It gives a communal, social aspect to mealtime.

While observing the mealtime rituals, the Navy chief in charge pointed out the residents of Whiskey Block and said, "We got wind of a plot there in 2005 to capture one of the guards and torture and kill him—or her. Some of those guys speak pretty good English. Omar Khadr was in Whiskey for a time. Hell, he grew up in Canada. They constantly try to strike up conversations with the guards, ask personal things, try to get inside their heads. Because these guys are supposed to be compliant, you know, wearing white and beige and all, the troopers might relax and let down their guard. That's all it will take. One minute of carelessness and suddenly we have a death on our hands." So far no one has been killed, but many attempts have been made on guards' lives and several plots have been uncovered.

What does he do about it? "We have to emphasize vigilance constantly," he said. "They [guards] get good training before they arrive at Guantánamo and we keep a pretty solid training program up for them after they're here. They can never forget these guys are our enemies. Treat 'em humanely, but never, ever trust one of them."[3]

While I was present, the Muslim call to prayer was chanted in each block by a detainee selected by his fellows. The call for prayer is sounded five times daily by the American staff over loudspeakers, but each block prefers to go on their own schedule. Today Whiskey Block starts off the call, in Pashto, and it is picked up around the large quadrangle by other blocks. At least three languages, maybe four, were evident in the noon call for prayer. It is a musical chant, punctuated by frequent repetitions of "Allahu akbar," carrying all of the exotic connotations of Central Asia, somewhat strange to hear in the Caribbean. Within minutes after meals are consumed ("Nothing gets in the way of these guys eating," a guard said, "including prayer time"), detainees in the blocks line up for prayer. Each, of course, has his rug, beads, and oil, along with a Koran provided by America for his use.

Within each block a particular detainee—usually the unofficial block leader—leads the actual prayer session. The identities of both the detainee who chants the call and the prayer leader himself are noted by the guards. This information is shared with detention administrators. Changes in personnel and functions may have significance for behavioral and compliance purposes and are duly noted.

Most of the inhabitants of Camp IV are Afghanis, we were told, though several other nationalities are included among the population. Here also for many months was the Canadian, Omar Ahmed Khadr, who is one of the Military Commission participants. In 2005, Khadr lived for a time in Whiskey Block with nine other detainees, mostly Afghanis.

We were also told that there are notably few Saudis in Camp IV, even though Saudis form a large portion of the overall population. "Saudis are less compliant," the guards tell us. "They fight more. They attack guards, and attack and intimidate other detainees who don't behave the way they want them to." The Saudis, who originate in the Bedouin-based culture that produced the virulent Wahabbist sect of Islam, are more intense in their commitment to jihad, and always ready and willing to eliminate any who do not conform to their standards. They tend to look down on the Afghanis, many of whom consider their form of Islam "purer" than the Wahabbism the Saudis preach. This provokes the Saudis to attack and threaten. Hence they are detained in camps with stricter security measures.

Conversely, bad behavior in a communal camp can result in privileges being taken away. Once I watched a detainee in Camp IV "test the fence" and continue to do so despite repeated warnings from guards. His behavior was reported to higher command and at the direction of the camp operational commander, and thus he was removed from his communal block, shackled, and escorted to Camp II/III, where he was placed in segregated quarters—a single person to a cell, under a much stricter daily regime than in the more relaxed Camp IV atmosphere. If he behaves there, he can regain his Camp IV privileges.

What was his motive for behaving in a manner certain to draw repercussions? "It's tough to say for sure," said Nicolucci. "Sometimes they seem to get tired of communal living and just want to be by themselves for a while. Most of the time we think that they are messengers, transferring information or instructions from camp to camp and playing the system in such a manner that they know they will be moved."[4]

During much of the time when the various detainee categories of designations were being formulated and put into action, Camp IV was under supervision of Donna Baptiste. A dedicated Navy officer from Newport, Rhode Island, Baptiste is a Desert Storm veteran who rose from the enlisted ranks to win an officer's commission, and despite serious medical issues volunteered for a tour of duty at Guantánamo. "She was superb with the guys in Camp IV," Bumgarner told me. "They thought so much of her that they would do anything she told them to do. Many of them cried when she left."

Baptiste showed a side that never gets reported. After the basketball court was completed, she bought several balls with her own money for the detainees to use. When she found out the detainees liked green tea, she bought them some. One night in the camp she discovered that one of the detainees had a bad cough that was keeping him up. She brewed some tea for him to quiet the cough.

She was adamant that the detainees "respect her guards" and vice versa. She accompanied one of the detainees, a young Afghan in his mid-thirties, on several trips to the dentist. Somehow he was still in pain that became especially acute one day. "The escorts called and said that they would be late," Baptiste said, "so my senior chief and I walked him over. The poor guy was still terrified of the dentist. My chief patted him on the leg to comfort him."

"Gladiator" was internal code for a detainee-on-detainee assault. Baptiste witnessed a couple of incidents and was careful to use a cultural interpreter to find out whether they were more than simple personality conflicts. If a conflict could be settled without punishment, she settled it.

Her comment about the perception of how Guantánamo is portrayed? "I get so damn mad at the media. They distort and lie about everything. No one knows the real picture down here."[5]

Are some of the guards too friendly at Camp IV? "We sometimes see what we call the 'reverse Stockholm syndrome,'" Brigadier General Edward Leacock said, "where the guards begin to think that the detainees are just innocent farmers or are their friends. Guards are told that these people are 'compliant' and may think they can relax. If they are on one post too long some of the detainees may try to buddy-up with them. A lot of these guys speak English better than the guards and have more education and experience. They are very manipulative." All it takes, Leacock emphasizes, is for one guard to relax too much, for one detainee to gain an edge, and tragedy can result.

Are there steps that can help alleviate this problem? "We train them hard when they're not on duty," Leacock said. "And constantly reinforce professional behavior. Also we like to rotate them through various positions and that keeps them from getting too complacent. It would be a shame if one of these kids got killed because he or she had an instant of carelessness. But it could happen very quickly."[6]

Interestingly, I was told by guards that despite the relative comfort of Camp IV, it is a common occurrence for some detainees to misbehave deliberately, violating instructions in a minor manner such as the "fence testing" I observed, and spend some time in a private cell. Some of this seemingly aberrant behavior could mean that a detainee has simply tired of the communal block living and wants to have some privacy. But it is also highly likely that the acting up is intentional, designed to force the Americans to move him and thereby facilitate intra-camp messenger servicing. A detainee on the move is an automatic conduit to other camps, carrying information, news, and messages back and forth. Life in Guantánamo is a constant cat-and-mouse game between detainees and guards, and as in any confinement situation, all things are possible. Both sides must learn to think out of the box. It is a skill at which the institutionalized detainees excel.

Following the incidents of May and June 2006, Admiral Harris began to rethink the policy of compliancy. "Most of my problems came out of Camp IV," he said. "So I had to ask if we needed to modify our attitudes towards these people. Were they taking advantage of our good nature—maybe our naiveté—in order to plot, gang up, and cause trouble?"

"We had big issues in Camp IV," Lieutenant Colonel Nicolucci said. "They were training each other on weapons, bomb-making, small-unit tactics, and Islamic jihad. Experts in certain areas would present instruction to the others. We were actually empowering these guys to work against us."

"Many of the really 'compliant' ones are simply hiding in deep cover," Paul Rester noted. "They are some of the brightest and in many cases, we think, the most dangerous. We were putting them in a position where they were underground leaders and trainers for much of the rest of the population."

One of the medical officers observed how two weeks prior to the May 18, 2006 disturbance, the detainees in Yankee Block (part of Camp IV) wanted more recreation time. "They get more rec time than any others," he said, "but they decided to make a big deal about it and started acting up big time. It made no sense. It was dumb. Or that's what we thought. Finally the OIC had to send in emergency reaction force teams to take them away to discipline block. Most were back after a couple of days, which is SOP." So what was the relationship to the May 18 incident? "Remember, the guys in Yankee Block didn't act up on May 18th. Prior to that they were testing the system: how long would it take for a response, who would come, what the timing was, and what our SOPs were. That wasn't anything more than an intel collection operation on their part. And it worked."

Something needed to be done, but what? After Wade Dennis took over detention functions he got involved. "The last thing we wanted to do was to give these guys a platform from which to attack us, but from hindsight it seems that is exactly what we were doing. We knew we had to change."

Concomitant with the plan to consolidate most of the population inside Camps V and VI, extensive remodeling of Camp IV was initiated. On a tour of the facilities, Nicolucci explained the changes Dennis was contemplating. "You won't see Camp IV configured as it was in the past," he said. "First off, we are going to have far fewer detainees here. No more of the 10-to-a-bay kind of arrangement. We decided that was giving them too much chance to organize and plot. At the most in the future we'll have five or fewer."

He pointed to the ceiling. "All the light fixtures and the camera will be recessed and protected so that they can't break out the bulbs and use them as weapons. The blocks will be air-conditioned so we can lose the fans, which were another source of weapons. The guards will be behind Plexiglas so that they can't be hit by anything thrown at them, and the bunks will be welded to the floor so they can't be torn up and used as clubs and spears."[7]

"We will probably use Camp IV as a contingency camp for the most part," Dennis said. "I don't see more than 30 or 40 detainees there at any one time and probably fewer. We trusted them and they showed that we were foolish to do so. They betrayed our trust once and we won't be fooled that way again."

CHAPTER 8

SEGREGATION AND SUPERVISION

CAMPS V AND VI

"It's a miracle my soldiers can deal with the constant abuse and assaults they receive from the detainees. They make it through the day because of training and discipline."

SFC ALLEN RICH, NONCOMMISSIONED OFFICER-IN-CHARGE, CAMP V

"THESE MEN ARE THE WORST of the worst." That's how commander of detainee operations Mike Bumgarner described the denizens of Camp V.[1] His evaluation is shared by his successor, Colonel Wade Dennis, and by both JTF commanders General Hood and Admiral Harris.

Major Timothy O'Reilly, who worked as operations officer for Bumgarner in 2005, said that he had never really encountered what he considered evil men before. "I worked as a defense attorney for years in the California penal system," he said. "But it wasn't until I walked those blocks and looked into some of those eyes that I realized what true evil was." Was this an exaggeration, perhaps, caused by an over-whelming sense of fear?

A broad-shouldered descendant of men who shoveled peat for a living and fought Black-and-Tans for amusement, O'Reilly was an anomaly: a trained attorney who eschewed what he considered the effete Judge Advocate General corps for the crossed-cannon insignia of Artillery. A Reservist, he returned to Newport Beach, California as a prosecutor, and his very appearance in the courtroom was said to make defense attorneys and criminals shrink.

"I knew the backgrounds on a lot of those detainees. I read the classified reports of what they had done in al Qaeda or the Taliban. These were people who had committed the most awful crimes, who lacked even the most basic humanity when it came to the victims of their actions. They weren't soldiers; they were stone, conscienceless killers. You could see it in their eyes."

How would he describe the look? "There was an emptiness of all humanity in those eyes. It was a vacuousness of a soul."[2]

Since camps have been numbered sequentially as they were constructed, Camps V and VI are the most modern. The two camps sit beside each other, connected by shared wire, and a bit distant from the original Camp Delta facility. They are sited on high ground overlooking the spreading Caribbean Sea. Under more benign circumstances the location would be a developer's dream. In Guantánamo it is a terrorist's nightmare.

Start with Camp V. As with all other camps, the outside world is separated by sally ports, double fences, concertina wire, and guard towers. However, Camp V is sleek, multistoried, and ultramodern in design and construction. Its architecture is based on lessons learned from prisons in the United States. Specialists in these matters flew down to Guantánamo to act as consultants. Their challenge was to produce a building that serves the standard detention mission—as do American maximum-security prisons—and has the additional capability of providing in-house interrogation facilities, medical facilities, and a meeting room for attorneys to talk privately with detainee clients.

The reason for Camp V is coldly simple: Some of these men,

despite being held in humane conditions, continue to threaten Americans by words and actions. They are the ones who regularly attack guards. They throw spit, urine, feces, vomit, and semen at guards at every opportunity.[3] They curse, threaten, and tell guards that they will have their al Qaeda friends rape and murder their families. They refuse to obey instructions, leaping from bunks onto guards when they need to be moved, or wedging themselves under bunks so that the guards have to pry them out. They claw under guards' protective masks, trying to gouge eyes and to rip and tear lips and ears. Nothing is easy with these men. They are the organizers and the motivators. When mixed with a more benign general population they may be enforcers—intimidating, attacking, and beating other detainees in order to bend them to their will.

A high percentage of the Camp V inhabitants are from Saudi Arabia. This is not a heavily advertised statistic because of America's bizarre relationship with the desert kingdom, a country that is billed as an ally but often behaves like an enemy. Just as a majority of the September 11, 2001 terrorist hijackers were Saudis, so are most of the noncompliant detainees in Guantánamo's Camp V facility.

The guards in Camp V—as befits the nature of the mission—are the most professional in the business. These men and women are trained corrections specialists, U.S. Army Military Occupational Specialty 31E, a subset of the Military Police branch. They enlisted in the Army and volunteered to be detention center guards. Many have served in correctional facilities within the United States and around the world.

The Noncommissioned Officer-in-Charge on two of my visits was the highly-squared-away Sergeant First Class Allen Rich, from Lakewood, Colorado. He has served at the military prison at Fort Leavenworth, Kansas, as well as others around the United States and in Germany. His last tour of duty was as a drill sergeant, a position reserved for the most promising and professional NCOs Army-wide. Rich is about six feet tall, with a wiry, tough physique that exudes enthusiasm and energy, and has encyclopedic knowledge of his area of responsibility. His standards of performance are reflected by the discipline, demeanor, and conduct of his soldiers. I was told on a later visit that Rich had been selected for Officer Candidate School.

During our tour we saw an interrogation team on break. A man in civilian clothes was napping in his chair.

"Sir," SFC Rich made the point, "that man is not one of my team. He's a linguist. I just wanted you to know. No one on my team would ever be permitted to lounge around like that."[4]

Every entrance into Camp V is a sally-port type. This is consistent with doctrine in all detention facilities. One door must be closed before the next door may be opened. In Camp V much of the oversight is electronic and computer assisted, permitting a lower manpower requirement compared to other facilities. A central control tower arrangement allows guards to monitor all entrances and internal spaces with cameras or direct line of sight. Guards on the floor communicate with each other and the tower using portable radios affixed to their uniforms or equipment harnesses. Camp V is a more secure facility, but because of high-tech advances it requires fewer guards and supervisors than a medium-security facility.

Camp V is essentially a core-with-spokes arrangement, having wings with sufficient individual cells to accommodate upward of 100 detainees. It also has a very modern medical/dental space in which all but complex procedures can be performed. A necessary addition is interrogation facilities that resemble more than anything else a small living-room ensemble—armchairs, a table, and a love seat or recliner for the detainee—with the provision that the detainee can be secured by a metal ring mounted in the floor. Some of these men have a history of attacking interrogators and interpreters. Securing them in place protects everyone concerned. As in other interrogation facilities there are two camera systems, one for the analysts who observe such things as detainee/interrogator body language and responses, and another for the guards in the case of an attack incident. There is a "panic button" on the wall within easy reach of the interrogator in case of untoward detainee behavior.

Having these additional facilities on site hugely reduces the need to move these "worst of the worst" long distances. Previously it was necessary to transport them from living facilities to medical, dental, or inter-rogation sites. It was during these moves that several attack incidents occurred, including punching, spitting, and scratching at nurses and doctors. By having them under a single roof, the temptation—and opportunity—to act aggressively is reduced.

Each cell in Camp V is highly efficient, ultramodern, and no frills. In a confinement scenario, "frills" can be converted into homemade weapons. In the past, detainees have used these weapons against guards and against fellow detainees they wish to intimidate. A collection of weapons includes springs removed from bunks, links of fencing straightened and sharpened, plastic shards from spoons, and a range of other items. In Camp V, much of the raw material for weapons has been removed.

Every cell contains a toilet and basin. In earlier constructed camps, the basins had extended faucets. The detainees jumped on the faucets, breaking them off from the wall and turning them into jagged-edged metal knives. In Camp V, basin water comes from a spout and there is nothing to break off. Bunks are solid, welded into position, with camping-type sleeping mats on top, not springs. Clothing hooks are short, blunt, and straight and will swivel with pressure, devices that preclude a detainee's ability to hang himself or rip them from the wall.

All detainees have space in their cell for a Koran and personal prayer items. A Belgian prison official, Alain Grignard, deputy head of Brussels's federal police antiterrorism unit, said, "At the level of the detention facilities, it is a model prison." At Guantánamo, "prisoners' rights to practice their religion, food, clothes and medical care were better than in Belgian prisons. 'I know of no Belgian prison where each prisoner receives its [sic] Muslim kit,' Grignard said."[5] He had "noticed dramatic improvements each time he visited the facility over the past two years." He was roundly castigated by certain European activist groups after making that statement.

Camp V detainees shower several times a week. There are individual showers in every block. Shower stalls are concrete all around and have no protruding parts that can be broken off. Heavy wire-mesh doors separate the detainee from the outside and three concrete walls are inside the shower. A shackled detainee enters the shower, turns around, and places his hands through the bean hole. His shackles are removed and the shower is activated on a 10-minute timer. Many detainees tuck clothing into the wire to form a privacy screen while they shower.

After finishing, the process is reversed. In one odd-appearing situation, an artificial leg protruded from the bean hole while a detainee showered. He had lost a leg sometime in his life and had a modern prosthetic leg provided by the United States. When showering, he kept the leg dry by shoving it out of the door.

In one of several tours through Camp V, I was standing in the first-floor hub area near the internal control room. SFC Rich was explaining one of the procedures when I had the uncomfortable sensation of being stared at. Behind me, on the second floor of one of the two showers, was a large man with an oversized head, jet-black unruly hair, and a tangled, water-soaked beard. But what was unnerving was the unwavering, hostile stare that penetrated through bulletproof glass down onto the floor.

Later, I told a few of the Camp V guards about the incident and mentioned that it "gave me the creeps." Rich agreed. "When I look at some of these people I can feel the sense of evil deep in my soul," he said gravely. "It's not what we run into in prisons anywhere else. These guys are not here to serve time, behave well, and get out. There's a big difference: these guys will kill us if they get the chance."[6]

Another guard, Staff Sergeant Raylon Miller, from Sacramento, California, responded with his own story: "I was here only a day or two. Just getting accustomed to walking the floor, and out on Delta block. All of a sudden one of the detainees began to yell 'Iraq! Iraq!' I didn't know what to make of it and went over to his cell. 'I know you from Iraq,' he said. 'You were in the prison there. Why aren't you wearing your combat patch from the unit you were with there?' It turns out we captured him in Iraq, released him, and re-captured him somewhere else. Either in Afghanistan or Bosnia, I guess."

How did the incident make him feel? "It really freaked me out. I mean, here's this guy who's probably seen a hundred Americans and he *recognizes* me? He even remembered my name and the unit I was with. He knows that we wear a combat patch on our right sleeves? Nothin' gets past these guys. I had to leave the block for a minute and go outside to regain my composure."[7]

Several detainees came from the battlefield with missing or injured limbs. Some were old injuries incurred years prior to capture by U.S. forces. Most had received, at best, cursory medical care from their own people. A few had homemade or primitive prosthetic devices. At Guantánamo they received the best, most modern prosthetics, as good as our wounded soldiers get returning from combat in Afghanistan and Iraq. There is a documented instance of a released detainee—one who was judged by the Annual Review Board process to be "no longer a danger to the U.S."—who had been fitted with a prosthetic leg during his Gitmo stay and was back on the battlefield fighting against American and Coalition forces.[8]

Many human rights organizations have vociferously condemned the Guantánamo facility as being "inhumane" and "abusive." One of the reasons they cite is that detainees are held in "isolation." They use Camp V as an example. It is therefore important to note that while detainees in Camp V are in fact segregated—one to a cell—they are not isolated. They see other detainees, and are permitted to converse across the hall and from cell to cell. "They talk to each other all the time," Rich noted, "and, of course, we don't interfere with that." It was reported that in Camp V, detainees also will yell into the toilet piping to communicate with their fellows.

Was this something that had developed over time, this detainee organization? "These guys were not a bunch of rabble coming together after they were imprisoned," said guard Sergeant Philip Shell, of Ketchikan, Alaska. "They were fully trained and cohesive *before* they got here. They are especially well trained in solidarity and cohesion. They know how to play us."[9]

"I call a couple of them 'Heavies,'" Rich commented. "They don't ever get involved in assaults themselves but they have enough authority to tell other, younger ones what to do. Sometimes they'll have one of these guys assault us to get moved to discipline block or to fake being sick to get over to the hospital. That's how they communicate and pass messages back and forth."

While I was present one of the detainees, apparently thinking I was from a media organization, began to lecture us loudly—in English—about his situation. Other detainees piped up in Arabic, shouting at him. During shower time, two detainees are in adjacent showers and are able to speak to each other if they desire. Several times weekly, Camp V detainees are permitted outdoor recreation. They are taken to the interior courtyard of the facility and unshackled into individual outdoor cages. Several detainees are outside simultaneously, each in a separate cage but sharing common wire-mesh walls permitting them to touch through the wire and converse openly. This is not isolation or solitary confinement by any definition, certainly not by the standards routinely applied in American prisons.

There are some tough characters inside Camp V and assaulting guards is common. "Sometimes they'll pretend to be friendly," Rich said, "to try to get the guards to relax. Then they'll toss a cup full of piss and shit at their faces or try to grab an arm to break it. I tell my people never, never lose your focus." Guards work long hours, and much of their time off the floor involves training. "We get refresher training every six months, and cultural awareness training more frequently."

Who are some of the tough ones? "They're almost all bad," Miller laughed. He has the unusual distinction of having served in Fallujah, Iraq, with his uncle, and has seen a lot. "David Hicks is one of the baddest. The other 'brothers' respect him because he left his woman and kids to go fight for Islam. They tell us how brutal he was on the battlefield and they admire that too. But lately Hicks has been flipping back and forth between Islam and Christianity. When he asked for a Bible one was given him, and word of that got out to the others. They are having trouble dealing with that."

What are the biggest problems on the blocks? "Medical, medical, medical." All three said it almost simultaneously.

"It's not their fault," Shell said. "The Navy medics don't get enough training in restraint procedures. They are trained to treat sick and injured people, not deal with killers like these. They don't have a sense when they get here about who is sick and who is faking. They get too close and get hit with a cup of crap or get busted up. By the time they learn they rotate out 'cause they're only on a six-month tour."

Rich quickly steps in. "You've got to know that these sailors and soldiers are among the most professional I've ever seen in my Army career. They bust their butts every day on the blocks and their only reward is to be insulted constantly—called the worst names you can imagine—and assaulted. We have at least one or two assaults a day here alone. And they still come back for duty every morning standing tall and proud. Tell your readers that for me."

Rich's comments are not isolated reports. In an October 2006 BBC interview, a former Guantánamo guard told of the threats and assaults on him by detainees. "They call me nigger, slave, they touch their necks and say 'We will kill you in Iraq.' I know why they do it, to provoke me, so that I will make a mistake. But I will just do my job, finish it, go and work out, or go fishing, or read my Bible."[10]

What about their relationship with the Joint Intelligence Group guys? "We have the utmost respect for them," Rich said. "They have miles and miles of patience. So do the cultural advisors. Whenever we're having a problem that we can't seem to fix we call on them. They're a big help."

Camp V detainees are aware that a greater degree of compliance—obeying guards' orders, not cooperating with interrogators—will reward them with more individual freedoms such as communal living in Camp IV. Some have been in more permissive environments and committed misbehaviors that earned them a trip back to segregated detention. How they decide to live in Guantánamo is a choice that individual detainees are free to make in an environment that by definition offers limited options. But it would be madness to mix these hard men into either a more benign general population or among themselves without intense supervision. Only deaths—most likely of cooperative detainees—and mob violence would be the expected results. Segregation of detainees is therefore necessary for eminently practical reasons, as well as for establishing a tiered arrangement that offers incentives for compliant behavior.

"We have responsibility for these people—safe and humane care. It's not about power," Rich said. "We're firm, fair, and consistent with them, give them respect and tell them the truth. We're doing the right thing."

Communal No Longer

Camp VI is an imposing structure, solid and modern. Its clean, crisp lines contrast incongruously with the tropical vegetation that grows just beyond the tall chain-link fence with the coiled razor wire atop it. The noncommissioned officer in charge, a U.S. Navy senior chief petty officer, says that the facility is modeled after a county prison in Michigan.

The latest and, at this point, final link in the chain of prisons, Camp VI was finished in November 2006. By mid-December almost 50 detainees had been moved into the various pods. It had been scheduled to open almost a month earlier, but ribbon cutting was delayed until the interior living space, designed for communal living, could be retrofitted.

The original concept for communal living was based on the hypothesis—strongly held by then–JTF commander General Jay Hood—that some, perhaps most, of the detainees could be trusted to live quietly and in relative harmony with the guards at some future time. The basis for Hood's hypothesis was that fair, humane, even generous treatment toward the detainees would be acknowledged by compliant behavior and a diminution of their jihadist ideology and mission.

When in the difficult May–June period of 2006 three attempted suicides were followed by a Camp IV uprising and ultimately by three successful suicides in Camp I, the whole theory of rating detainees for compliancy and the practice of rewarding better compliancy by increased trust—the rewards conveyed by more communal living—was called into question.

"It didn't take us long to realize that most of our problems were originating from the groups we labeled 'compliant,' primarily in Camp I and in Camp IV," Wade Dennis said. "Therefore the Admiral changed the plans for the new Camp VI facility." How so?

Admiral Harris had been convinced from the start that the medium-security camp, Camp IV, and Camp I, together housing the "most compliant" detainees, posed the greatest threats. In both camps, detainees who had been rated compliant were permitted the most communication with each other along with the most mingling. Unfortunately, detainees violated the trust placed upon them and plotted to kill American guards and harm themselves. In reviewing the outcome of the previous policy, Harris concluded that "there is no such thing as a medium-security terrorist."[11]

Camp VI is a $37 million structure originally designed as a communal facility in which maximum recreation time, co-mingling, and socialization among detainees was permitted. Camp VI has eight separate pods surrounding common areas. Each pod is two-story, with a high-ceilinged, roughly circular interior, and contains 22 individual cells plus a common area. Pod interior space is very open and well lit, with both skylights and protected fluorescent lighting. Cells have protected fluorescent lighting and are painted a light, neutral color.

Each cell measures 6 feet, 8 inches in width by 12 feet in depth, for an 81-square-foot capacity. Both Camps V and VI meet or exceed the American Correctional Association standards of 80 square feet space per cell. When filled, single-bunk Camp VI holds 176 detainees. If double-bunking is necessary—and that is not being considered unless need arises for emergency shelter, such as in an approaching hurricane—that number rises to 220 (not all cells are fitted with the second bunk space).

Inside, many of the cells have two single metal bunk racks welded into the walls, a stainless-steel Western-style toilet and sink, and a stainless-steel desk/table and bench also welded into the walls. On the walls are two special low-weight-bearing hooks for hanging clothing.

The second floor of each Camp VI pod is of a mezzanine-type design, with low metal bar railings protecting an open walkway onto which cell doors face. Detainees access the second floor by way of metal stairwells. Handicapped cells are available if needed on the first floor. These cells are identified by a wider-than-normal access door and special toilet.

The pod communal space is occupied by several metal picnic-style tables and benches welded to the concrete floor and by a series of storage units and wire baskets. These were originally intended as a place for board games, books, personal possessions, and the like. Shower stalls are located around the common area.

Also located within Camp VI's central area, around which the eight pods are built, is a very modern medical and dental facility, administrative offices, and guard break areas. There are also a few private rooms within which a detainee may meet with his attorney. Each of these rooms contains a camera but no sound equipment, so that client–attorney privilege is respected but guards can monitor against passing of contraband items or in case of assault.

After the difficult summer of 2006, the interior pods of Camp VI were retrofitted at an approximate million-dollar cost. Those nice balconies inside the pods were just too convenient a place for a mass suicide by hanging, or by a detainee launching himself into the air to break a neck or fracture a skull on the concrete floor below. A proclivity to incite a mass uprising would place guards in jeopardy of facing a large number of detainees—20 or more at a time—that they would have to subdue.

Given that the committed jihadists, especially among the so-called compliant groups, have demonstrated that regardless of how leniently they are treated they will harm themselves or guards, the command had no choice but to clamp down and revise the policy on communal living. "If they are segregated individually and kept in a place where the ability to harm themselves is minimized," Wade Dennis said, "then my troops will be able to complete their mission of safe, humane care and treatment that much more effectively."[12]

It is important to note a vital distinction between prisons designed to house criminals, who for the most part are simply serving time, and jihadists who are sworn to kill Americans and would welcome death as a consequence. As the Navy senior chief at Camp VI told us, "To these people we are not simply jailors, we are the enemy that they are committed to kill. I warn my people on the blocks never to forget that fact."[13]

As a result of the revised threat evaluation, a thorough refitting was undertaken. Two railings were added atop the original railing and heavy mesh chain-link fencing was run the entire length of the elevated walkways, wall-to-wall right up flush with the ceilings. It is now impossible for a detainee to harm himself by jumping or hanging.

The ideal of a happy detainee community playing board games, eating communal meals, and chatting around the picnic tables has also been shelved, probably permanently. The haunting potential of 20-plus simultaneous suicides or a mass uprising from detainees who were "trusted to behave properly" gave the lie to Hood and Bumgarner's original bucolic vision. The stainless-steel picnic tables will remain in place—it is cheaper to leave them than rip them out—but will not be used by detainees in the foreseeable future. Storage units are being utilized, but personal contents have to be brought up to a detainee's cell when he requests them.

Detainees have been shifted into Camp VI on a planned, measured, highly considered basis. Joint Detention Group commander Colonel Wade Dennis, who replaced Colonel Michael Bumgarner in August 2006, wanted to "have most of the detainee population in camps IV, V, and VI as soon as practicable."

Dennis is of average height and commands any room he enters with the force of his personality. Polite and affable, he is restrained in speech and considers his words before vocalizing them. One senses immediately that an ass-chewing from Wade Dennis would be a memorable experience but one that few would wish to repeat. Concomitantly, you know in your heart that he has administered more than a few in his day.

Dennis intended to use Camp I for "residual" detainees, if there are any. That would include men waiting for return to host countries after release or whose transfer is approved by the ARB. At present detainee movement orders occur on an irregular, intermittent basis; hence the overall census is slowly declining. As a result, the number that may not be accommodated under Dennis's plan to consolidate everyone into Camps IV, V, and VI may be few indeed.

Will all this consolidation pose a problem? Possibly. Before Dennis even came to Guantánamo, SFC Allen Rich spoke about population numbers in Camp V. "When the census increases," he said, "you can feel the tension and stress rise." He's not certain as to why but knows it happens. "Below 79 or so things are okay, but when it gets up to 85 or more things get tense." It is an issue that will have to be determined by trial and error over time.

As internally secure as Camp V appears to be, the detainees have at least once beaten the system. In June 2007, on the anniversary of the three 2006 suicides, a detainee, 34-year-old Abdul Rahman Ma'ath Thafir al Amri, managed to hang himself during afternoon prayer. Fully aware of the "quiet time" imposed by the JDG commander—during which guards' movements are restricted, prayer cones encouraging low-voiced conversations are placed out, and detainees are left unobserved—the Camp V detainee leaders decided that would be the best time to act.

Amri was coached by internal Camp V leaders on how to proceed. He was in many ways a typical Saudi detainee: The disaffected late-born son of a middle-class family, he'd dabbled in alcohol and drugs before finding salvation in virulent Wahabbist Islam, trained in Afghanistan's al Qaeda camps, and eventually became a mid-level AQ operative. He had been a hunger striker and at one time was precariously thin, then was given supplemental nutrition to regain his health.

According to unofficial accounts, Amri collected plastic food wrappings and braided a short rope from them while the rest of the block prayed. He then used a rolled mattress to reach the air-conditioning vent, threaded the handmade rope through the grill and around his neck, and hanged himself. He was found almost immediately, but by then he had succeeded. Despite frantic resuscitation efforts he was declared dead at the detainee hospital.[14]

O NE OF THE STATED GOALS achieved in relocating the detainee population into Camps V and VI was that with their in-house medical, interrogation, and attorney meeting areas, the intra-camp traffic that had been the norm was greatly reduced. Prior to this consolidation, it was a common sight to see shackled detainees riding four-wheelers with two escort guards almost any time of the day. They had to be escorted to the dispensary, hospital, or dentist. They were taken to see their attorneys, and they were moved into Camp Delta for interrogation. With consolidation into Camps V and VI, much of that kind of extraneous movement has been mitigated. If they need to go to interrogation, booths are available in Camp V. Dental? Camp VI has full-up dental support and sophisticated medical care for all but the most serious cases. If the meeting room for attorneys is full, they can be moved a short distance across the road to Camp V or in a pinch down to Camp Iguana. All in all it is a much better solution.

Why is this detainee movement reduction so important? In a large percentage of the cases, movement facilitated communications between camps and among detainees. Common areas like the detainee dispensary and the detainee hospital were favorite meeting places to exchange camp-to-camp information. The medical personnel were told not to refuse a detainee the right to go on sick call, so the local camp or block leader might designate one to complain of stomach cramps and diarrhea that day or to wake up with a headache. Once at the hospital, he could converse with fellow detainees, trade news and information, and pass along instructions. Many think that orders to engage in hunger strikes, to act hostile toward guards, or other instructions were commonly passed by this method. With less movement, some of that traffic will be reduced.

Impeding communications is another reason Dennis took time to move detainees into Camp VI in a most deliberate manner. It is also a reason for him to reconsider the policy of moving detainees who "act up" into a disciplinary block. "We won't need to move them because of the existence of camps V and VI," he said. "When we took them out of Camp IV or Camp I and moved them to Camp II/III for discipline, all we were doing was permitting messages to be exchanged between the leaders of the various camps. One reason that hunger striking was able to spread so fast, for example, is that the orders went out from the in-house leaders and were conveyed by detainees who deliberately assaulted a guard or tried to harm themselves. These guys were taken to a discipline block, then returned with new instructions to their old blocks. Now that I've got the capacity to house them individually and separately with minimum movement we're going to put a stop to a lot of that nonsense."

Dennis intended to "mothball" Camp II/III (and even Camp I if possible) in order to reduce needed manpower but still have the camps available in the unlikely event a contingency arises. He also recognized that keeping the vacant camps well maintained, clean, and ready for use is a better use of taxpayers' money than simply closing them down and allowing the tropical elements of wind, rain, and corrosive salt air to take their toll.

Such a contingency could arise apart from detention needs associated with the war. Given the unsettled nature of regional politics, some planners are anticipating a future large refugee flow into Guantánamo. This is a legitimate concern based on past experience when Haitians, Cubans, and Jamaicans have sought refuge in the Guantánamo facility. But there are no expectations that the Camp Delta detention facility would be used to house any of those people should they come. The detention cells wait in case a new enemy combatant need arises, given the nature of the current war.

Because ethnic and personal chemistry among the detainees is of principal concern, much thought is given to housing certain groups, nationalities, and individuals. Since 2002, incidents of detainee-on-detainee violence have occurred regularly. Stabbings, beatings, and fistfights between different ethnic groups or between al Qaeda and Taliban followers are the most frequent. Consequently, assignment to Camp VI is anything but capricious. Dennis and his staff have worked with the

Joint Interrogation Group and other staff entities to determine which mix of detainees lends itself best to mission support. For example, some nationalities such as Saudis and Yemenis tend to look down on Afghanis, Africans, and others they consider inferior. A lot of the Saudis are well-educated, often well-traveled al Qaeda jihadists who are not above referring to the Africans—in English—as "stupid niggers," "ignorant wogs," or other pejorative names.

So personalities among the residents are of primary concern as pod and cell assignments are made. "I'm not just going to throw these people into empty cells simply to move them or to fill up the cells," Dennis stated. "We're being very deliberate and contemplative in our cell assignments. We're taking our time and allowing the detainees to become accustomed to the newness of the place. We constantly evaluate, analyze, and tinker with the situation. Eventually we'll have what we think is the best mix. But if we find we have issues, we're flexible enough to reevaluate and rearrange living quarters for them."

Moreover, according to Dennis, "everyone is going to start with a clean slate." When the initial transfers were made into Camp VI late in 2006, Dennis was determined to give every detainee a fresh start. "We're moving them into Camp VI with a beige jumpsuit—even if they're wearing orange now—and giving them all of their comfort items." The concept, he said, was to "give them something that I can take away in the event of inappropriate behavior." What exactly did he mean?

"If they get transferred wearing orange—the sign of non-compliancy—and having no comfort items, then I figure they have nothing to lose by acting up in the new place. This way—by giving them beige clothes, which they all prefer, and a full CI allotment—then there's a good chance that they'll respond and behave." And if they don't? "Then I've got something I can remove to show that there are consequences for bad behavior."

Even though the objective was to empty Camp II/III fairly quickly, Dennis refused to be rushed. "We have the opportunity to take our time with this move in order to do it right," he said. "In some cases we're even shifting detainees from Camp V into Camp VI simply because we think it a better fit than bringing in someone from II/III. The net result just opens a cell in Camp V for a new transfer so we lose nothing by it." Most of all, Dennis was pleased that he could be deliberate with his move. "If we rush this thing and do it half-assed it could result in a high discomfort level for detainees and guards, and disrupt the mission," he said. He planned that the pods in Camp VI would be filled in a measured, timely basis. As always, the emphasis with the JDG commander is "safe, humane care and consideration for the detainees."[15] And, of course, expeditious accomplishment of the mission.

CHAPTER 9

CAMPS ECHO, IGUANA, AND A "SECRET" CIA INSTALLATION

*"You're lucky to see this camp. Very few people
from the outside ever set foot in this place."*
NAVY CHIEF IN CAMP ECHO

IN AN ODD FOOTNOTE TO the unfolding saga of the Guantánamo facility, there was a small group—approximately 20 or so—of men who had been found not to threaten the United States, but were still confined for many months. How could this have happened? And what steps, if any, were taken to rectify the situation?

As part of the ongoing system of detainee evaluation, two boards hear information and evidence from each case. The first is the Combatant Status Review Tribunal (CSRT), which determines whether the detainees are in fact enemy combatants. "Only those determined to be enemy combatants remain detained." The second, the Administrative Review Board (ARB), "will review every detainee at least once per year to determine the continuing need to detain."[1] The term "need to detain" is defined by focusing on two primary areas: intelligence value and threat potential. Therefore, ARB members must satisfy themselves on both of these accounts.

Officers on the three-member ARB ask two necessary questions: First, is this detainee a potential source of useful intelligence information? Second, does this detainee pose a continual, real threat to the United States or its allies? As part of this continuous, ongoing process, more than 400 Guantánamo detainees either have been released outright or have been transferred to their home countries.

"We do not want to hold anyone any longer than necessary,"[2] has been official U.S. policy since enemy combatants were first captured on the battlefield. This policy was affirmed by Matthew Waxman, former deputy assistant secretary of defense for Detainee Affairs, who cited "moral cost" along with the fact that "unnecessary detentions would undermine our message of freedom and democracy." "Long-term detention is not a sought-after mission," Waxman noted, "but we'll do what we have to do."[3]

Regarding the turnback of detainees to their governments, Waxman was adamant that certain points had to be clarified. In many cases, foreign governments may complain publicly that their citizens are being held by America but may say privately, "We don't want them; you keep them." Nonetheless, numerous detainees have either been transferred or released to a dozen countries including Afghanistan, Pakistan, Saudi Arabia, Russia, Australia, the United Kingdom, and France.[4]

America, Waxman noted, is "looking for ways to accelerate transfer of detainees to their home countries . . . This is," he added, "the right course [for] coalition partners effectively [to] share the burden." Prior to transferring any detainee to another country's jurisdiction, he said, "we must be assured of two things. First, receiving countries must commit to credible and effective steps, consistent with their own laws, to prevent transferred combatants from re-engaging in hostile activity." Basically, this means U.S. authorities do not want to contribute to a terrorist catch-and-release program whereby they send a committed jihadist to a national government that will cut him loose to reemerge on the battlefield.

"Second," Waxman continued, "receiving countries *must pledge to treat transferred detainees humanely*. Consistent with the Convention against Torture . . . the United States will not transfer any detainee to a country where he is likely to be tortured."[5]

This is a straightforward, easily understood policy: America refuses to transfer a person to a place where he may be tortured or executed. "We cannot compromise our commitment to humane treatment or U.S. efforts to promote human rights." This says exactly what it is intended to say: that America consistently treats detainees humanely and insists that other custodial agencies do likewise.

That presented an odd quandary for 20 or so detainees held at Guantánamo who had been designated by the ARB as no longer posing a threat to the United States and not possessing sufficient intelligence value to be held.

Primary among this group were Muslims from the People's Republic of China. These people inhabit the far western Xinjiang province, a location that is predominantly Islamic. A majority are from a Turkic ethnic group known as Uighurs. Physically they resemble Central Asians much more than Han Chinese. Most are of medium height or taller, stocky, and strong. With a bit of imagination one can see them crossing the barren steppes on ponies, armed with bows and swords, looking for new worlds to conquer. Today's Uighurs seek nationalism and independence from the PRC.

They are called "wei-wu-er Zu" in Chinese history books, or more commonly, "wai fan"—barbarians from outside. In the old days they were considered ignorant, uneducated, and of lesser status in the eyes of the imperial court and the educated Han people. They often had to offer their princesses as ransom to keep peace with the Han emperors. There are still many romantic stories told about the Uighur nomads that are Shakespearean in nature: beautiful, but brutal. Popular Chinese television dramas today glorify those tragedies.[6]

But to the security-minded Chinese government officials, the Uighur community has a darker side. Within the Uighur community are extremist groups who are radical Islamist fundamentalists dedicated to using terrorism to achieve their goals of independence.

China, according to some observers, "had been using the war on terror as carte blanche to step up its 'Strike Hard' campaign in the Uighur Xinjiang Autonomous Region in the northwest, resulting in unprecedented numbers of executions of political prisoners, a suspension of free religious worship, and a general decline in respect for human rights."[7]

Such reports gave U.S. policymakers pause when considering the fate of the nine Uighurs captured in Afghanistan, who had been deemed no longer of intelligence value and not a threat to America by the ARBs.

Just to be clear, these men are not choirboys who strayed on the path home from church services. They were captured in al Qaeda camps in Afghanistan, in which they were by their own admission undergoing training so that they could return to China to be terrorists supporting an independent Uighur Islamic nation. In several cases they were captured by the Northern Alliance or its supporters and eventually screened by U.S. forces. Some reports on anti-war websites claim that the Uighurs were "sold" to Americans for $5,000 apiece, but this is an unconfirmed rumor.

Nevertheless, the nine Uighurs along with several other detainees from countries, such as Egypt, that have egregious human rights records were literally stuck in Guantánamo. Since America refused to release these people to their home countries (or in one case was unable to substantiate a home country), the U.S. diplomatic community tried for several years to find a place to transfer them. During that time they resided at Camp Iguana, confined, but with an ocean view, communal living, good food, and satellite TV.

But even there problems arose. In a fit of "frat-boy" anger, two Uighurs at Camp Iguana trashed their living room, including smashing a wide-screen television set. This earned them a prompt return to November Block, a tougher, segregated facility where they spent a few weeks in a cell with restricted recreational facilities. As then-commander of the guard force Mike Bumgarner said, "If anyone busts their facilities up they have to be held responsible. They broke a $500 television set. I'd have punished one of my troops harshly for such actions."[8]

Not all Uighurs, by the way, were in Camp Iguana. At least two have been found by the ARB review process to pose a danger and have potential intelligence value. They remain with the detainee general population. But what about the Camp Iguana Uighurs and others deemed ready for release? In 2005 a federal judge bemoaned the situation, noting that the U.S. military was "violating the law" by continuing to hold them, but agreeing that "the military has no other choice."

Rather an easy judgment from the court, but a tough proposition for the military and diplomatic staffs trying to be fair to these people.[9]

If a handoff to China, Egypt, or another potential human rights violator is rejected by policy, then what alternatives exist? State Department representatives asked at embassies and missions worldwide to see if any other country might wish to accept these men. For several months there were rumors that a Scandinavian country, possibly Finland, might accept the Uighurs. Eventually they were welcomed by the government of Albania, where, to much surprise, there exists a healthy Uighur community. Whether Albania can keep the Uighur terrorists from returning to Xinjiang Province is now a problem for China.

Some have asked whether America has the right to question how returnees will be treated. After all, we typically demand extradition of terrorists and major criminals from the European Union, Brazil, and other countries and are publicly angered when they decline because of their opposition to capital punishment. What right do they have, we ask, to tell us how to run our internal affairs? Doesn't similar logic apply here? Is it really our business to tell China, Egypt, Russia, or any other countries how to handle the terrorists when they are repatriated? After all, we don't refuse to turn detainees over to those countries that are notoriously lax with them.

Some countries like the United Kingdom give perfunctory attention to the Guantánamo detainees and set them free within hours. Others, like Pakistan, Bahrain, or Morocco, may free some and hold others. If we accept the fact that some detainees we consider to be enemy combatants are allowed to walk free to return to the battlefield, then ought we not be equally sanguine with the fact that certain countries may adopt a harder line than ours? The bottom line is that the United States, and particularly the commander and staff at JTF GTMO, were delighted to see the Uighurs and other nonthreatening detainees shipped off to a suitable home.[10]

Nor was this issue put to bed when the Uighurs were shipped out. A Libyan detainee, Abdul Rauf al Qassim, has what Jennifer Daskal of Human Rights Watch describes as a "credible fear" that if returned to Libya he will be tortured. Supported by Human Rights Watch and the

Center for Constitutional Rights, Qassim was judged to be eligible for release. Plans were made to send him home to Libya.

Now the same organizations that vociferously protested his detention have been equally dissatisfied about his release. Even though the United States has received word from Libya that Qassim will not be tortured, "such assurances from countries known to torture are worthless," according to CCR director Vincent Warren. Those assurances, Warren insists, are "fig leaves for the U.S. government."[11]

C AMP IGUANA AS OF THIS writing sits empty but not neglected. Lawns are kept clipped and work is going on inside the few buildings in the small camp. Sitting on the picnic benches looking south, the views from the fenced-in yard are stunning. The broad Caribbean spreads out before the onlooker and gentle waves lap against the rocky, low cliffs at the base of the camp. Sited on a small peninsula jutting into the crystal-clear blue-green ocean, it is easy to imagine a resort villa occupying this spot.

A picnic table sits near the fence. Occasionally, attorneys and their clients are dropped off here to speak privately. But when the camp was occupied, the Uighurs and others would take meals here. In a central block building they had their own refrigerator, stove, microwave, and washer and dryer. They made clever cabinets from remnants of MRE crates, decorated them with marking pens, and used them to hold supplies that the cadre purchased for them.

Inside the two main buildings there was a dayroom, a communal recreational facility that had satellite television hookup, a Ping-Pong table, exercise machines, bookshelves, and other paraphernalia. A couple of large couches and some overstuffed chairs offered convenient places to relax, watch TV, or read.

By the time you read this, the old dayroom will be divided into two separate areas by a soundproof wall. Tables, shelves, and other facilities will be available for client–attorney meetings designed to take some of the pressure off Camp Echo when the Military Commission proceedings resume. Conceivably detainees could be housed in the other main building, but at this point in time such thoughts are mere contingency plans.

In the yard, iguanas that were made into pets by the Uighurs still creep into the wire seeking the food handouts that were given by the previous occupants. And outside the Camp "Iggy" wire, as the troops refer to it, the Caribbean beckons with some of the best snorkeling and diving in the area.

The Mysterious Camp Echo

Camp Echo receives relatively few visitors. It is somewhat mysterious, sited near but decidedly apart from all other links in the original Camp Delta chain. Echo sits across the macadam road from the new Camp V–Camp VI complex. Camp Echo is a multifunction camp. First, it is surprisingly large, occupying several acres in contrast to tiny Camp Iguana. It is hot. The chain-link fences topped with razor concertina wire are also covered with hunter-green plastic sheeting that keeps the breezes out.

Fortunately for detainee comfort, Echo is comprised of modular structures similar to those in a quickie housing unit. Known as containerized housing units or CHUs, each modular is approximately 60 feet long and divided into two spacious cells. Additional reinforcing was put into the modulars to permit hard points for securing a detainee if needed and for holding the wire cells inside. Detainees here might be called "special category" inmates. Some have proven to be extraordinarily cooperative, including more than one who has recanted jihadist activity. Some have given incredible amounts of information to interrogators including identifying other detainees, usually "hard cases" who were in many instances close to Osama bin Laden. One detainee identified 11 of his fellows who were part of bin Laden's special bodyguard unit.

Al Qaeda bodyguards are a very special bunch. All have proved themselves as committed, ideologically pure, completely trustworthy jihadists. All have pledged personal *bayat* to bin Laden, meaning not only that they are willing—indeed eager—to die for him but that they will unquestioningly undertake any mission that he assigns, including suicide missions.

Nor are they merely "guards" in the Western sense, although they certainly perform a personal security function. They are acolytes, confidants, even being sought for opinion or advice on occasion. They were trusted with the intimacy of being close to the emir, of food preparation, cooking, shelter, movement, and security. To be an al Qaeda bodyguard meant that a jihadist had reached a very selective inner circle. Bodyguards would hear of future plans, of distant sleeper cells, and foreign recruiting efforts. They would learn of money laundering, explosives design and manufacture, weapons transfers, troop movements, and high-level strategies. In short, an al Qaeda bodyguard provides a potential gold mine of intelligence information to interrogators. Hence, anyone who exposes them must be protected even in detention from the reprisal that is certain to come. Camp Echo offers the ideal place to both reward and protect those who are cooperating.

It is also a good place to hide someone from the general population who may be considered too dangerous.

Detainee ISN 239, Shakir Ami, is a classic example. For almost two years, Shakir and Michael Bumgarner competed for leadership over the camp. Shakir was pushing to control the camp. Bumgarner wanted above all to keep his troops safe and to prevent injury—especially suicide—among the detainees. Bumgarner calculated that he could strike a gentleman's agreement with the detainees, negotiated and agreed to through natural leaders like Shakir.[12]

One of the things Bumgarner did not anticipate was that ostensible leaders might not be the real thing. Perhaps their comfort with English or the desire of the higher-ranking al Qaeda operatives to remain hidden from sight allowed them to feign overall leadership. And even if they really had a following inside the camp, could they seriously enforce their directives? This was the key question and the point that was ultimately tested by the true leaders inside the wire.

A CIA Installation at Guantánamo?

"We called it 'Secret Squirrel,'" a former Army enlisted soldier told the author in an interview after he had completed his tour of duty in Guantánamo. "It was over by the Windmill Beach area [on the relatively isolated southern coast of Guantánamo between the Camp Delta complex and the mountain cliffs that drop into the Caribbean] and was guarded by the Infantry battalion that pulled security for the entire Camp Delta/Camp America installation."[13]

Exactly what was Secret Squirrel? "It was a CIA-run camp for detainees," he said. "And unlike our detainee movement operations, which were huge productions, these guys would be brought in and out virtually without military escort. All the movements were at night and they came in wearing orange jumpsuits, hoods, and ear muffs. In some cases they would be carried into the camp rather than risk them tripping and falling."

This soldier left months prior to the announced movement of 14 high-value individuals into Guantánamo from camps in Central Asia that had been secret until the *New York Times* reported their existence. Among the group were Khalid Sheikh Muhammad, Abu Zubaydah, Ramzi bin al-Shibh, Majid Khan, and others considered to be "extraordinarily dangerous" top al Qaeda leaders. Many of these leaders had talked to interrogators. That much was known. It was a safe bet that some of the Camp Delta detainees were wearing orange, eating from Styrofoam boxes, and praying in metal boxes five times a day because of things that KSM, Zubaydah, and others had told interrogators. So it was unlikely that they would be transferred to the general population anytime soon.

Meanwhile, the existence of the 14 became a short-time fixation of the media. Admiral Harris was besieged with questions about them. Most sessions began and ended with one question: Where are the 14 being held? Harris answered firmly, "They are being held in Guantánamo." That was his answer for every other question, too. Are they treated well, are they being tortured, does the CIA have control, are they receiving mail, do they have legal representation? All got the same shut-out answer. After awhile, even single-minded reporters lose interest in the game and change the subject.

We know from late news reports that Secret Squirrel is designated as Camp 7. It is somewhat removed from the Camp Delta complex west down the road to Windmill Beach. Only ultra-high-value detainees are kept there, top al Qaeda leaders. As one senior staffer commented, "recreational water activities down that way have been put off limits."

If the CIA-held 14 are not being integrated into the general Camp Delta population or being made available to JIG interrogation (this is a strong supposition, not confirmed), then what was the point in moving them to Guantánamo in the first instance? There are solid reasons why this might be a good strategic relocation. First, sufficient diplomatic heat might have been generated to have the governments of various countries get cold feet about keeping these high-profile characters in custody. Second, and this seems more likely, with the progression of time al Qaeda has been able to buy, intimidate, coerce, or force its way into prisons all over the world, springing some of the worst cases back into circulation.

Finally, with the way cleared by the Federal District Court of Washington, DC for resumption of Military Commission proceedings, the decision was made to prepare some of these men for trial and judgment. Several, including KSM at the time of this writing, are well into the Military Commission queue.

To date, no one has escaped from Guantánamo. That is a remarkable record considering that escapes by high-value terrorists from other locales have been fairly common. In January 2002, an al Qaeda fighter in Kandahar attempted to escape along with six of his fellow terrorists from a hospital where they had been hiding for about a month. According to an Associated Press report, "The escape attempt underscored the difficulty of capturing hard-core members of Osama bin Laden's terrorist network."[14]

In October 2003, a report from China noted that "some 30 members of Afghanistan's ousted Taliban movement have escaped from a prison in the southern city of Kandahar." A local reporter, Duad Khan, is quoted as saying that "their escape in fact was their release, which took place under a deal [with local officials]."[15] This is proof positive that in tribal societies like Afghanistan, conflicting loyalties are legion and opportunities to circumvent the central government's desires are ripe for the taking. In this case, a little grease purchased freedom for known terrorists.

In July 2005, four Arab terrorists (in Afghan jargon, "Arab" or "foreign" equals "al Qaeda," as opposed to Taliban) escaped from Bagram, a primarily U.S. facility. The four reportedly cut through the barbed wire and made their escape.[16] Several months later it was learned that one of the escapees was a high-value detainee by the name of Omar al Faruq, described as "one of Osama bin Laden's top lieutenants in Southeast Asia."[17]

Faruq is a Kuwaiti who was the key link in Indonesia between al Qaeda and the local terror network Jemaah Islamiah, which was responsible for the Bali bombings and other attacks. He was a key al Qaeda player in the region, having set up terrorist training camps in Mindanao working with the Philippine terrorist group Abu al Sayeff. Faruq had reportedly been captured in Indonesia in June 2002, turned over to U.S. custody, then evacuated to Bagram. A U.S. military spokesman said that Bagram had "shortcomings identified in the physical security of the facility that have been corrected."[18]

Within Indonesia, Farouk was described as "dangerous" by Major General Ansyadd Mbai, the region's top antiterror chief. The Indonesian authorities were acting to "co-ordinate security" because they were certain that the bloody-handed terrorist would return. General Mbai expressed anger and frustration that he had not been told immediately about Faruq's escape.[19]

On January 24, 2006, seven Taliban prisoners, described as "mid-level detainees," escaped from Policharki Prison near Kabul. Afghan general Salam Bakshi, who is director of prisons, spoke of launching a "manhunt" for the escapees but said that "there's no sign of them so far." Policharki is undergoing improvements in order to facilitate transfer of detainees from Guantánamo who have been found to continue to pose a threat but have been determined to possess no further intelligence value. Meanwhile at Policharki, 10 prison guards who apparently assisted the seven Taliban to escape have been arrested.[20]

In what will certainly not be the last of these egregious escapes, in February 2006, 23 al Qaeda terrorists escaped from a Yemeni prison on the outskirts of Sanaa, the capital of Yemen, by means of an 80-yard tunnel. Fifteen of these prisoners were scheduled for trial the following day. According to Michael Halpern, "this particular prison is used almost exclusively to house security prisoners connected to terrorist activities." And not just low- and medium-value targets. Inside the wire was "the most notorious, the scariest, the person we should most worry about," who escaped with 22 of his henchmen. His name is Jamal Badawi al Ahdal, and he was charged with masterminding the suicide boat attack on the USS *Cole* that killed 17 American sailors.[21]

These were all tough, hardened al Qaeda terrorists. And they escaped without a trace. Three years ago, three al Qaeda prisoners walked out of that same Yemeni jail and disappeared. The tunnel, it has been said, is "longer than a football field" and ran "into a nearby mosque." Yemeni authorities have yet to send a "red notice" to Interpol, alerting them to the threat of the escapees. Frequent Guantánamo critic Senator Barbara Boxer said she was "troubled" by the escape. "I feel uneasy about [the escape]," she said. "How do 23 people escape? It raises some terribly difficult questions."[22]

CHAPTER 10

DAILY LIFE AT GITMO

"You can bet on one thing: the detainees will
always have better chow than we get."
ARMY SERGEANT, CAMP AMERICA

A MERICAN READERS ARE OFTEN TOLD that detainees in Guantánamo are kept in terrible, inhumane conditions. They lack privacy, basic sanitary facilities, recreational time, exercise opportunities, and decent medical care. Further, the detainees are fed "slop" unfit for their personal and religious requirements. They are kept in tiny spaces, blasted with unpleasantly loud music, and forced to live like animals.

Is there any truth to these widespread beliefs? In my extensive investigation, none of these charges was verifiable.

In the early Camp X-Ray days, confinement conditions at Guantánamo were considerably more basic than they are today. As we have seen, confinement and interrogation facilities had to be established urgently based on the requirements of war. The detainees were kept in the best conditions possible at the time. Even though those conditions were not necessarily pleasant or comfortable, the detainees always had better living conditions than their guards. While detainees ate cooked, hot food, American guards ate MREs. As discussed above, there was a very brief time, in August through September of 2002, when a part of the camp was reopened and two high-value detainees were kept in undeniably harsh conditions at Camp X-Ray; but that was an isolated incident, and was quickly addressed by authorities. Moreover, Camp X-Ray as a primarily holding facility was in operation only four short months, from January to April 2002.

Since then, the changes that have taken place are dramatic. Increasingly permanent, modern facilities have been constructed, modeled on the experience of the U.S. federal prison system. It has been a growth and learning process. For example, every time weapons are found on a detainee's person or hidden in a cell, those weapons are studied for ways in which the material can be withheld or substituted with material that has less dangerous potential. Standard in any tour of the facility is a layout of the weapons discovered. Some of these weapons are highly creative. Some techniques were obviously learned in the training camps. All the homemade weapons can be deadly if used forcibly.

Detainees have access to a reasonable amount of personal space. In the maximum-security section every cell has built-in sanitary facilities, a comfortable bunk, an arrow permanently placed pointing in the direction of Mecca, and clean blankets and jumpsuits. The cells are well lighted for reading and every detainee has a personal copy of the Koran, a prayer rug, beads, and oils, and hears the five-times-daily call to prayer announced over loudspeakers throughout the various camps. The call for prayer is repeated in several of the 17 languages represented in the facility by various self-appointed detainee prayer leaders.

Food service at the Guantánamo facility received a lot of public attention. After especially adverse reports, Guantánamo meals actually were prepared and demonstrated in congressional offices. Amid a series of reports of poor-quality food, food that was incompatible with Islamic religious proscriptions, or inadequate food supplies, the straight facts emerged: These guys are eating better than they ever did in Afghanistan. During a visit with the Guantánamo-based medical team devoted to detainee medical and health issues, the senior medical officer, a Navy commander, chuckled that one of the increasing health issues now is *fat*!

"When these detainees were first brought here," he said, "most were definitely underweight. They had nutritional health issues as well as other problems that we were tasked to address." Of late, he said, "during periodic health checks we noted that they are gaining weight at a rapid pace. Many are now confronted with the problem that plagues most Americans: losing weight!"[1]

While visiting the Guantánamo facilities, I had the opportunity to lunch on detainee food. "This is the meal that they are being served right now," said the contract food service specialist, Ms. Sam Scott, originally from South Korea, now a manager for Pentad Corporation out of Las Vegas. "You mean this is the day's ration?" I asked, looking at two large Styrofoam boxes—the kind you get at restaurants to take food home—packed with rice, vegetables, bread, meat, and other items.

"No," Scott reassured me, "that is just one of the three meals they receive daily." It was, I learned, rather typical of the day. "These detainees consume about 4,200 calories daily," Command Sergeant Major Anthony Menendez told me.[2]

The food service preparation facility is a huge complex, responsible for preparing meals not only for the 500 or so detainees but also for the guard and support staff of several thousand. Interestingly, the detainees eat better than the guards. "Menus for the soldiers rotate on 35-day cycles," said Seabee lieutenant Daniel Sym, who was in overall charge of the facility. "For the detainees, menus rotate on a weekly cycle."[3] That translates to much more variety and interest for the detainees.

The cooking center itself is in almost constant motion. Baking— all detainee bread is fresh-baked—and food prep begin at 0200, and the kitchen staff goes well into the next night on multiple shifts. All equipment is modern and sanitary, placed in a space that is clean, well lighted, and well ventilated. Most of the staff is comprised of Filipino and Jamaican third-country nationals who are contract workers at Guantánamo.

"Inspection teams from the medical side are on site almost continuously," Sym said. "They oversee and make snap inspections not only here at preparation site, but after food is transferred to thermos containers, and at the delivery point in the various camps. They test for proper temperature, quality, hygiene, and freshness." For example, food temperature at the serving point has to be within a seven-degree window.

What happens if the food fails to meet the medical inspector's standards? "It gets tossed out on the spot," Sym replied flatly, "and replacement food is prepared."

"We order a lot of special food from the States for the detainees," Scott said. "We don't have *halal* capability here," she observed.[4] "All halal food comes from the U.S. along with many specialty items." As an example, she holds up a date so large that it normally could not be found in an average American supermarket. The dates, stacked crate by crate on stainless-steel tables prior to preparation, are huge. Each is about two inches or more in length. They are pitted and extraordinarily sweet.

"These are *very* expensive," Scott noted. The dates were ordered as "treats" for the detainees. "After Ramadan, they have a feast," she said, "and we really worked hard to prepare a very special meal for that feast."

During the 28-day period of the Ramadan observance, Muslims are expected to refrain from taking anything by mouth, including water, from sunrise to sunset. Guantánamo detainees were each day offered the choice of observing Ramadan—a "fasting menu"—or being served the regular menu. If they selected fasting, they were fed an early, pre-dawn breakfast and a late, post-sunset dinner. About all but 40 detainees stayed with fasting, but every detainee could make his choice. Many switched back and forth. Some detainees opted to fast for a few days and then go back to regular eating schedules. Whatever they decided was an individual choice and was honored by the command.

Eid is an Islamic feast day celebrating the conclusion of Ramadan. The list of foodstuffs included in the menu for the Eid feast in 2006 was extensive: parsley salad, chicken kabsa, Saudi rice, grilled shish kebab, dates, honey, yogurt, fruit, orange juice, and milk.

"In some cases," added Jay Hood, discussing overall food concerns, "detainees are served special individual meals. This may be in response to food allergies discovered by the doctors in examinations, or in pure individual preference." One of the more dangerous detainees, I learned, was served his own individual meal three times daily because he had expressed special preferences. How did he make these preferences known, I asked? "He threw his food containers at the guards," Hood replied.

Whether at one of the camps, the hospital, the interrogation centers, or the food service facility, Hood would stick his head in anywhere, anytime. Personnel were usually not surprised to see their commander dragging along one of the too-frequent visitors to Guantánamo, even a congressman or high-ranking officer.

There is an old saying in the military that "the troops do well what the Old Man looks at." At Guantánamo the troops made every effort to do *everything* well, because they knew Hood was a hands-on leader who demanded perfection or close to it in every endeavor.

Why did Jay Hood insist on these almost unattainable standards? "Because we must remember at all times that this is a critically important mission," Hood said, "and that the eyes of the world are on this operation and this facility." He took stories of possible abuse very seriously, investigated each one, and insisted on the truth coming out.[5] No one wished to end up castigated, slandered, attacked, and tossed out with the trash like former commander Geoff Miller, least of all Hood. So he watched everything with a microscopic intensity.

What about those individual meals? When the detainee population was approximately 500, about 90 meals were individually prepared. The ratio remains roughly the same. These may be designated by medical personnel because of need for certain minerals in a detainee's diet—low potassium and calcium levels, for example—or they may eliminate proscribed items because of clinical conditions such as diabetes or coronary issues, or because of food allergies.

Detainees are medically checked with great frequency and care is taken to make certain that they receive a proper diet. A list of each of these meals is faxed or hand carried weekly (it arrives usually about 0200 hours, when kitchen staff is setting up) and details exact specifications for these medically ordered meals. Some meals may be vegetarian, fish only, soft foods only, or designed to meet other special conditions. Each meal is prepared individually, placed in clamshell Styrofoam containers, and marked for the particular recipient by detainee ISN and camp number. Additionally, the meal is labeled so that inspectors at the distribution point will be able to double-check it.

Other special meals are offered simply at the request of the individual detainee. These meals may exclude some items that would ordinarily be included. If a detainee doesn't like carrots, to cite a not-exaggerated example, food service specialists must make certain that no carrot-containing items are included. No steamed carrots, no peas and carrots, no carrot cake, no carrots in his salad . . . you get the idea. Other detainees might not like to receive their meals with certain items touching other items. Regardless of the inanity of the request, Guantánamo supervisory officials honor it.

It costs the U.S. taxpayer about twice as much to keep a detainee fed at Guantánamo as it does to feed an American soldier in Iraq or Afghanistan, roughly $34 a day versus $17 for a soldier in combat. Bottom line: When you hear about the suffering that the detainees endure at Guantánamo, know that it is not for lack of food or quality thereof.

There are many reasons to treat detainees humanely, not least because this is what America is and what America does. Good nutrition and feeding is a part of that. But humane treatment does not mean catch and release. It may cost a lot to keep detainees confined, but the price of allowing more attacks against the United States is too high to pay for capricious release.

In April 2006, Rear Admiral Harry Harris replaced Brigadier General Jay Hood as commander, Joint Task Force Guantánamo. Harris, a Navy pilot, came to Guantánamo from the Pentagon, where he was formulating current operations and antiterrorism/force protection policy for the Chief of Naval Operations. A 1978 graduate of the Naval Academy with a master's from Harvard's John F. Kennedy School of Government, Harris brought with him a keen intellect and a marked predilection toward action with measurable results. His style differed sharply from Hood's: Harris delegated more, and was content to allow subordinates to take responsibility for their actions. He stood behind them as long as they remained within certain agreed-upon boundaries.

When the May 2006 incident erupted in Camp IV in which the officer ordered OC gas deployed and use of nonlethal munitions, Colonel Bumgarner was outspoken in his praise of Harris's command style. "He told me calmly that he would support the use of the nonlethals," Bumgarner said. "I think General Hood would have relieved me on the spot." Why so? "Hood was more acutely concerned with possible adverse public relations and congressional reactions," Bumgarner said. "Remember, he took over when the Abu Ghraib scandal was at its height."

Indeed, Harris's calm reaction to the report that nonlethal munitions had been fired—"That's what we issue them to you for"—accurately captures the style of leadership that he brought to the command. Unlike Hood, who would certainly have rushed to be on the scene, and would likely have taken over from subordinates and begun to make decisions on the spot, Harris, confident in his unit and himself, remained in his headquarters—removed but easily available—and kept his superiors at SOUTHCOM and in Washington informed while allowing his officers and troopers to do their jobs.

Medical Care—Too Much and Too Lax?

Most of the detainees brought with them to Guantánamo a health crisis if not a health catastrophe. Combat wounds, diseases, malnutrition, exhaustion, lack of immunization against disease, absence of dental care, and poor health habits were among the general issues that had to be addressed. The specifics in each category—festering wounds, traumatic amputations, tuberculosis, hepatitis, vitamin and mineral deficiencies, dental emergencies, and a plethora of other problems—would easily fill this chapter.

Almost from the start, the medical support has been provided from U.S.–based Navy assets, primarily from the Navy hospital at the Pensacola, Florida base. They deploy to Guantánamo, typically on a six-month tour, with a complete staff ranging from a hospital commander and Navy captain through surgeons, physicians, nurses, technicians, corpsmen, and general support staff. The morale, motivation, and professional qualifications of the medical staff are unquestioned.

Their training for this most dangerous duty, on the other hand, has been sorely deficient.

Medical care at Guantánamo has been a frequent focus of complaints by outside critics. To my surprise, I learned that the detainees have their own complete medical setup including a small hospital with two operating rooms. Backing up the doctors is an array of modern, elaborate diagnostic equipment including MRI, CAT scan, X-ray, and ultrasound machines. The detainees have ultramodern digitalized X-ray equipment in their hospital that is not available to the soldiers and civilians at the Guantánamo Base.

Full-time doctors, physicians' assistants, and nurse teams are on duty to handle detainee health issues 24/7. Full dental-care facilities can handle everything from routine dental work to oral surgery to implants and dentures. Detainees have at least semiannual health checks and can see the doctor more often as needed. They have an opportunity to go on sick call daily. If a detainee complains of what could be a health-related issue he is immediately taken to the hospital, or in the case of Camps V and VI, first to the in-house dispensary for examination and evaluation.

In June 2005, Navy Commander Cary Ostergaard, then commander of the detainee hospital, summarized his approach in testimony before the House Armed Services Committee: "A military doctor gives every detainee a full medical examination upon arrival at Guantánamo. Our most common complaints are intestinal, respiratory and musculoskeletal. The detainees are also given dental and mental health screening examinations, and tests for HIV/AIDS, tuberculosis, malaria and hepatitis." Further, from a preventative medicine standpoint, "Detainees are given a tetanus immunization and an influenza immunization in season." He added that his staff had developed several medical surveillance programs to monitor the weight and nutrition of the detainees.[6]

Not long afterward a group of physicians that included Susan Okie, a doctor who is contributing editor to the *New England Journal of Medicine*, visited Guantánamo. Okie was troubled that she did not get to interview or examine detainees, though that has long been stated

Department of Defense policy. "Had I known that I would not have access to prisoners," she wrote, "I might have declined the invitation to visit Guantánamo, as United Nations representatives have done." Nonetheless, Dr. Okie, clearly what would be called a "hostile witness," noted that the floors were "spotless" and that she saw physical therapy equipment, an X-ray room, a glass-windowed nurses' station, and a supply room full of surgical kits and medical equipment. She also inspected the hospital's "empty" operating room.[7]

Dr. Okie was not present long enough to see routine screening and triage of daily sick calls and emergency cases. Had she been, she would have learned that after an evaluation when it is decided to keep a detainee as an inpatient, there are specially designed beds available in which he is comfortable but kept secured. This is necessary because instances of detainees slugging nurses and doctors are common, as is exposure of genitals, masturbation, spitting, and clawing at medical personnel. If a detainee puts deep scratches in a nurse's face while trying to gouge her eyeball out, she doesn't rate a Purple Heart for wounds received in combat, but she ought to.

Dr. Okie quotes attorney Kristine Huskey, saying that "some of her clients had complained about their medical treatment. 'Often the only medical person who comes around is a corpsman. They complained that they want to see the doctor and they don't get to. I know that some guys have really serious health issues. I know they're not getting the care.'" A Washington, DC attorney formerly with Shearman & Sterling and presently a practitioner-in-residence with American University's Human Rights Clinic associated with its Washington College of Law, Huskey represented several Guantánamo clients and participated in the *Rasul v. Bush* case that went to the Supreme Court.

Yet Dr. Okie herself writes that "detainees should receive medical care similar to that provided to U.S. soldiers," and documents the fact that "for one Guantánamo detainee that meant bringing in a team to perform coronary catheterization and place stents; for another, it required bringing in a thoracic surgeon to remove an anterior mediastinal thymoma. Other specialists are available . . . A prostheticist visits quarterly . . . The hospital has a mini-ICU and two negative-pressure laminar-flow rooms for patients with communicable diseases."[8] That doesn't sound like a pattern of medical neglect. And it no doubt exceeds the quality of care any of these men have received in the past.

Although not specifically mentioned in her catalog of exotic medical procedures available at Guantánamo, Dr. Okie was probably aware of the voluntary colonoscopy program offered to detainees over age 50, the extraordinary dental care, and the almost obscene proliferation of prescription medications. This is not intended to single out Dr. Okie for special criticism, but simply to note once again that the Guantánamo facility is routinely held to impossible standards.

Another critic, Carol Williams of the *Los Angeles Times*, took pride in her "scattershot" style of "interrogating officials" while she was on what she considered a "rare" inside-the-wire tour of the camps. Williams learned that "prisoners are force-fed through a nasal-gastric tube if they refuse to eat for 3 days and that 1,000 pills a day are dispensed to treat anxiety and depression." Perhaps the tour was "rare" for Williams, but Public Affairs officers like Colonel Lora Tucker will tell you that it happens "every time we get media at the base."[9] Williams appeared unaware that her "exclusive" report yielded facts that were posted regularly on the Guantánamo and Department of Defense websites for all to read.

Beginning with the reasonable presumption that the detainees are dangerous people, the medics at Gitmo have tried to take adequate precautions. They are determined to safeguard everyone, medical personnel and detainees alike. But sometimes they slip. Unlike guards who are alert to attack, medical personnel often have an expectation that since they are there to care for the detainee, the detainee will appreciate that and respond positively. One of the detainee hospital commanders, a Navy captain skilled at family practice medicine, remarked somewhat naïvely that "we take pride in the fact that we treat these people just like our patients back in Pensacola and not like prisoners."[10]

But this permissive attitude can lead to laxity and carelessness, and imputes a degree of trust that is entirely one-way. Detainees brought into the hospital were shackled to the beds with two-point restraints. Shackling detainees alleviated concerns about a detainee using on-hand equipment to injure medical staff or attempt an escape. Then the detainee would moan about the pain in a foot or hand and ask that the restraints be loosened. Often sympathetic medics would comply with the request.

On one such occasion, while being treated by a female nurse, a detainee with no provocation drew back and punched her so hard that her nose was broken and splashed across her face. Blood spattered profusely. She withdrew to get medical attention herself. Meanwhile the detainee loudly complained for his clothing and sheet to be changed. "The infidel whore's blood has defiled me," he shouted. "Change my clothes!"

In an amazing performance of duty, the nurse returned after she was patched up.

"Why do you come back and care for me?" the detainee demanded.

"Because you are my patient," she replied calmly. This time he was four-point shackled, with both hands and both feet restrained.[11]

The hospital was the scene of at least two major insurrections during the height of the hunger striking in 2004–2005 (see below), in which detainees slipped restraints or were able to grab metal poles that held intravenous bags and swing them like clubs, break glass and use the shards as knives, and generally tear the place apart. A quick reaction force was dispatched to put down the disturbance. But the hospital continued to be a source of concern.

"Look around this place," former U.S. Air Force lieutenant colonel dentist John Rudisill said in May 2006 when he first visited the facility. Walking around the hospital he rapidly pointed to storage cabinets, shelves, and wall hangings. "Everything here is a potential weapon: poles, cords, bottles, syringes, scalpels, even these clothing hooks. You've got an assortment of clubs, spears, knives, and garrotes, all looking like normal hospital paraphernalia to a doctor, nurse, or corpsman. They don't have the trained eye to spot this stuff. Suppose a detainee ripped one of these hooks from the wall—they're barely attached—he could drive it deep through an eye or a temple into someone's brain."

Rudisill had done a clinical rotation in the Texas Department of Corrections and was well versed on prison culture. "My dental assistants were a murderer and a serial rapist," he said with a grin. "I found out quickly how expert inmates become on figuring out how the system works and playing it to their advantage. And how dangerous it can be to let your guard down, even for a moment." Rudisill had learned his lessons well inside the walls of some of the state's toughest prisons. "The biggest mistake the medical staff can make is to think of these people as patients," Rudisill said. "They are prisoners first, and patients second."[12]

By late 2006, a new hospital commander and staff seemed to have modified their permissive attitudes. "We no longer dispense prescription medications like we did previously," the commander, a thin, no-nonsense Navy captain, said. "And we have instituted new protocols whereby the corpsman or PA must watch the detainee consume the medications. Also whatever can be liquefied or powdered has been done."

The purpose was to reduce hoarding of dangerous medications so that they could then be given to a suicide candidate in lethal doses. Prior to the suicide attempts in May, well-intentioned but naïve corpsmen had simply dropped off pills in cups and not monitored consumption. And as later reviews would reveal, the quantities of medications offered to the detainees—particularly of the antidepressant, mood-enhancing type—were off the charts. "We probably gave out more psychological drugs than we needed to," a Navy hospital commander said.[13]

"In my opinion," Rudisill commented after extensive personal interviews with medical personnel during two visits to Guantánamo, "the medical staff wanted to be extra nice to these people, and expected them to be kinder, gentler prisoners in return. That is nonsense as anyone who ever worked in a prison can tell you. And these guys aren't just criminals, they are killers who were smart enough to play games with the young corpsmen and bend them to their will."

The hospital commander, who requested anonymity, in late 2006—who took the position after the suicides—ruefully agrees, saying, "We had to train our people to be a bit tougher and demanding and not to trust the detainees. Nor do we allow the kind of loose actions we did in the past. When detainees come here in the hospital they are restrained as needed now. We learned the hard way."[14]

What about operating procedures, disease control, and other preventative medicine issues? "We no longer have any active TB among the detainee population," the hospital commander said. "Several had active cases when they arrived here and we have been able to control that." Tuberculosis may have been the most dangerous communicable disease. "We did not uncover any cases of HIV/AIDS, or any exotic tropical diseases. There were cases of hepatitis and other disease but nothing life-threatening."

Does the hospital still perform as many surgeries as in the past? "Most of the immediate, combat-related stuff has been taken care of. We do a lot of health maintenance stuff, the kind of procedures you might expect to find in a general community hospital. Gall bladder, appendix, colonoscopies, hernia work, that kind of thing. Any really serious stuff we can use the Navy hospital here or call in specialists."

I heard about a major heart bypass procedure that had been scheduled and then cancelled. I had been told that the patient, Saifullah Paracha, ISN 1094, a Pakistani national, was diagnosed as requiring multiple bypass surgery and with his concurrence had been placed on a special surgical schedule. The hospital commander would not confirm the name of the patient, which I had learned from the JDG personnel, for "confidentiality reasons," but explained the sequence of events:

"The procedure was to be performed at Guantánamo. We were going to do it at the main hospital OR and had arranged for a team of specialists to fly down from Bethesda. They came with a complete crew, equipment, backup, the entire package. After they got here—and by now the patient had received innumerable examinations, we had discussed the surgery at length, gone over recovery times—everything. After the team got here and was ready to go, he abruptly changed his mind and refused the operation. Nothing we could do, so everyone went home."

Colonel Wade Dennis showed anger and exasperation when he amplified the incident: "It probably cost the American taxpayer half a million dollars to get that team flown down here on special aircraft with all its equipment. Plus there was all the time lost that they could have been performing work up at Bethesda. It was a huge waste and as far as I'm concerned a victory for al Qaeda. I think he [Saifullah Paracha] had no intention of going through with the operation at any time and was just jerking us around. It worked."[15]

By the way, I asked the hospital commander on the way out, repeating a question that I had asked three of his predecessors, "What part do you play in the interrogation process?"

"None. We keep detainee medical records completely private. Rarely JIG may come to us with a specific issue like 'this detainee complains of lower back problems' and we'll let them know that it is a valid complaint so they will seat him more comfortably. But other than that kind of thing we have no interaction with the JIG people." It was the same reply I had received every time I asked the question.

While many of the earlier problems with the detainee dispensary and hospital appear to have been ameliorated post–summer 2006, some people-to-people issues continue. One of the major problems is that the medical personnel with the most interaction with the detainees are the youngest, least experienced, and most vulnerable. In a group meeting with a physician, nurses, and several corpsmen—men and women—much of this anguish surfaced.

"I've never been so terrified in my life when I walked through the blocks at Camp I," a doctor said. He is from the Midwest originally, and with dark skin and soft, Subcontinental features appears to be of Indian descent. "I knew in my head that they couldn't get to me physically and that all they could do was threaten, but the hostility, the shouting, the noise, was almost overpowering. Emotionally it was devastatingly frightening. And these are supposed to be compliant ones."

"They always call the doctor racial names when he's only trying to take care of them," one of the female corpsmen chimed in.

"They change completely when they come into the dispensary," said another female corpsman. "When I'm on the blocks they call me names like 'whore,' 'bitch,' and 'infidel.' Sometimes they insist that a man come to them."

"They won't look at me directly or speak to me," said another female corpsman. "They will talk to the male guard as if I'm not there but the content of the conversation is for me."

"Then when they get back here," the first corpsman said, referring to the detainee dispensary, "they are totally changed. "They are friendly, kind, almost flirting sometimes. It's much nicer to have them here."

Had any of them been targets of abuse? "Constantly," replied one of the male corpsmen. "I've done a tour in Afghanistan and two tours in Iraq. It's much worse here. I'd rather be in the Sandbox than here."

What kinds of things do they do? "They throw stuff all the time— feces, urine, semen, spit, and vomit are their specialties. They try to get it into our mouths and eyes 'cause they know that can do some damage. Then they laugh at us."

"I've had them punch me and try to feel my breasts," one of the female corpsmen said.

"They say that I'm not a good corpsman," one of the youngest females said, who appeared to be near tears. She looked young enough to be worried about selecting dresses for the junior prom rather than attending to enemy combatants' medical needs. "And I think I *am* a good corpsman. I really try to take care of them but they don't seem to care how hard we work."

"Please don't use my name in your book," one of the nurses, an experienced officer in her mid-forties, said. "I'm constantly threatened with death and rape. They tell me that they will give my name to their friends in America who will come and find me. I'm scared to death." Her hands shook uncontrollably as she recounted story after story of abuse from the detainees.

I was unable to take notes fast enough to keep up with the outflow of pent-up stories from the group. And they still had two months left on their half-year rotation.

After the group meeting, Rudisill commented: "These people are excellent medical staff. But they were not prepared to deal with prisoners, particularly as virulent a crowd as these guys are. Look how the detainees play mind games with them, particularly the young women. And they're only here for six months! By the time they learn how to deal with the system they're gone and a new group has to learn.

"The command would be better off bringing down teams from military prisons like Leavenworth and Portsmouth or even hiring contract medical help that would have experience working in the American prison systems."[16]

On the mental health side, things appear better, especially since the volume of psych-related drugs has been reduced. "It looked to me like any time any of these guys came in saying he felt bad they slapped an antidepressant on him," Rudisill commented. "Hell, its prison, you're not supposed to feel good."

The mental health clinic is up and running and has a few inpatients. "We estimate that about 10 to 18 percent of this population has mental issues. Most we can treat as outpatients and do," the resident psychiatrist said. It seemed to a nonprofessional that treating mental illness in such different cultures would be difficult if not impossible. Imagine hearing "in my village the men have been warriors for 2,000 years," or "I am the third son of my father's eighth wife." How does Freud, Jung, or whoever construct a bridge? "We manage," the psychiatrist laughed. "We use interpreters when necessary and what we call cultural interpreters who help us cross these barriers." Is it effective? "We think we are doing the best we can." Interaction with interrogators? "Zero."

In summary, despite myths of collusion between medical personnel and interrogators, about mental health professionals using their skills against the detainees, the truth is that medical facilities at Guantánamo are highly supervised, tightly controlled, and all involved are concerned about the health and welfare of the detainees. They also take their unique mission very seriously and are determined that it be carried out in a most efficient, humane manner.

CHAPTER 11

MEET THE AMERICAN MILITARY

"Honor Bound to Defend Freedom"
MOTTO OF THE JOINT TASK FORCE GUANTÁNAMO

THE SPECIAL DEMANDS OF GUARDING a sensitive facility like Guantánamo call for concerted, coordinated effort by all branches of the military. Because it has both land and water approaches, defense of the facility necessarily includes specialists in ground and sea combat. The working relationship among services is as professional as can be found anywhere in the world.

Patrolling Guantánamo Waters: The U.S. Coast Guard Takes Charge

One of the big terrain-related surprises at Guantánamo is that there is an awful lot of water out there, much actually within the boundaries of the base itself. An impressively large inlet approximately one mile across divides the two land sections, so the only way to travel from the east to the west side and back is by ferry or fast boat. Add to the mix a Cuban government that might turn a blind eye to a third party hostile to U.S. interests, and it makes sense to have regular security patrols on the waters.

On the west side, the Guantánamo River flows into the bay. Some of the Coast Guardsmen have been up the river, which they say reminds them of tropical adventure films because of the way the mangrove swamps encroach on the passageway. Two miles or so upriver, a fence barrier lets them know that Cuban territory lies just beyond.

The Coast Guard runs 24-foot Boston Whaler fast boats, called Vipers, with twin 150-horsepower outboard engines. Given the power of these sleek boats, they can close in on an intruder faster than anything not flying. Add a little chop on the bay and much of the ride is airborne. Passengers are told to "hold on" before the chief pours power to the engines.

Mounted on a swiveling tripod forward of the Whaler's mid-ships control console is a venerable M-2 .50-caliber machine gun, the famous "Ma Deuce" so beloved of soldiers and sailors who want to shoot really big bullets at a target and tear it to pieces or blow it out of the water. Just aft of the control console on port and starboard sides are two U.S. M-240 machine guns, firing 7.62–millimeter NATO rounds. Nothing fancy, just reliable, proven weapons designed to bring smoke on waterborne intruders or terrorists who might decide to attack the camp through the bay or river.

Individually, the Coasties are rigged like seaborne infantrymen. They carry Beretta 9-millimeter automatic pistols strapped low in leg holsters with pouches containing extra magazines. Each wears a black nylon equipment vest complete with knife, strobe lights, emergency survival equipment, flotation device, and first aid pouch. They wear desert camouflage battle-dress uniforms with Navy/Marine Corps–style blocked covers ("hats," for you landlubber grunts). On one of the trips, I chatted with the chief in charge of the boat. He had been on station three months. How did he like being assigned to Guantánamo? He grinned proudly with the spontaneous smile that conveys volumes to a fellow soldier: "I'm on my second tour."

Many of the Coast Guardsmen hail from the Midwest. There is something about kids from prairie towns and cities that makes many of them fall in love with water. A lot of the Coasties at Gitmo have served tours in Iraq, primarily down south around the Umm Qsar seaport area, running patrols against terrorists who have nefarious designs on wharves, oil platforms, and merchant shipping.

How serious is a possible attack on Guantánamo? It would not be easy, which was a primary reason for selecting such a secluded, difficult-to-approach installation. But it would be foolish to dismiss the threat. The ultimate objective of the attackers must also be taken into consideration. One scenario might envision them assaulting the camps with the idea of breaking out detainees. There have already been escapes from prisons in Afghanistan. Even a minimal breakout from Guantánamo would be trumpeted as a huge al Qaeda victory. Attackers could also engage in a "martyrdom" operation. They might try to kill American soldiers and civilians, blow up facilities, and create general mayhem. Merely setting foot on the soil at Guantánamo and causing a reaction would be of inestimable propaganda value for al Qaeda, giving them an opportunity to claim success in a war that has gone very badly for them.

Regardless, military planners do not live in a world of wishful thinking. By definition they occupy a dark, pessimistic, Murphy's Law–driven world where whatever can go wrong inevitably does; and they make a variety of contingency plans accordingly. Their task is to counter intruders, whatever their intentions might be. Since it is fairly well known that al Qaeda possesses a fleet of merchant ships, it might be possible—albeit difficult—for terrorists to launch an attack offshore from a freighter, coming ashore in small inflatable boats.

These types of operations have been conducted by irregular agents on various shorelines for years. North Korean merchant shipping consistently drops infiltration teams off the rugged coast of South Korea. For years Taiwan did the same to the People's Republic. More recently in Yemen, al Qaeda used small craft to bomb the USS *Cole*. It is hardly a stretch to imagine a similar al Qaeda operation at Gitmo, particularly given the fact that they would likely be content with a one-way, suicide mission.

That makes the challenge of defending the installation even greater. Hence the Coast Guard, specialists in brown-water operations, accepted the mission to defend Guantánamo from the sea. And to judge by the morale and professionalism of the crews who are meeting this difficult challenge, they are doing a great job.

The Navy Guards: Life Inside the Wire

In U.S. Navy parlance, masters-at-arms are equivalent to military policemen in the Army and air police in the Air Force. They are usually assigned to typical base policing duties, though in time of war their duties may expand to include handling of prisoners, traffic control, and other related assignments. Today, many Navy MAs are pulling detainee guard duty at Guantánamo. As Ryan Camp of Grande Island, Nebraska said when I asked him why he came to Gitmo, "I thought I was going to be a military cop. Then I ended up here." He is young, and marvels at the contrast in his life: The previous year he had been a senior in high school.

His partner, a three-year-plus Navy MA from Flint, Michigan named Daniel Kosiba, is more accustomed to Navy ways. "I'm happy here to be doing my job," Kosiba said, though he feels underappreciated by critics who "are not living" his life.

Camp chimed in, "Our motto is 'Honor Bound to Defend Freedom.' We're defending their right to say bad things about us."

Both these MAs were on escort duty when I interviewed them. Unlike camp guard duty, which puts a guard at a specific camp, usually for a fixed period of time, escort teams are on call to go to any and all of the camps. They are routinely called upon to take detainees to the hospital, dentist, or interrogation, to deliver them to an attorney during periodic visits, or for any other movement requirements. Each trip can be boring or exciting, depending on the detainee.

"One of these guys speaks six languages," Kosiba noted, ticking them off: English, French, German, Spanish, Arabic, and Pashto. "These people are not stupid. This particular detainee lived for years in Europe. He attended college there."

Occasionally a detainee will try to "get into their heads," a tactic I also heard about from a Navy MA guard in charge of the shift over at

Camp IV. In that particular case he was speaking of Omar Ahmed Khadr, the Canadian prisoner, who he said "likes to screw around with us." All guards and escorts must exercise extreme caution about allowing the detainees to develop a casual relationship around them. They are instructed to avoid unnecessary conversation and never, ever release personal details to the detainees. Some of the detainees are smooth talkers. "They like to use English language proficiency as a way of softening us up," Camp said.

"We have to work to stay alert all the time," Kosiba said. "Sometimes waiting for the detainee to finish his business can be a dangerous time for us." Detainee medical appointments or interrogation sessions can last hours, and the escorts are tempted to relax and let their guard down. "That is the time we must force ourselves to be extra alert."

"Sometimes they make sexual advances at us," Camp added. Ryan has the kind of youthful, boyish face that would make him a natural target for such advances. It's not hard to imagine him still back in high school. "They may try to rub their genitals on our hands or masturbate openly. Some will try it with us, other times they may do it to a woman, a nurse, for instance."

Do detainees threaten them? Regularly, they both said. "It is disturbing to know that the detainees' highest priority is to do you harm when you're working so hard to take care of them," Kosiba said. In my discussions, I learned that the terrorist detainees want more than anything to capture a guard.

They are plotting to capture an American guard or administrative person, hold him hostage, and leverage that kidnapping for the most widespread exposure possible. The kidnapping would undoubtedly be followed by a beheading. Both Kosiba and Camp agreed that the detainees are just waiting to make a move.

Does this sort of behavior anger them? "We know they're terrorists but every day we have to treat them humanely and in a professional manner," Kosiba said. "I'm here to do my best."

Camp nodded in agreement. "We spent three weeks of intense training at Fort Lewis, Washington prior to coming here learning how to act and react. The training was hard work but really prepared us for this. When we got here and it seemed easier than the training, then we knew we had really done something," he added with a laugh.

Two other Navy guards spoke with me. Fire Controlman Daniel Thayer, originally from Durango, Colorado, has eight and a half years in the Navy. He came to Guantánamo in September 2005. Thayer was on escort duty at the time of the interview and had previously been assigned as a camp guard. His partner in the escort job was Master-at-Arms Second Class Timothy Gilbertson, originally from Ontario, California.

When asked what they thought was the "greatest myth" about the Guantánamo facility, they both answered promptly: "The greatest myth is that detainees are abused!"

"We exercise an incredible amount of restraint," Thayer noted. Both guards recounted that they have been punched, spat upon, and had their genitals touched.

"I watched a guard get punched in the face once, at the hospital," Thayer said. "He had his glasses knocked off, and his face scratched and bruised. I was amazed at how he slowly, carefully, put the detainee's arm back onto the bed, secured the man's arm firmly and gently with straps. He walked away very calmly with no harm done. He had no anger on his face, no show of emotion during the entire episode. It was awesome."

Tim Gilbertson said that the "most stressful, challenging moments are in the middle of a move—when we are escorting a detainee someplace—and suddenly he refuses to move." What does he do? "At first we try to persuade him, find out if something is bothering him. We move him physically only after everything else fails." Do they twist his arm or inflict pain in any way to move him?

"Absolutely not. We're trained not to do that," Gilbertson said emphatically.

Both of them found the Fort Lewis training excellent. "We learned how to react in a number of special situations," Thayer said. They noted that learning and training continue on a daily basis.

"The translators are very good at explaining cultural specifics," he added.

What do they think when they hear themselves compared to brutal SS guards or Cambodian mass murderer Pol Pot?

"We don't let it upset us. Those people are speaking out of ignorance," Thayer said. His partner agrees. "Those people haven't walked these blocks, they haven't had to deal with the daily grind of the job and they don't know what we have to go through or what we are accomplishing here."[1]

Watching the Fence: Marines Defend Guantánamo from Land Approaches

Since their predecessors stormed the hilltop fortifications that made up the original Spanish defense of Cuba, U.S. Marines have played a key role in defending the installation from all comers. During the turbulent Cold War period of the 1960s and 1970s, when tensions with Cuba were high and fence incidents common, it was the practice for the Marines to have a reinforced brigade at Guantánamo. In those days they had a mere five tanks available to repel any sort of Cuban land incursion. Rear Admiral John D. Buckeley, one of the tough, character sailors that the Navy occasionally produces, was then in charge. Buckeley made his reputation as a PT boat commander in the Pacific and won the Congressional Medal of Honor in 1942 for spiriting General Douglas MacArthur and his staff and family out of the fortress at Corregidor Island under the noses of the attacking Japanese.

Under siege again at Guantánamo, Buckeley demonstrated equal imagination and aplomb. Every day he had his five tanks roll along the inside of the perimeter wire, knowing full well that they were under intense observation by Cuban military. He would then have the tanks run into cover, where the individual identifying markings were painted out and new numbers painted in. Those same five tanks, bearing different unit identification numbers, would then roll the perimeter road under Cuban cameras. The deception convinced Cuban intelligence analysts to calculate a much larger armor capability than really existed.

Relations with the Cuban military occupying positions outside of Guantánamo are far different today. It has been years since there was an incident between the two forces. However, the fence lines remain in place and tall Cuban watchtowers look down at the facility. One of the things they can see is minefields that were laid during a more confrontational time. These mines still exist and are active. They are buried shallow in the fields. Occasionally an animal, usually one of the large indigenous rodents known as "banana rats," trips a mine.

When that happens, the Marines will check the situation just in case. There are also concrete barrier obstacles placed for detonation on the sole road that enters Guantánamo from the Northeast Gate. In the unlikely event of Cuban military forcing the gate these obstacles would block the road, diverting vehicular traffic into the adjacent flooded ditches and wetlands. And into the minefields.

Fortunately the military-to-military relationship between Cuban and American forces is very professional and cordial. Frequent meetings are held at the Northeast Gate facility—where a large sign in Spanish on the Cuban side reads "Welcome to Free Cuba"—to exchange observations, ideas, issues, and—one suspects but cannot confirm—excellent Cuban cigars and coffee. Unless there is a remarkable, unanticipated deterioration of relations, any friction between the two is unlikely. What is more of a possibility would be terrorists— individually or in a cell—pretending to be tourists or even demonstrators and then attempting to breach the fence line in order to create an incident.

For this reason and others, the Cuban military assiduously maintains a separation zone for several miles outside the fence line. This extreme eastern section of Cuba is relatively infertile and sparsely inhabited anyway, so isolating Guantánamo Base does not pose a special hardship for the Cuban people.

Despite heated rhetoric generated by Havana, the Cuban military commander wants no trouble locally. He has told the American side that the Cubans do not want these people, referring to the Guantánamo detainees, and that if one were to escape they would "give him back to you."

On one occasion a primarily American anti-Gitmo group had

assembled in nearby Santiago with the intent of marching to the Cuban side of the Northeast Gate and staging a protest. When the Cuban commander learned of their intent, he stopped them several miles short of their goal and told them that "for their own safety" he could not permit them to come closer to the base. "We don't want to be bothered by these people and I thought you would not want to either," he told the American commander at their next meeting.[2]

National Guard Units Protect the Camps

At least since 2004, U.S.–based Army National Guard units have been assigned the duty of camp protection. Imagine if you will an inner perimeter, distant from the Camp Delta, Camp America (the guards' barracks and admin area), and Camps V, VI, and Echo complex, but well inside the normal boundaries of U.S. Naval Base Guantánamo. On the ground at any of the above facilities, it is easy to pick out guard towers dotting the ridgeline that wraps itself around the mini-base on the northern land side. To the south the Caribbean Sea provides a boundary. These facilities are manned by the National Guard.

In April 2005, 1/18th Cavalry Squadron, commanded by Lieutenant Colonel John J. Lonergan, deployed to Guantánamo to assume the mission of force protection. They deployed from California as part of the 40th Division. They brought several hundred Cav Troopers, who made up three ground troops and a headquarters troop. The unit rotated out in March 2006 and was replaced by units of the 29th Infantry Division, of Omaha Beach fame, headquartered in Maryland and composed primarily of units based from that state and from Virginia. In 2007, the 29th Infantry was replaced by a similar unit.

The Guard units, according to Colonel Lonergan, "perform a variety of missions here to include mounted and dismounted patrols throughout the Joint Operational Area." These are the areas that contain the detention camps themselves and housing areas for the American guard and support force. The Cav mans two traffic control points, four observation posts, and all of the sally ports at Camp Delta.

The Guard troopers are also tasked to provide a Quick Reaction Platoon in case of "contingencies" either in or out of the camps. In the event of a detainee riot, for example, similar to what happened at the Koje-do camp in the Korean War, the QRP would be the first line of defense to control the riot. If any terrorists from outside decided to attack the facilities over water and managed to get past the Coast Guard, they would face perimeter defenses in the form of the QRP.

Military Commission activities are considered one of the most dangerous times. There are hundreds of strangers from outside the facility, most from the media and legal communities, but also relatives and friends of the detainees. As a consequence, units elevate readiness status to a higher level during these periods. For example, during the January 2006 Military Commissions proceedings, a special unit designated Task Force Patriot was formed with Colonel Lonergan as commander. At that time he had Army MPs and Navy MAs assigned to his security force. When each additional round of commission hearings takes place, a similar ad hoc unit will be formed and tasked with the security mission.

From late 2005 through the present, detainee movement operations—outward flights of detainees either for release or transfer to other countries—have played a big part in trooper duties. Detainees have to be moved from the Camp Delta area under guard to the harbor, where they are loaded onto a U-boat (not the German submarine but a Navy version of a utilitarian launch that regularly ferries passengers and freight across the bay). On arrival at Leeward Dock they are placed on buses for the short ride to the airport. There they might be loaded on special Air Saudi 747s or into USAF C-17 Globemaster III cargo aircraft. The C-17 can hold more than 100 passengers and has a 2,400-nautical-mile range with internal fuel. Give it a drink of gas from midair refueling and it truly spans the globe. Once aboard and under control of special guards on the C-17, the DMO mission terminates.

Another contingency especially appropriate for Cuba is that in case of an impending storm, detainees must be evacuated to what the command refers to as a "safe and secure location." Typically this will be done at the last minute to avoid the sort of mishaps that are always possible when moving a large number of detainees. Camps V and VI are suitable hurricane refuges and with the double bunk capability have the capacity to hold most of the remaining camp detainees safely. With Colonel Dennis's plan complete to consolidate detainees in those modern camps anyway, future contingency movement operational requirements have also been materially reduced.

The Army Guards the "Worst of the Worst"

Soldiers in maximum-security Camp V are among the most highly trained, dedicated people on the installation. Unlike many of the Navy masters-at-arms or Army military policemen, or the National Guard unit providing overall security to the various detention camps, these soldiers are trained confinement specialists, carrying the military occupational specialty code of 31E, prison guard. Most have volunteered several times: for the Army, for their specialty, and for service at Guantánamo.

The troops are professional from head to foot. Their uniforms and grooming are impeccable, their bearing soldierly, and their demeanor all business. They are men and women who come from experienced backgrounds of working difficult detention centers in America, Europe, and Asia, wherever American forces are stationed.

During my several visits to Guantánamo, at which time I was allowed to walk almost every square foot of the various prisons, camps, and blocks, I observed absolutely no evidence of torture of detainees or the sort of equipment that might have been used in such coercive techniques. However, it was clear that the daily atmosphere is rife with harsh abuse: *The prisoners are constantly assaulting the guards!*

Our young military men and women routinely endure the vilest invective imaginable, angry words laced with racial epithets and sexual threats and slurs. Detainees fluent in English—and they are many— throw curses at the troops constantly, including death threats that also involve the guards' families. Because of these specific threats, all soldiers and sailors working inside the wire have taped out their name tags. Before that step was taken, the terrorists were threatening to reveal guards' identities to their al Qaeda colleagues still at large. "We will look you up on the Internet," the detainees said. "We will find you and slaughter you and your family in your homes at night. We will cut your throats like sheep. We will drink the blood of the infidel."

Secretly fashioned weapons intended for use in attacking guards or fellow detainees are confiscated regularly. When food or other items are passed through the bean hole in the cell doors, the detainees have grabbed at the wrists and arms of the Americans feeding them and tried to slash their wrists or break their bones. On one occasion a female medic was asked to come close by a detainee that she had treated frequently in the past. When she asked him his problem, he indicated that it was private and he did not want to discuss it loudly. He asked her to lean over so he could whisper his problem to her. When she did, canting her head toward him, his hands darted through the bean hole, seized her face, and smashed it against the cell door several times before guards were able to break her free. The bones in her face were so badly shattered that she required multiple reconstructive surgeries to correct the damage.

No retaliation or punishment was taken against the detainee. In the U.S. prison system, prisoners who attack guards are routinely charged with criminal assault. One wonders if such charges will emerge from Guantánamo or whether aberrant detainee behavior will be overlooked.

When a detainee will not voluntarily leave the cell for a medical check or shower, displays inappropriate behavior, or for any number of other reasons, guards are required to perform a forced cell extraction. For the record, detainees are rarely forcibly removed for interrogation purposes. "What's the point?" Paul Rester asked. "If you have to drag him into the interrogation booth he's not going to tell you anything anyway."

Keep in mind that our soldiers—young men and young women— are absolutely forbidden from responding in kind. They are required to maintain absolute discipline and to follow humane operating procedures at all times, at risk of serious punishment.

In one incident, an MP doused with filthy toilet water responded by spraying the offending inmate with a hose. For this he was charged with assault. Another American soldier was disciplined for cursing at inmates. One guard punched a detainee after being struck and spit on while placing the man in restraints in the detention facility's hospital in October 2004. ("My instincts took over after the hitting and spitting," the soldier wrote in his report.) He was recommended for a reduction in rank to E-4, loss of a month's pay, and extra duty for 45 days.[3]

Ever wonder what it's like to be a guard at Guantánamo? They receive, on average, 450 assaults annually. Most of these involve being drenched with a noxious "cocktail"; others involve actual physical attack. Verbal assaults are so constant and commonplace that they are not even counted. More than half the assaults, approximately 250 a year, require some sort of medical attention. This ranges from on-the-spot cleaning and bandaging at the infirmary to major plastic surgery. This number does not count the "cocktail" assaults, because as a matter of SOP, every trooper who is hit with one must go to the medics to determine whether the detainee may have anything communicable if the substance was ingested through the nose or mouth. As one deputy commander said emotionally, "It was very difficult to stand by and do nothing when I watched the young people in my command who were trying to be nice to these guys end up with a mouth and nose full of shit."[4]

Would any of us be willing to put up with such treatment, while being required to stand there and do nothing? I seriously doubt it. Further, to perform such intense duty for a pittance in compensation and benefits, while enduring the most scathing criticism from fellow Americans and much of the rest of the world, actually doubles and redoubles their stress. This is what American soldiers and sailors face every day when they come in to pull their 12-hour shifts at Guantánamo.

A MERICANS IN GUANTÁNAMO ARE FOR the most part faceless, nameless people who are hardworking, dedicated soldiers, sailors, airmen, coast guardsmen, marines, and civilians deployed on behalf of the American people. They perform important, essential duties and exercise exceptional restraint where the vast majority of us would fly off the handle and lash out in justifiable rage. They voluntarily submit themselves to an intense oversight and scrutiny by the chain of command, and work under a code of iron discipline that would stress any soldier and break most civilians.

They are not allowed to respond to insults, assaults with noxious bodily fluids, or physical and verbal attacks. Instead they remain locked into a well-defined code of acceptable responses that must be adhered to without deviation.

Incidence of post-traumatic stress disorder have been anecdotally reported from Guantánamo at an alarmingly high rate. In 2007, one African-American Navy lieutenant committed suicide after pulling a tour in Guantánamo. "I knew him well," Lieutenant Donna Baptiste wrote me. "He was sensitive and dedicated. I'm convinced that the volume of racial and physical abuse he suffered at the hands of the detainees contributed materially to his depression." Baptiste herself underwent extensive psychological counseling post-Guantánamo. "My PTSD was rated off the charts," she wrote. "Now it is under control but I have terrible nightmares."[5]

In addition to the physical and mental abuse they receive from the detainees, the Guantánamo soldiers are subject to an avalanche of outside criticism. In February 2006, the United Nations Commission on Human Rights issued a long report thoroughly condemning the Guantánamo facility for torture and abuse as well as violation of civil and political rights. This is not the place to evaluate the efficacy or moral qualifications of the UN Commission, except to point out that some of the world's worst human rights violators—Eritrea, Saudi Arabia, Libya, Cuba, North Korea, and others—occupy prominent places on it. The UN Commission decided, strictly based on hearsay evidence, to issue a report condemning Guantánamo. Although the members had requested and been granted permission to visit, they demurred because they were not allowed to be face to face with individual detainees. Consequently they prepared their report based on adverse comments made by the released British detainee Moazzam Begg, and detainee defense attorneys like Clive Stafford Smith and his colleagues.

Nevertheless, the Commission members felt sufficiently qualified to condemn the United States for what it considered improper behavior, concluding that "the United States should close the Guantánamo Bay detention facilities without further delay."[6] It goes on to say that "all special interrogation techniques . . . should immediately be revoked." In point of fact, these issues were dealt with years ago by responsible authorities. The UN's criticism is late, irrelevant, and gratuitous.

Working in Guantánamo is a thankless, frustrating experience. In other places in the world, troops get to shoot back at the enemy. They can curse, complain, and throw hand grenades, and can see the results of their efforts. They get the recognition, accolades, and awards they deserve. At Guantánamo the professional forces—be they regular, reserve, or National Guard—can do none of this. Instead they stand to their posts daily while serving under a torrent of the most vicious, underhanded, and irresponsible allegations.

CHAPTER 12

HUNGER STRIKES

ASYMMETRICAL WARFARE IN ACTION

"There can be no reward for being on hunger strike."

COLONEL MICHAEL BUMGARNER, COMMANDER,
JOINT DETENTION GROUP

THE HUNGER STRIKE IS AN old tool, but one that is effective only when the captor or occupier has a moral conscience. Hunger strike in a Soviet gulag, an Iranian prison, or as a prisoner of al Qaeda terrorists and you will be left to die. But apply hunger strikes as a form of civil disobedience to a government that has moral fiber and a free media and it can be a very effective tool.

Irish Republican Army operatives used hunger strikes in 1981 as an effective tool to achieve their objectives. The British government did not administer supplemental feeding. Ten IRA strikers died, including Bobby Sands, who had been elected to Parliament while on strike.[1] During these hunger strikes dozens of civilians, policemen, and soldiers were killed by IRA bombs and during IRA-inspired riots on the streets,[2] yet public sympathy nonetheless shifted to the IRA prisoners. More than 100,000 turned out to honor Sands at his funeral. The hunger strikes became the driving force that brought Sinn Féin into mainstream politics.[3]

Hunger striking at Guantánamo has a history that predates the current Joint Task Force operation by six years or more. In the mid-1990s Guantánamo became an involuntary haven for Haitian refugees fleeing an oppressive government. Overloaded from the start, Guantánamo authorities placed the Haitians in quickly constructed camps within the installation. One issue was the prevalence of HIV/AIDS among the population. Special holding areas were constructed for those so affected, and this drew the ire of organizations like the Center for Constitutional Rights. Attorney Michael Ratner, now representing many of the Guantánamo terror detainees, prides himself on having "closed Guantánamo" back in the mid-1990s primarily through coaching in civil disobedience, particularly hunger striking.[4] It therefore came as no surprise that shortly after attorneys like Ratner began to show up in Guantánamo in 2004, organized hunger strikes began in earnest.

The attorneys from CCR and other organizations are consummately adept at manipulating a malleable media and are able to generate many condemnatory headlines as a result. Consequently the sympathy—and hysteria—over hunger strikes fed an insatiable media appetite for bad news from Guantánamo. The false reporting from Europe, especially virulent by summer of 2005, hit new lows with staged photos cut-lined "forced feeding of detainees at Guantánamo" portraying a bearded man in an orange jumpsuit bent backward over a bench, held in place by a chain around his neck heavy enough to deter a Manhattan bicycle thief. Meanwhile, scruffy "soldiers," clothed in uniforms that suspiciously resembled something you could pick up in a Serbian discount Army-Navy store, gleefully stuck a garden hose up his nose.

Several of the attorneys involved in those confrontational days also currently represent Gitmo detainees. There is strong suspicion that some of these attorneys may have violated their agreements and coached their clients to launch a hunger strike. The rationale behind this hypothesis is speculative but compelling.[5]

Over the first year, a hunger strike that began with a few detainees swelled to a point where 131 detainees were participating. Shortly after the first hunger striker began to fast, General Hood made the statement that "no detainee will die on my watch!" He instructed his staff, particularly medical experts, to take necessary steps to guarantee that detainees on hunger strike received proper treatment and care. Initially the hospital ward filled to accommodate administration of nutritional requirements to the detainees. Meanwhile, activist propaganda groups launched immediate, coordinated media attacks against the United States.

The Guantánamo medical staff was committed both by their professional dedication and by General Hood's orders to do everything necessary to make certain that detainees in their care did not die. Hunger strikers were weighed daily. Once their body weight fell below an accepted benchmark percentage or when they missed three successive days of meals, they were designated for supplemental feeding.

What does this involve? According to an October 2005 Reuters report, courtesy of Al Jazeera, "Amnesty International and human-rights lawyer Clive Stafford Smith, representing 40 detainees, said on Thursday that U.S. authorities were keeping 21 alive by forcing food into their stomachs through tubes pushed up their noses." The well-known activist attorney further stated that "the prisoners are shackled to their beds 24 hours a day to stop them removing the tubes."[6]

This burgeoning myth was fed by Center for Constitutional Rights attorney Julia Tarver, who passed on accusations from her client, Saudi Arabian detainee Yousef al Shehri. Shehri said that "U.S. [military] forces—not doctors or nurses—have brutally inserted and removed feeding tubes, and on one occasion yanked a bloody tube out of one prisoner and put it up the nose and into the stomach of another." Tarver went on to paint a wild scene of detainees "vomiting blood after doctors pumped too much liquid nutritional supplement into them."

Meanwhile, according to Tarver, vicious American soldiers "mocked and cursed them," using statements like "look what your religion has brought you." Tarver further stated that Shehri told her that for punishment, the military inserted "oversized tubes, 'the thickness of a finger' . . . through his nose, down his throat and into his stomach."[7]

Tarver's comments were picked up by many without challenge, including the usually quite sensible Nat Hentoff of the *Village Voice* in a piece with a photo captioned "Guantánamo: Abandon Hope all ye who enter here." Hentoff repeated Tarver's report of what her Saudi client told her as though it were absolute truth, never doubting that U.S. soldiers would abuse detainees in the way Shehri described.[8]

TIME magazine chimed in with a report about Shehri in which it claimed that he was fed with "a plastic tube that is 50% larger, and more painful to insert, than the commonly used variety." The result, *TIME* concluded, was "a state of high anxiety . . . nausea, bleeding, vomiting, and diarrhea."[9] Though *TIME* cited "medical records" obtained by its reporters, the magazine did not make these records public, nor for patient privacy purposes has the U.S. government released detainee medical records. Suspicion is heavy therefore that *TIME* relied exclusively on Shehri's testimony. A few reports from other publications did add contradictory and explanatory testimony from other unnamed sources, but in no case were al Qaeda training documents such as the Manchester Manual cited, in which terrorists are taught to fabricate stories of torture and abuse.[10]

When Moazzam Begg and two fellow Brits arrived in the United Kingdom from Guantánamo, they immediately complained of "beatings and abuse by American soldiers." When General Miller was asked about their statement, he replied, "These people have a number of cover stories. I can say with certainty that the British detainees were here for an appropriate reason."[11] Paul Rester, not hiding his disgust, said it even more plainly: "They were hard-core al Qaeda. We hoped when we turned them over to [British] custody, that the Brits would at least check them out." These al Qaeda fighters are smart, in many cases well educated, and extremely aware of American sensitivities.

Did Shehri fabricate his stories on his own? Were they teased out of him or suggested by others? Were these allegations, as several have suggested, given to the detainees by their attorneys? After the Lynne Stewart case in New York, where she was convicted by a federal jury in Manhattan of aiding Islamic terrorism by smuggling messages out of jail from a terrorist client,[12] stories of attorneys colluding with hardened terrorists do not seem as far-fetched as they once might have.[13]

A UN report on feeding hunger strikers noted that captors should "not force-feed any detainee who is capable of forming a rational judgment and is aware of the consequences of refusing food." One wonders what the UN's reaction would be if a detainee actually starved himself to death while in the hands of the U.S. military. Further, the Commission demanded that the United States "invite independent health professionals to monitor hunger strikes."[14]

So let us sweep aside accusation and hyperbole and investigate exactly what is happening with the hunger strikers.

To begin with, detainees have told authorities at Guantánamo that their motivation was a protest against continued detention, not complaints about abusive treatment.[15] In other cases, as we have seen, some who have been released appear to be following chapter and verse of their al Qaeda training manual by insisting that they have been tortured and abused.[16]

Media firestorms to the contrary, the hunger strikers were treated humanely and with all the care that the medical staff could muster. Contrary allegations, according to Lieutenant Colonel Jeremy Martin, former JTF GTMO public affairs officer, "come from totally unsubstantiated claims made by a small handful of detainees to their habeas attorneys."[17]

General Hood had already declared that no detainee would die from hunger striking while he was boss. Up and down the chain of command that became official policy, and it continued so through subsequent commanders. (When Assistant Secretary of Defense for Health Affairs Dr. William Winkenwerder, Jr. was asked how we could deny a person the right to decide to eat or not, he replied, "Do you allow a person to commit suicide? Or do you take steps to protect their health and protect life?"[18]) The issue was how to do it most efficiently, especially when the numbers began to creep up from a dozen to over 100.

At first the hunger strikers were brought to the hospital for their daily feedings. The hospital commander at the time, Navy Captain Stephen Edmonson, reviewed the standards by which a detainee was fed. "We watch body weight—if it falls by 15 percent we begin assisted nutritional processes. Also if he refuses solid food nine meals in succession."[19] With slight modifications, those standards hold to this day. They are based on consultation with federal corrections systems experts who deal with hunger strikes in the American penal system on a daily basis.

The strikers, counseled by camp leaders such as Shakir Ami, Ghassan al Sharbi, and others, were also, it is believed, well coached by their lawyers. Ratner, Joshua Colangelo-Bryan, Stafford Smith, Gitanjali Guiterrez, Thomas Wilner, and others made certain that the detainees called the shots when it came to feeding.[20] Hospital personnel, ever eager to assist their "patients," were easy to manipulate. "When we didn't do what they wanted," one corpsman said, "they would say that they were going to tell their brothers that we defaced the Koran and start an incident. So we gave them what they wanted."[21]

What they wanted was just the minimum amount of liquid feeding—the staff used Ensure at the time—to keep them alive but looking wan: about 1,000 calories daily. "Just give me enough to keep me alive," one detainee told the nurses attending him. "No more."[22]

"The hunger striking population will pick up when they know the time for attorney visits is getting close," Rester said. "That way they'll look really awful when the attorneys are here—and some media is around. Once the lawyers leave then they'll start eating again."

"They want to make the worst impression possible," Hood confirmed. "If they can get the world thinking that we're abusing them or harming them, they've won. They know how to play the public relations game and are doing a damn good job of it."

"Not only will they try to look bad, but sometimes a detainee will actually harm himself right before a lawyer visit and claim the guards beat him," a Navy guard said. "One of these guys is notorious for it. He'll run into the wall of his cell to bruise and skin up his face. Scratch himself with his fingernails, punch himself. The attorneys love it."

By fall of 2005, the hunger-strike numbers were beginning to rise sharply. "They were recruiting more strikers. The word went out from the leaders to join the strike," Jeremy Martin said. "By the anniversary of September 11 there were 131 detainees officially hunger-striking. That was where it peaked."

The hospital was quickly becoming overworked, as were the escort teams required to move striking detainees to and fro for their twice-daily feedings, weigh-in, and medical evaluation. "They got to where they knew it was wearing us down," an Army major in the JDG said. "It had turned into a game with them and they were winning. They got to go to the air-conditioned hospital for a few hours,[23] hang out with the brothers and talk all they wanted, get a feeding, and have their feet rubbed. Not a bad deal."

What's with the foot rub? "Hunger striking leads to poor circulation in the extremities. So the nurses and female corpsmen rub their feet."

Meanwhile, the overload on the hospital staff was beginning to tell. Incidents of detainees striking or clawing nurses and corpsmen rose sharply, due in part to a failure to restrain the patients properly. Some were moved into the newly constructed mental health facility for feeding due to overcrowding at the hospital, which was set up for only 20 beds and had just a small overflow area. Angry incidents rose to a peak and culminated with two detainee uprisings in the mental health area.

"They tore out the IV bottles, swung the poles like clubs, ripped up the cots, and threw everything they could at us," one of the medics reported. "Finally the guards came in with an ERF [emergency response force] team and quieted them down."

The hunger-strike feeding had turned into a comic opera. "They were telling us what flavor of Ensure they liked, putting the NG tube over an ear to talk to the other brothers more easily while getting a feeding, and generally having a great time," a medic said.

"It was highly organized," the Army major said. "They would designate 10 guys to go on a hunger strike for a week. After it was over most would come back to eat. Some of the guys would say 'I can hang in a few days more,' and the leaders would tell them to 'go for it.' You could see them rotating teams in and out. Sometimes they'd eat for a few days, then go back. It was all designed to jerk us around."

"It was purely political," Rester confirmed. "Not that there weren't some of them, like Juma Dossari, ISN 261, who really wanted to commit suicide. Most of them were faking, but Juma, that boy really wants to kill himself. But the others were playing a game along with the lawyers to try to break us."

"We wouldn't break," Hood said.

The first response came from Bumgarner. "I said, why in the hell are we letting these detainees tell us how much nourishment they get? If we're in charge we'll tell them." Nutritional specialists were brought in from the West Coast. The consultants advised the command on how to increase nutrition safely.

"Over time," one of the hospital commanders said, "we brought them up from about 1,000 calories daily to approximately 2,500. We replaced the Ensure with a special formula that was particularly nutritious. Suddenly instead of looking wan, they began to have rosy, plump cheeks. They were actually putting weight back on while hunger striking!"

It wasn't all easy. Some of the hard-core detainees had gamed the system and began to vomit up the liquid—"purging," the medics called it. Others figured that if left alone for a few minutes they could suck on the NG tubes and siphon the liquid back out of their systems. Again, the federal prisons consultant assisted.

"We ordered special restraint chairs from the States," Bumgarner said. "The docs told us that it took about 45 minutes or more for a person to digest the liquid feeding. So the ones that were notorious got to sit in the chair for about an hour plus until they got fed."

"We also used a dry cell to cool them off afterwards. With no toilet or sink we knew if they were purging," a medic said. "And if they persisted then they were placed in the restraint chair until they digested."

Bumgarner came up with another innovation: If the hospital is such a pleasant experience for them, then deny them that pleasure. "We decided that it was getting to be a logistic and morale nightmare to do the hospital feeding of each striker twice daily. Just too dangerous with the assaults and incidents, too. Plus we thought hunger strikers ought not get rewarded for what they are doing. So we arranged a small setup in Camp II/III and began to do the feeding right in the block. The medics brought the equipment down, set everyone up for feeding—my guys kept strictly hands-off other than to move them—and they got fed here in the camp. That wasn't nearly as much fun as the trip to the hospital."

"That broke the strikes," Donna Baptiste, the Naval officer then in charge of Camp IV, reported. "Once they saw that there was no point in striking, that we weren't going to let them starve, or even look pitiful, that they weren't going to get pampered in the hospital, then most of them gave it up."

By the spring, the number of strikers had fallen from 131 to less than a handful. "It is clear," said Thomas Wilner, who represents six Kuwaiti detainees, "that the government has ended the hunger strike through the use of force and through the most brutal and inhumane types of treatment. It is a disgrace." Department of Defense officials "strongly disputed" any allegations that they were using "punitive measures." They insisted that they were "sensitive to ethical issues" and that the procedures used to feed the detainees were "consistent with those of Federal prisons in the U.S."

Legislative and court rulings in the United States empowered DOD officials to make the correct calls, based on protecting the health of the detainees. Habeas lawyers were disappointed. "Because of actions in Congress, the military feels emboldened to take more extreme measures vis-à-vis the hunger strikers," said Sarah Havens of Allen & Overy.[24]

Harry Harris followed Jay Hood's original guidance—"No detainee will die during a hunger strike"—and medical personnel assiduously follow that directive.[25] Detainees are monitored continuously while on hunger strike, with weights, blood, and vital signs evaluated at frequent, regular intervals. Numbers fluctuate, but at the time of writing there are only a few detainees still on hunger strike, down from the very highest number of 131 on the anniversary of September 11, 2001, when the detainees celebrated that attack.

All hunger strikers are clinically stable and receive excellent medical care. Initially they were fed by a nasogastric tube that is soft, flexible, and only four millimeters in diameter. That narrow tube has since been replaced by an even smaller-diameter tube of three millimeters. This is very small and comfortable. It is an apparatus commonly used in American hospitals. Of interesting note is that in the U.S. federal prison system—which has developed settled policies and procedures for addressing hunger strikes—a slightly larger tube is standard use.[26] A lubricant with a mild painkiller in it is used to reduce any discomfort.

Detainees are fed twice daily only if they refuse a standard meal that is always offered first. They will remain in the chair if considered a purge risk just long enough to digest the food. In order to test the system shortly after his arrival in spring 2006, Admiral Harris directed that medical personnel set him up with a tube feeding exactly as they do a hunger-striking detainee. He went through the entire process, including actually being given liquid nourishment, without discomfort.[27]

On one of my visits, I asked Harris if I could be set up with a tube feeding also. "You did it," I implored. "So could I." I argued strenuously that it would add verisimilitude to my report. Shaking his head firmly with a typical wry grin, the admiral offered me a drink and cigar instead.

Only qualified medical personnel—a doctor, nurse, or physician's assistant—are permitted to administer the feedings. "It is that way now and was that way when we had more than a hundred," insisted the hospital commander. "We would never allow an unqualified person to touch one of these detainees. It would be unethical and unprofessional. We had to supplement our staff with TDY [temporary duty] personnel from outside for a few weeks but got through it okay."

Some detainees are hostile to assistance of any kind and require restraint. These are the type that punch and lash out at nurses and doctors, trying to scratch eyes and break bones. They are restrained during feeding times twice daily (not shackled to the bed 24/7 as attorneys have alleged) and then escorted back to their various blocks, where they can walk about or rest. In no instances were nonmedical personnel in any manner permitted to feed, handle apparatus, or become involved in the process other than in their security role. Tubes are never exchanged from one detainee to another; new tubes right out of sterile wrappers are always used. I saw medical lockers in the hospital stacked with sterile containers of the three-millimeter tubes, readily available for use.

What about ethical issues of feeding people who didn't want to be fed? "That's for those higher up the policy chain to decide," the hospital commander said. "I'm a physician and am charged with keeping these people as healthy and comfortable as is consistent with the detention mission. That's exactly what we did—and so did our predecessors—during the hunger strike. I'm extremely proud of the job we did and of my people."

The Habeas Attorneys

Almost before the dust of battle settled in Afghanistan, American attorneys rushed to defend the detainees at Gitmo. The attorneys came from advocacy organizations like the American Civil Liberties Union, academia, and various nongovernmental organizations, and included trial lawyers on the make and highly skilled professional litigators hired by unnamed Middle Eastern backers to represent same-country nationals detained at Guantánamo. There is informed speculation that the governments of Kuwait, Bahrain, and Saudi Arabia are paying the rapidly escalating fees for attorneys to defend their citizens at Gitmo.

In January 2007 the Department of Justice, in response to a Freedom of Information Act request filed by radio and television host Monica Crowley, released a long list of attorneys ("Lead Petitioners' Counsel"), the names of their law firms or agencies, and the DOJ case number. The released information did not tie each detainee to an attorney, nor did it list all attorneys.[28]

A review of the released material shows that attorneys fall into three broad categories: federal public defenders from several jurisdictions, all volunteers for this particular task—but who are paid by taxpayers' dollars; nonprofit and advocacy groups such as the Center for Constitutional Rights; and established law firms, such as Dorsey & Whitney LLP, Debevoise & Plimpton LLP, Jenner & Block, and many others.

For background purposes, as of this writing more than 153 petitions of habeas corpus have been filed covering about 250 detainees. In layperson's terms, a habeas petition asks the court to rule that a person held in custody must be made available to a court with jurisdiction. In an admitted oversimplification, this is an attempt by attorneys and supportive groups and foreign governments to try to have the Guantánamo detainees moved from military to criminal jurisdiction and accorded the same rights that an American citizen would expect under the Constitution. The departments of Justice and Defense have argued that the detainees are unlawful enemy combatants more properly tried under military, not criminal, systems. Further, they do not fall under provisions of the Constitution since they are aliens. The latter point seems self-evident but was contested.[29]

There is ample evidence of U.S. legal interest in Guantánamo. By January 2007, at least 500 lawyers from more than 120 American law firms represented Guantánamo Bay detainees.[30] The October 2008 edition of the Center for Constitutional Rights *Guantánamo Newsletter* stated that CCR alone "coordinates the representation of detainees at Guantánamo Bay with a network of over 500 pro bono habeas counsel." A coalition calling itself the "Guantánamo Bay Bar Association" lists 385 attorneys in its directory.[31] At least 300 law schools, universities, and seminaries are shown on the "partial list" of participants in the Seton Hall Law "Guantánamo Teach-in" program.[32]

Let's meet a few of the attorneys representing clients confined at Guantánamo.

The most prominent among them is undoubtedly habeas attorney Clive Stafford Smith. British by birth, he practices in the area of civil rights in the United States and is admitted to the Louisiana bar. He is a vocal opponent of the death penalty. Since 2002, Stafford Smith has represented detainees at Guantánamo on a volunteer basis. He represents some of the rougher clients, including Benyam Mohammed. At least one of his clients, Moazzam Begg, who was released by authorities, returned to the United Kingdom and has since become a poster boy for anti-American activists, filling the airwaves with extravagant claims of torture. He is a regular on the BBC and is a key board member of a nonprofit organization known as Cageprisoners LTD, which he helped found along with Stafford Smith.

In August of 2005, Stafford Smith told attendees at a major Christian gathering in Britain, the Greenbelt Festival, that the second hunger strike had begun in Guantánamo and that prisoners were likely to die soon. (No prisoners have died from hunger strikes at JTF GTMO.) In September of that year, he told a *BBC Evening News* audience that the genesis for the second hunger strike was to protest continuing imprisonment of children in Guantánamo Bay. (In light of this charge, it should be noted that the youngest Gitmo detainee, Omar Khadr, was captured at age 15 after throwing a grenade that mortally wounded a Special Forces medic.)

A rising star in progressive legal circles is Joshua Colangelo-Bryan, a New York City–based attorney who began to represent some of the Bahrainis held at Guantánamo in 2005. In a visit that year one of his clients, Essa al Murbati, was reportedly "so frail that he could not sit up."[33] (This may well have been the time that the Guantánamo command grew impatient with the detainees maintaining a "hunger strike" that kept them alive but looking emaciated and ordered a gradual but steady intake in calories.) Colangelo-Bryan is young, having graduated from Washington School of Law in 1999. He works for the upscale Park Avenue law firm of Dorsey & Whitney. The firm has been hired since summer of 2004 by an unknown client or clients to represent six of the Bahrainis detained at Guantánamo. Some speculate that it may be the government of Bahrain, others that one or more Gulf emirs may be contributing to the fund to get their people out of Guantánamo. More than a few of these old-line aristocrats are closet Wahabbists and secret supporters of al Qaeda and other terror groups.

Recent Miami law school graduate and author Mahvish Khan visited Guantánamo frequently as a linguistic and cultural translator and later as counsel for some of the Afghani detainees. Her book, *My Guantánamo Diary: The Detainees and the Stories They Told Me*, recounts how she was quickly won over by their stories of abuse and injustice, and she has been a vocal advocate for their release. During her visits, she took pride in treating U.S. soldiers with disdain and contempt. She boasts about nagging a guard about the "Soldiers Creed" posted in his guardhouse. Khan referred insultingly to one female soldier as "Rodent Face," while trumpeting the innocence of those confined in the facility.

Khan—an Afghani by heritage—was limited to interviewing fellow Afghans. Yet she did not question what they told her, nor did she hesitate to extrapolate from their purported experiences to the camp in general. Thus she readily accepts detainee stories of torture and systematic abuse, and goes so far as to suggest that the three detainees who committed suicide in June 2006 "may have been murdered" by U.S. authorities.[34] Even the *New York Times Book Review* suggested that she may have been too willing to believe what she was told by detainees playing on her sympathies.

While the preponderance of attorneys representing Guantánamo detainees quite likely are motivated by idealism, there are some bad apples. Stephen Yagman was the very first American attorney to file a lawsuit on behalf of the detainees. His initial suit—he filed many, including some involving CCR attorneys—was filed on January 21, 2002, just 10 days after the first detainees arrived at the detention facility from Afghanistan. According to the Associated Press, Yagman was a civil rights attorney specializing in what his website called "police brutality and other government corruption" and had already "filed dozens of lawsuits claiming that Los Angeles police abused and framed suspects and made false arrests."

Yagman has a sordid history. His mother, aunts, and uncles lived in the Southbridge apartment complex in New York, just five blocks away from the World Trade Center. He was later suspected by authorities of bilking them out of $776,000 from their low-interest-earning bank and Treasury-bill accounts so he could invest their money in the stock market in the late 1990s, but these accusations were not pursued.[35] In November 2007 he was convicted on one count of attempting to evade his taxes, one count of bankruptcy fraud, and 17 counts of money laundering. He was sentenced to three years in prison for "trying to avoid paying more than $100,000 in federal income taxes while living a lavish lifestyle replete with expensive suits from London, Aspen vacations and fine dining . . . When Yagman filed for bankruptcy in 1999, prosecutors said, he failed to disclose that he lived in a 2,800-square-foot home near the beach in Venice . . ."[36]

But while most habeas attorneys are undoubtedly motivated by idealism, there are questions as to whether they are actually helping their clients. As Hood noted, some of the detainees, acting on advice of legal counsel, were actually hurting their cause. "They have been told 'whatever you do, don't talk to the Americans. Don't tell them anything.'" That silence merely hampered the disposition of many cases.[37]

While a silent strategy might make sense in a criminal case, in several instances Guantánamo detainees who spoke freely were later adjudged by Annual Review Boards to be nonthreatening and no longer holding important intelligence information. Many were therefore recommended for transfer. By remaining incommunicado during interrogation, detainees who might otherwise have been released or transferred were manipulated by counsel advice into needlessly prolonging their confinement.

By mid-2006, many of the detainees were becoming aware that the machinations of their legal representatives were keeping them confined longer. They actually began firing their habeas lawyers. "They realized," Commander Patrick McCarthy said, "that some of their attorneys were dragging out the process through endless motions, legal actions, and other maneuvering that made the lawyers look good and played well to whatever agenda they were pushing. But it wasn't getting the detainee anywhere. Many of these detainees would have been transferred or released if it wasn't for all the blocking filings the lawyers made. Once the detainees realized that their lawyer had interests other than theirs they fired him."[38]

How widespread was this action? "It's happening a lot. Even some of the big names like Clive Stafford Smith have been fired by their clients," McCarthy noted.[39]

While Pentagon officials such as Brigadier General Thomas Hemingway actually welcome high-quality defense of the detainees ("It tests our system and proves its fairness"), there is legitimate concern, inside the Pentagon and in the Joint Task Force, that attorneys follow proper, agreed procedures for interacting with their detainee clients.[40] Naturally, it is the advocate's task to provide a defendant in a criminal case with the best defense possible, including discrediting the court, evidence, venue, or presiding officials when possible. However, when officers of the court promulgate stories that they know to be alleged or untrue, when they disparage processes that are values-driven and widely accepted, and when they deliberately circumvent processes and agreements to which they have willingly acceded, then they must be held accountable by proper authorities.

It has become so common to hear certain canards about Guantánamo broadcast by those who should know better, such as former president Jimmy Carter, that it no longer makes news. Comments about detainees "languishing about, devoid of hope, with no way out of Guantánamo" fly in the face of events.[41]

During a BBC radio interview I was challenged by attorney Stafford Smith, who claimed that "the Guantánamo detainees have no legal recourse." When I mentioned the CSRT and ARB processes, he derisively commented that this amounted to no more than a legal façade. When I countered with the fact that because of those processes several hundred detainees had been transferred or released outright, the host cut me off and terminated the interview. In point of fact, however, the detainee population has been reduced by more than 50 percent. CSRTs and ARBs have taken place for years. The Military Commissions would have taken place also on a more widespread level if habeas attorneys had not frozen all movement by the commissions with endless filings and suits. So where is the "lack of due process"? At least two detainee cases have been raised to the Supreme Court level, and numerous others have been argued at the District Court for the District of Columbia.[42]

Many attorneys attack the process itself. Some attack it endlessly. Attorneys representing David Hicks, ISN 002, have been especially vociferous in proclaiming his innocence or, in a racial twist, that as a white Australian he ought not to be treated similarly to Arabs and other Middle Easterners. The New York City–based Center for Constitutional Rights represents a large portion of the detainees. The CCR website and statements consistently challenge the legitimacy and fairness of the processes and even the basic right of the United States to hold enemy combatants.

One universal theme of the attorneys regardless of their origin is that the war against al Qaeda and radical Islam is not a war at all, but a series of criminal actions that must be adjudicated in a courtroom. Many profess to believe that America is the real criminal and that they are defending "revolutionaries," "militants," or "freedom fighters."

When attorneys come to Guantánamo to visit clients, they must sign a court-ordered affirmation with the U.S. government acknowledging their willingness to abide by certain clearly delineated rules and regulations. High on the list is that communications concerning matters other than the actual material of the detainee's case are prohibited. Not discouraged, not "something we hope you don't do," but flatly prohibited. The actual language says the following:

> Written and oral communications with a detainee, including all incoming legal mail, shall not include information relating to any ongoing or completed military, intelligence, security, or law enforcement operations, investigations, or arrests, or the results of such activities, by any nation or agency or current political events in any country that are *not directly related* [emphasis added] to counsel's representation of that detainee; or security procedures at GTMO (including names of U.S. Government personnel and the layout of camp facilities) or the status of other detainees, not directly related to counsel's representation.[43]

Part and parcel of the agreement is that all matters discussed with a detainee, either written or oral, shall be treated as classified information, meaning that it must be treated in the same manner as other government secrets. Unfortunately, however, in the highly charged atmosphere of recent years, even safeguarding of classified information has become politicized. Cases such as former National Security advisor Sandy Berger purloining documents from the National Archives, CIA leaks to the press, disclosure of highly sensitive war-related information from other agencies, and a plethora of other violations have been treated as insignificant misdemeanors at best by authorities regardless of political affiliation.

Unless a leak is supportive of the media's particular agenda, as was the case in the "Scooter" Libby/Valerie Plame incident, it is typically ignored or excused. But the District Court was highly specific in regard to treatment of classified information by habeas attorneys, going so far as to specify exact procedures for handling of material, methods for transporting notes to and from Guantánamo, and proscriptions of discussing classified material obtained from one detainee client with another. The Court uses the language that "the Protective Order shall survive the termination of this case and is permanently binding," and that "failure to comply with the terms . . . may result in the imposition of sanctions."[44]

The terms of the attorney agreement are equally stark and encompassing, and state clearly that "this Memorandum of Understanding and any other non-disclosure agreement signed by me will remain forever binding on me."[45]

These are not terms imposed by the departments of Justice or Defense or by some executive agency of the Bush administration. These are terms argued before a sitting federal judge and imposed by her on the participants. They ought to be sternly enforced as the law demands.

Communications between the attorney and his or her client are privileged. While cameras observe the meetings for security purposes (for example, if the detainee decides to gouge out the attorney's eyes the guards can intervene), their conversations are not monitored nor is their correspondence read. This is the correspondence specifically designated as "legal mail" by the Court. Clear procedures have been outlined for processing this paperwork, because it seems like a trivial detail but can quickly become troublesome.

During attorney Joshua Colangelo-Bryan's defense of a detainee client—in early 2004, when the entire process was just getting under way—the military authorities realized that conversations between detainee and attorney that were both classified and privileged presented problems. For example, Colangelo-Bryan needed to send his notes from an interview back to his office in the States. The DOD people responsible took far too long handling the notes and finally got them mailed to the wrong address, and for a time the notes were lost. This was clearly unsatisfactory. Better, more efficient procedures were devised in response, and there have been no repetitions of this error.

Suppose a detainee tried to use counsel—wittingly or not—as a conduit to transmit coded or even open messages to cohorts. Such an eventuality is not unheard of, and the case of attorney Lynne Stewart and Sheik Omar Abdel Rahman, the "Blind Sheik," is an example of how far some activists are willing to go.[46] On the other hand, by exposing his notes to the "opposition," is the counsel jeopardizing his defense and compromising his position as an officer of the court? These and other quandaries, so often overlooked in setting up a process and only discovered as it unfolds (or unravels!), were issues that demanded address.

A solution, roundly approved by the Court, was to appoint a Privilege Team to review such material, primarily notes taken by the attorney during his or her interview with the detainee. Each Privilege Team is comprised of one or more Judge Advocate General officers and one or more intelligence specialists or law enforcement personnel. The key point specified by the Court is that they must "have not taken part in, and, in the future, will not take part in, any domestic or foreign court, military commission or combatant status tribunal proceedings involving the detainee." Further, that "the team may include interpreters/ translators, provided that such personnel meet the same criteria."[47]

The latter personnel are clearly necessary if the counsel is carrying notes written by the detainee in Arabic, Pashto, or whatever. The Court also established a "reasonable" time line for outgoing transmission of the sensitive papers, allowing for them to be reviewed, translated if necessary, and examined if suspicion of code use was present.

What about incoming traffic? That is an issue, because more than messages can come in. Potential weapons, drugs, and other contraband are easy to smuggle in envelopes and packages. The Court made a smart decision using standards from U.S. criminal prisons. Everything is opened and examined for contraband and then forwarded to the detainee. Incoming mail is read only if there are compelling security reasons, and mail labeled "legal mail" is not read at all but is simply examined for contraband.

Despite the precautions, sworn affirmations to adhere to court-ordered agreements, and contraband inspections, there are many instances when papers from outside have been received through legal channels—either transferred by face-to-face meetings or in the mail—and ultimately passed among the detainees. The content and nature of the papers makes it certain that they could only have originated from a habeas lawyer. They include newspaper articles or magazine pieces from publications just out in the States but not yet arrived at the Navy Exchange in Guantánamo, for instance.

When these things occur, the lawyer can be criticized or even forbidden to see his or her client. But what about when communications are oral? If no one listens—as the protocol insists, to preserve attorney-client privilege—then if counsel passes contraband information to the detainee authorities would not know about it, and if they suspected could not prove it.

Officials, present and past, at both the Joint Detention Group and the Joint Intelligence Group affirm that a major part of the news detainees receive originates from unauthorized attorney communications. "Three to four days," Mike Bumgarner said flatly. "That's how long it takes a piece of information to get from a detainee–lawyer conversation to spread throughout the camps. Sooner if it is a major event."[48]

Events like the capture of Saddam Hussein, his execution, the killing of Abu Musab al Zarqawi, bombings in Madrid and London, and Islamic riots in France and Holland tend to make the "hot news" circuit within the camp. So do Supreme Court decisions, American elections (the election of November 2006, in which the Democrats won both houses of Congress, was praised as a "great victory for Islam" by the detainees), and other major events.

How do we know that the news comes from the lawyers? "You can just about time it from the visits," said Lieutenant Colonel Michael Nicolucci. "The attorneys meet on one day and by the next the entire camp is buzzing with the news." What about the effect the lawyers have on behavior inside the wire? "They contribute to a lot of unrest," Nicolucci said. "I'm certain that much of the 'acting up,' the hunger strikes, the attacks on guards, are all a result of encouragement and training they receive from their attorneys. Or one hears it and passes it to his 'brothers.' It's a constant threat to us all."[49]

What is the command response? "We can act if we can prove that they violated something specific," Admiral Harry Harris said, "but most of the time we know what is happening but can't prove it."

Why not? Because of attorney–client privilege. "We give them privileged areas in which to speak and communicate. It's during those meetings that messages are passed and prohibited news and coaching takes place. As long as the courts say that they get that privacy then we must grant it to them."[50]

Nonetheless, there is widespread speculation within Gitmo and the Pentagon that many of the habeas attorneys have violated their agreement with the U.S. government for what can only be described as political purposes.

There have also been concerns expressed on issues other than attorney ethics. On January 11, 2007, senior Pentagon official Charles "Cully" Stimson, then the deputy assistant secretary of defense for Detainee Affairs, gave a radio interview pointing out that many of the pro bono attorneys representing Guantánamo detainees worked for law firms that also represented some of the largest corporations in America. "I think, quite honestly, when corporate CEOs see that those firms are representing the very terrorists who hit their bottom line back in 2001, those CEOs are going to make those law firms choose between representing terrorists or representing reputable firms," Stimson told Federal News Radio.[51]

Attorneys from Center for Constitutional Rights, the American Bar Association, the National Lawyers Guild, and other activist groups were immediately enraged, portraying Stimson's comments as an effort to deny legal recourse to detainees. "His egregious comments gave us a great educational moment," said Karen Mathis, president of the ABA. "Every accused person should receive adequate legal representation, and it's encouraging to see that his comments were universally rejected."[52]

The Defense Department, the Bush administration, and Attorney General Alberto Gonzalez reportedly distanced themselves from Stimson as well. Within days, he apologized and voluntarily resigned from his position. However, the situation he described remains: Top U.S. corporations are, perhaps unwittingly, indirectly financing significant detainee legal costs.

On October 14–16, 2007, Hofstra Law School held a conference on "Lawyering at the Edge: Unpopular Clients, Difficult Cases, Zealous Advocates." Attorney Clive Stafford Smith, author of *Bad Men: Guantánamo Bay and the Secret Prisons,* who has represented over 100 detainees, gave a presentation entitled "Ethical Challenges at Guantánamo." Hofstra received more than 50 e-mails in protest from people from around the country because attorney Lynne Stewart—who was found guilty of helping a terrorist client, the blind Egyptian Sheik Omar Ahmad Ali Abdel Rahman, pass messages to his supporters—was scheduled to serve on one of the panels.[53] Similar concerns have been expressed about attorneys working with Guantánamo detainees.

A *Washington Times* article by Tim McElhatton published in July 2008 noted that "three U.S. law firms and a public relations company have received millions of dollars from a Middle Eastern organization partly financed by the Kuwaiti government to work for families of Kuwaiti men detained at the U.S. Naval Base Guantánamo Bay, Cuba." The legal work done—paid for in large measure by the Kuwait-based International Counsel Bureau—has led to significant results, including cases heard by the Supreme Court and the controversial ruling that accorded detainees the right to have their cases heard in U.S. courts.

McElhatton reported that the ICB gets some of its funding to hire U.S. lawyers through the Kuwaiti government, a fact acknowledged by attorneys. "We understand that the government of Kuwait makes financial contributions for the legal fees and expenses of the International Counsel Bureau," DC lawyer Thomas B. Wilner said. The Kuwaiti government has neither confirmed nor denied these reports.

Shearman & Sterling LLP, at which Wilner is a partner, reportedly received more than $1 million from the Kuwait-based group. According to Justice Department and U.S. Senate lobbying records, ICB has paid nearly $4 million overall to American firms. Wilner denied financial motivation. "This is not a case where the firm profited financially. We put more time and effort in this case than all the other firms combined."

These and similar arrangements were condemned by Debra Burlingame, co-founder of 9/11 Families for a Safe & Strong America. She challenged the propriety of U.S. attorneys involving themselves at foreign expense in matters of national security. Though in 2007 the National Legal Aid & Defender Association lauded firms for doing pro bono work, among them Shearman & Sterling, "The idea that all of the lawyers here are working pro bono isn't true. It just makes the cause look more noble," Burlingame said. She deplored "millions of dollars in fees in furtherance of acquiring the release of committed [jihadis] from U.S. custody while men and women of the U.S. armed services are under fire in Iraq and Afghanistan."

The firms of Arnold & Porter LLP and Pillsbury Winthrop Shaw Pittman LLP have received funds from ICB, according to the *Washington Times*. The article states, "Arnold & Porter has lobbied Congress, the Justice Department, the State Department and the Defense Department on 'issues related to efforts to obtain due process for the Kuwaiti detainees in U.S. custody in Guantánamo Bay.'"

Nor have legal firms been the only recipient of Kuwaiti funding. According to Justice Department memoranda, the firm of Levick Strategic Communications, a public relations company, was engaged in promoting the cause of the Guantánamo detainees. Levick, according to Justice, had contacts with the American Civil Liberties Union to explore "possible collaboration on the orange-ribbon movement to shut down Guantánamo." Levick senior vice president Gene Grabowski replied, "We were engaged to make the case . . . give them a real trial. It was never about freedom. If they're found guilty, they should be punished. We're not arguing for their blanket freedom."[54]

Some might find Grabowski's point disingenuous, if not for him in particular then certainly for the anti-Guantánamo effort in general.

Thus attorney Clive Stafford Smith told an interviewer that if sufficient political pressure were applied by the UK government, "all his clients would be released."[55] Meanwhile, the press of legal initiatives continues unabated. It is a rare day when some new court action does not make headlines—and petrodollars or unwitting corporate clients pay the sharply mounting legal fees. Former CIA director James Woolsey notes with irony that "except for the Civil War this is the only war that we have fought where we are paying for both sides."[56]

It appears unlikely that complex, emotionally driven legal issues will ever be solved to anyone's satisfaction. Whatever the eventual outcome of the myriad legal struggles surrounding Guantánamo and its detainees, it is important to keep in mind that precedents set in resolving these cases will continue to influence military and law enforcement authorities and defenders of those held far into the future.

CHAPTER 13

THE VALUE OF INTELLIGENCE

WHILE NO MORAL, CLEAR-THINKING PERSON condones torture, there are indications that many outside the military community misunderstand the differences between military and police interrogation. In fact, some of the FBI agents in Guantánamo's early days had difficulty separating the need to make a criminal case from determining strategic information. TV crimes are solved by confessions; real cases are made with the popularly maligned but more convincing use of circumstantial evidence. As a result, anything that involves interrogation of a "suspect" that does not include attorneys present, reading of rights, protection from self-incrimination, and the entire list of constitutional protections in a criminal affair is considered beyond the pale.

Even the relatively soft type of strategic interrogation that takes place at Guantánamo does not sit well with the media. Witness the *Washington Post* editorial of December 11, 2005 that decried "waterboarding, painful stress positions, forced nudity and other methods" as equivalent to "Torquemada and the Spanish Inquisition." The *Post* editors seemed especially exercised over "waterboarding" and compared "suffocation by water" to techniques "such as the Pinochet dictatorship" used that the State Department "didn't hesitate to call torture." In essence, the editorial board accused the Bush administration of "accepting in principle" that the FBI may use these methods in American prisons.[1]

As the interrogators at Guantánamo say repeatedly, torture simply doesn't work. This is widely acknowledged even among the most hawkish supporters of the war on terror. Author Jed Babbin, for instance, has noted that "you are as likely to get [Khalid Sheikh] Muhammad to confess to the Kennedy assassination as you are to get useful information from him under torture. People will say anything to stop the pain."[2]

Other experts, such as former CIA undercover agent to the drug cartels Wayne Simmons, who has been, as he says "both the interrogator and the subject," differ: "The very idea that severe methods are off the table allows the terrorists to say F-you to the lead interrogator. Most terrorists will crack quickly if the right combination of interrogation methods are either threatened or used, including second-generation drugs like Propofol."[3]

Babbin tends to agree with the statement on chemical inducement: "So-called 'truth serums' are not foolproof, and do not guarantee success. But chemically assisted interrogation can significantly increase the interrogator's chance to get the facts without descending into barbarism."[4]

Military analyst Chuck Nash makes the point that "uncertainty is what scares people the most. If the prisoner knows what the U.S. can and cannot do, much of the uncertainty is removed and thus the element of fear that can be an instrument that wears down the prisoner much sooner than cold and lack of sleep. It is ludicrous that we publish what we are prepared to do. It exposes critical elements to our enemies that they use in their training."[5] But in preserving the transparency of the Guantánamo operation, that is exactly what happens.

The odd point is that the primary debate is over what defines torture. According to the UN, simply being detained at Guantánamo is "tantamount to torture."[6] Former Army Muslim chaplain at Guantánamo James Yee made the outlandish claim that "Islam is smeared and demeaned" because Muslims are detained by Christian captors even though the latter may be doing everything possible to treat them decently.[7] Habeas attorney Clive Stafford Smith cites twice-removed claims that detainees are subject to "systemic humiliation and torture, encouraged by military higher-ups." He writes of "a Yemeni prisoner recently beaten and his Koran trampled because he asked to finish his prayers before responding to a guard's demand."[8]

Mahvish Khan bought into the stories the detainees told her with naïve acceptance. She repeats the most outlandish tales of forced feeding, routine beatings, and isolation with certainty, strongly implying that such treatment was general and routine, yet recounts an interview with a released Afghani detainee named Badr Raman who said "neither he nor his brother was tortured at Gitmo."[9]

Regardless of the often hyperbolic nature of some allegations, every charge, including the beating and stomped Koran story along with Korans being flushed down toilets and otherwise defaced, is taken seriously by the command. Investigations are immediately launched, and in the rare cases when an infraction did take place—intentionally or accidentally, as in the case of a Koran possibly being soiled by wind-blown urine—soldiers are invariably disciplined. In the majority of incidents, however, investigations return a conclusion that the alleged abuse did not occur. At that point the easy course for disbelieving critics is simply to accuse the command—or the secretary of defense—of "dissimulation," and of "hiding its hypocrisy behind a smokescreen of secrecy and semantics."[10]

Analyst and Middle East expert Brigitte Gabriel dismisses these charges. A former news anchor of *World News* for Middle East television and now a contributing editor of FamilySecurityMatters.com, Gabriel maintains, "Gitmo is a joke as far as Arabs are concerned. Let me tell you what some of the prisoners call Guantánamo, 'Al muntazah al-dini lilmujaheden al Muslimin,' The Religious Resort for Islamic Militants."[11]

For the record, I deplore torture. Because I was outraged and upset by reports of wholesale torture and abuse, I visited the installation to find out what was really happening. After that initial fact-finding trip, a major reason for my accepting the challenge to write this book was to inform readers of the truth about blanket allegations of misbehavior by American soldiers. As the Church Report, the Schmidt-Furlow Report, and other investigations referenced in this book disclose, highly isolated, limited instances of inexcusable abuse have occurred at Guantánamo. These abuses took place in a time of organizational chaos exacerbated by superheated pressure from the American public transferred through governmental institutions to prevent further attacks on the country.

That these abuses took place at all is terribly unfortunate. Critical to note, however, is that the abusive practices were corrected and offenders disciplined according to the Uniform Code of Military Justice. Lessons learned from those investigations led directly to improved policies and guidance and to upgraded oversight protocols to prevent recurrence.

Most important, I learned through my investigations that torture and abuse are simply not part of the cultural makeup of the American soldier and are not tolerated at any level of the chain of command. Nor should they be. Simply stated, torture is unacceptable from both a moral and a practical aspect: In addition to being inhumane, torture does not work and is an ineffective means of obtaining valid intelligence information. Further, history shows, as in the case of the French military in Algeria, that a culture of torture ultimately erodes the very institution that permits or encourages it. I learned through my queries that torture is categorically rejected at every level of the military community.

That said, I am equally appalled by the ease and frequency with which hostile critics accuse the U.S. military of engaging routinely in torture and abuse. The core issue is that in attempting to address conspiracy theorists and cover-up accusations, Guantánamo authorities cannot prove a negative. Consequently they must continue to labor on, upholding professional standards in the face of unrelenting slander. Fortunately there are third-party, objective agencies present in the facility.

Almost from the onset, the International Committee of the Red Cross (separate entirely from the American Red Cross) has had unlimited access to the detainees. Not once have any of its administrators alleged that torture, maltreatment, or abuse of detainees is taking place. In fact, the ICRC representative frequently makes recommendations to the camp commander that are often accepted and implemented. This collegial atmosphere has resulted for the most part in accusations levied against the ICRC representative as being complicit with Guantánamo authorities.

As part of its charter, the ICRC handles detainee communications with the outside world and has transmitted letters from the detainees to addresses abroad. These letters have first been screened by the authorities at Guantánamo, a completely acceptable process under international rules, for information that might refer to future terrorist operations, organizations, or money laundering, along with directions or instructions to sleeper cells. The letters are reviewed, discussed, and pulled or censored as necessary.

Responding to accusations regarding detainees being cut off from the outside world, Admiral Harris noted, "Over 40,000 pieces of mail have come in and out of here. If you chose to write one of them a letter, all you'd need to do is put their name on it, say 'Guantánamo Bay, Cuba,' put our ZIP code on it, and they will get that letter."[12]

Over time, intelligence analysts discovered that many letters contain repetitive patterns of words, passages, and drawings. Analysts surmised that these are coded messages to terrorists on the outside. In some cases, drawings of flowers or mosques have been discovered to have tiny messages written in the detail work of the petals and mosque façades. Linguistic specialists and intelligence analysts are cooperating to decipher the possible coded messages leaving the camp by ordinary mail.[13]

While the letters and drawings themselves have high intelligence value, so do some of the more seemingly prosaic aspects of the external communication process. For example, comparison of outgoing, destination addresses among the thousands of pieces of mail and return addresses on incoming mail has uncovered some interesting facts. In many instances, letters that originated from an identical address are mailed to several different detainees. In other cases, many different detainee letters are sent to the same address, and a lot of the replies to different detainees originate from identical addresses. Often these are in places like Hamburg, Germany or Liverpool, England—addresses that by themselves might not raise suspicion. What does all this mean to intelligence personnel? Certainly it points to al Qaeda efforts to orchestrate communications in and out of Guantánamo. It also means that information that interrogators would prefer not be released to detainees often gets through to them. On the other hand, the source could be as innocent as a Dear Osama service for the lonely and forlorn. More suspicious types might sense the existence of a sleeper cell, a convenience address, or a filter through which instructions, information, and orders can be passed into the Guantánamo detainee population. Undetected, this might be a dangerous phenomenon, but once aware of it counterintelligence officers can move decisively to thwart plans, uncover cells, and foil plots.

Sorting all this traffic is a formidable challenge. The mail is probably impossible to screen completely, but authorities make the attempt. Surprisingly to many, not all of the traffic is from European or Middle Eastern addresses. "The detainees receive a large amount of mail from the U.S.," said Colonel Lora Tucker, JTF GTMO Public Affairs Officer. "Especially around the holidays the detainees get packages, cards, letters, and expressions of sympathy from thousands of Americans."

The first time I heard this I thought it was a joke. Americans are really sending well-wishes to radical Islamic terrorists? On Christmas and Easter, our largest Christian holidays? "It's strange but true," Tucker affirmed. "Sometimes it looks like they get more holiday mail than the troopers."[14]

It is easy to imagine that the holiday mail is a perfect screen for more insidious traffic. There is no doubt that al Qaeda sleeper cells are present and active in America. Even some of the top al Qaeda operatives have traveled to the United States at one time or another. So intercepting and tracking possible high-value targets that may be hiding inside the States is a high priority in intercepting and analyzing communications.

Information obtained recently in Afghanistan has assisted in breaking the stoically held cover story of one high-level detainee. In another instance, a cooperative Guantánamo detainee has assisted with issues involving an Afghan tribal leader working with the Coalition forces.

Many critics, including some who support the detention of the terrorists, question the utility of continued interrogation. In a front-page story on June 21, 2004, *New York Times* reporters Tim Golden and Don Van Natta dismissed Bush administration claims about high-value detainees: "Contrary to repeated assertions . . . none of the detainees at Guantánamo Bay rank as leaders or senior operatives of Al Qaeda, and only a handful are sworn Qaeda members." They cited "dozens" of "high-level military, intelligence and law-enforcement officials in the US, Europe and the Middle East." These unnamed officials are convinced that "only a trickle of intelligence with current value" has been produced on the island, and "none that has enabled intelligence or law-enforcement agencies to foil imminent attacks."[15]

Oddly, three months prior to Golden and Van Natta's exposé, *Times* reporter Neil Lewis uncovered a "stream of intelligence" coming from Guantánamo. It included detailed information on "al Qaeda's recruitment of Muslim men in Europe," and about "chemical and biological weapons efforts . . . training of suicide bombers, and use of charities to raise money for its aims." Lewis interviewed involved officials. "We have been able as a result of information gained here to take operational actions, even military campaigns," he quoted Steve Rodriguez, then JTF GTMO intelligence chief. Another official, Lewis pointed out, said, "There are instances of learning about active [al Qaeda] cells, and we have taken action to see that the cell was broken." Analysts have been able to "understand a kind of network" that al Qaeda uses in Europe to recruit young Muslim men. Further, this information had been "sent on" to Europe's intelligence counterparts.[16]

Similarly, some former military officers are confused about the intelligence value of the Guantánamo detainees. Some think that any pertinent information they possess must certainly be dated by this time. But the interrogators at Guantánamo know differently. "We're just beginning to get to some of these people," JIG chief Paul Rester said. "Some of them have been silent for years and finally just say, to hell with it, and begin to talk. Some want to get things off their chests, others are bored or lonely, some have developed a conscience, and others may have been caught in a lie so give it up."[17]

There have been occasions when information came in from the

field that blew the cover story that a detainee had stuck to for months. Perhaps a fighter picked up in Iraq or Afghanistan had identified a photo of a detainee held in Guantánamo and said that he had trained with him at al Farouk, or met him in Hamburg and passed some travel money to him. Or maybe information from interrogators identifies the detainee as the expert bomb-maker that al Qaeda chatter said was confined in Guantánamo. Often when a detainee is faced with hard information that compromises his cover story, he caves and tells all.

So what kinds of information can someone held in Guantánamo that long possess? "Some of it is surprisingly good stuff," Rester said, "and occasionally very timely." It turns out that cells have indeed been busted up—particularly in Europe and the United States—as well as money trails cut and terrorist activities stymied by information coming out of Guantánamo's interrogation booths. In the multiple-aircraft hijacking planned from the United Kingdom in summer 2006, many of the plotters had already been identified by intelligence sources in Guantánamo as possible terrorists and placed on watch lists by British intelligence.

In late 2004 through early 2005, intelligence sharing from Guantánamo scored spectacular results in Europe. The *Boston Globe*'s Charlie Savage reported that "700 police swept through mosques, homes and businesses in six [German] cities and arrested 22 militant extremists." Why? "Information obtained through the interrogation of a Guantánamo Bay detainee" led to the busts. These January 12 raids were considered "the most extensive intelligence coup attributed to the [Guantánamo] operation," and give credence to statements that the "hard core group still provides valuable intelligence."

What came out of these raids? "Police seized computers, cell phones, large sums of money, counterfeit identity documents, and literature espousing jihad." The terrorists arrested came from Egypt, Tunisia, Algeria, Libya, Palestine, Morocco, Bulgaria, and Germany. German prosecutors said that they "worked collaboratively, highly professionally, and conspiratorially, misusing mosques and other Islamic establishments as cover" for "political violence."[18] Further, they were linked to "militant extremist groups Ansar al-Islam and El Tauhid."[19]

Additionally, Savage noted, "Jay Hood . . . confirmed . . . that there had been a previously unknown terrorist cell in another country recently uncovered by information" from Guantánamo. Backing Hood's statement, Savage interviewed a "senior Defense Department official" who "confirmed that the intelligence breakthrough led to the arrests in Germany." These were considered "particularly significant because the terrorists involved in the Sept. 11, 2001 terrorist attacks on the United States had roots in Al Qaeda cells in Germany."

"It's not like *24*," Rester said, referring to the popular TV series. "We're not going to have someone lay out chapter and verse of a plot against America complete with ticking nuclear bombs. Our successes are measured on a much less dramatic level. We get a piece there, a piece here, and put part of the puzzle together. We'll run it past other agencies and occasionally get a great hit." Nor does it happen overnight. "After years of questioning . . . the sessions continue to yield useful information," Steve Rodriguez affirmed.[20] "Not every detainee is a plethora of information," Rodriguez said. "But many had good placement and access in a worldwide terrorist network. Financiers, engineers, bodyguards, recruiters for al Qaeda—all these people have lots of valuable information."[21]

So what kinds of things have we learned? Rester was thinking about some of the interrogation reports one day and had an idea. He told his staff that they were going to construct "fantasy hijack teams." First they assembled the profiles of all known 9/11 hijackers, including Muhammad al Qahtani, Zacarias Moussaoui, and the 19 who suicided with the aircraft. Then they applied these derived standards to detainees in Guantánamo. To their surprise they were able to come up with four additional hijack teams: trained pilots, aircraft engineers, committed muscle, and presence in the United States on 9/11. It is highly likely that these men—some, if not all—were among other hijack teams aloft on the morning of September 11, 2001. Perhaps they did not have sufficient time to launch their attacks because of the quick grounding of all civilian aircraft by national authorities and were thus prevented from making a terrible event that much worse.

One of the primary fantasy hijackers is ISN 682, Ghassan Abdullah al Sharbi. Sharbi, 32, is a Saudi who brags of his jihadist nature. "I'm going to make it easy for you guys," he said in fluent English at his ARB hearing. "I fought against the United States. I took up arms. I'm proud of what I did."[22] On another occasion he told Mike Bumgarner, who teased him about being a mechanical engineer, "Knock it off, Bumgarner. You know I'm an electrical engineer. I'm a bomb maker!"[23]

Sharbi is a graduate of Embry-Riddle Aeronautical University in Prescott, Arizona. He majored in electrical engineering and took extensive flight training. He was a friend of and shared lodging with Hami Hanjour, whom the 9/11 Commission refers to as the "Fourth Pilot" in the attack. Hanjour flew American Airlines Flight 77 out of Washington Dulles Airport and crashed into the Pentagon on September 11.

During his time in Phoenix, Sharbi associated with many terrorists and their enablers. He was friends with Hamdan al Shawali, and trained with him in al Qaeda's Afghanistan camps. In 1999, Shawali and fellow Saudi Muhammad al Qudhaein were detained by the FBI for trying twice to get into the cockpit of a passenger airplane flying from Phoenix, Arizona, to Washington, DC. They claimed later that they thought the cockpit was the bathroom. After 9/11, the FBI calculated that this may have been a rehearsal for the September 11, 2001 attacks. The FBI also reports that the two were plotting a "Khobar Towers" type attack in Saudi Arabia that was later scrubbed.[24]

By focusing interrogators on Ghassan al Sharbi and other potential hijackers, we may be able to learn more about how the 9/11 plot was put together and how others—such as the foiled September 2006 London plot to hijack up to 10 airliners—can be thwarted. Indeed, there are indications that significant information leading to the London terrorists also came from Guantánamo.

Unquestionably, intelligence information gleaned in Guantánamo has been used by law enforcement agencies in the United States to unearth and arrest terrorist cells. The Lackawanna Six,[25] the Cleveland sleeper group,[26] and several others were intercepted in large part as a result of information obtained in Guantánamo interrogations.

The Lackawanna Six, all U.S.–born men of Yemeni extraction, trained in summer of 2001 in the al Farouk camp, where they became friends with Guantánamo resident David Hicks and other English speakers. They no doubt talked about their hometowns and what actions they hoped to undertake on their return to America. The Afghanistan camps—along with battlegrounds in places like Chechnya, Somalia, and the Balkans—became terrorist meeting places and fostered acquaintances and friendships that would span continents and time. Detainees telling of their meetings and experiences in these camps have provided much material for intelligence agencies to follow up, as well as crime-oriented agencies such as the FBI and Interpol.[27]

Guantánamo-derived information has been material in intercepting terrorist money-laundering operations, breaking up plots, destroying training bases, and capturing or killing additional terrorists. But it is not the proverbial "magic bullet," Paul Butler noted. "The point is not to be able to stop an impending attack, but to construct an intelligence net and process information. Also we must recognize that there are many different terrorist groups and offshoots represented at Guantánamo."[28] Because of classification and compartmentalization (the term usually defined by "need to know"), the public may never know the extent and magnitude of the actionable intelligence that has been extracted in Guantánamo.[29]

Paul Rester strongly underscores the enormous value of Guantánamo-derived information: "The production of strategic-level intelligence information out of Guantánamo—stuff dealing with money laundering and phony Islamic charities, with recruiting and vetting processes, with training, bomb manufacture, ways that they obtain forged documents, methods of international travel, who supports them in Europe and America—all this and more has come out of these guys and more continues to flow. We have some who are only now beginning to talk to us. There's a lot to be learned here."

The Joint Intelligence Group at JTF GTMO sends interrogation analysis up the intelligence food chain to the National Command Authority, passing along the way through Southern Command, the Defense Intelligence Agency, and the Pentagon. Other agencies such as the Central Intelligence Agency, Federal Bureau of Investigation, National Security Agency, and various other federal and local agencies who may be concerned are in the loop for distribution. Pertinent— need-to-know— information is shared with major military commands that might be affected. Certainly, Central Command and Pacific Command receive steady traffic flow.

Information is also shared with allied intelligence agencies, most particularly with NATO country agencies including those of France, Italy, Germany (all reported to be surprisingly cooperative at the intelligence services level), and the United Kingdom. Close allies and active coalition partners such as Australia, Japan, and South Korea are included in information sharing when the need-to-know criteria apply.

For the record, Rester categorically denies the use of torture and abuse in interrogating the detainees. "That's B-movie stuff," he said dismissively. "Any interrogator worth his pay has to establish rapport with the subject, gain mutual respect and trust, and work over a long time to extract information that would be of strategic value."[30] As we have seen, tactical intelligence—the stuff of battlefield locations and actions—is highly perishable and fades after about 48 hours. Strategic intelligence, on the other hand—the locations and methods of money laundering, recruiting terrorists, media and propaganda, training and indoctrination, chain of command, sleeper cells, future operational plans, bomb-making, and many other specialties—has value long after the battlefields are cold.

Some note that "people change, but terrain and villages don't," a reference to the fact that many held in Guantánamo can discuss with topical lucidity the use of terrain (for example, Tora Bora, Waziristan, or certain Taliban-sympathetic villages) and people (local terrorists and warlords, officials who are al Qaeda supporters). So there is an acute need for strategic interrogation at Guantánamo, and that, as every specialist in the field will agree, cannot be obtained by Hollywood methods of abuse, torture, or drugging.

CHAPTER 14

THE FUTURE OF GUANTÁNAMO

CRITIQUES AND RECOMMENDATIONS

C LOSE GITMO. THAT WAS THE position of both presidential candidates in the 2008 election, and it will undoubtedly be high on the agenda of President Barack Obama and his allies in Congress. Yet even some of the camp's harshest critics are beginning to recognize that closing it down is not a simple matter and will raise a host of thorny administrative and legal issues that may take months, if not years, to resolve.

Now that we've had an overview of Guantánamo—detainees, facilities, operation, and opposition—it's the proper moment to look at the positives and negatives associated with its continued operation, including options that must be considered if the facility is closed. Let's start with the basics.

Detention and Interrogation

There is an inherent institutional conflict between the necessary dual functions of interrogation and detention. Over time at Guantánamo, the pendulum has swung toward detention, sometimes hampering interrogation efforts. The emphasis is a natural one. The public, including oversight agencies and the media, sees a lot more of detention than of interrogation. One can tour the camps, the hospital, and adjunct facilities and see what is happening, unlike the shadowy, classified world of intelligence-gathering and current operations.

The critics who complain about the "poor intelligence value" of Guantánamo detainees are simply not in the loop. They are not aware of the successes, because in most instances follow-up investigations continue long after the immediate information has been obtained. If information is passed to German intelligence, for example, that a certain cell is located in a given area, they would not immediately bust it up but would observe and expand the investigation hoping to net bigger prey. Given the closed nature of that world, we probably never will be fully apprised of what has been accomplished as a result.

People on the ground try to do best what is most visible, and that clearly is detention. For the commander, whose rating is heavily weighted to the detention side (it is a lot easier to measure good detainee health, for example, than to quantify actionable intelligence), it is natural to focus primarily on that function. Commanders and their superiors must take steps to facilitate expeditious, efficient interrogation processes while ensuring safe, humane care and treatment.

How to do this practically will of course be left to the initiative of individual commanders and staff.

One of the most widespread popular misconceptions about the interrogation process is that a successful interrogation means the subject has disclosed details of a pending attack, which authorities are then able to thwart. Such scenarios lend great suspense to films and novels. In reality, however, normal interrogations are almost devoid of such thrilling escapades.

What in the trade is called "actionable intelligence" does not mean SWAT teams in full combat regalia kicking down doors and flex-cuffing suspects who were arming digital clock–rigged dirty bombs when the Feds burst in. Rather, the term means that information is gleaned that can be used to fill in blank spots and, ideally, to generate more questions and avenues to explore. If we think of intelligence as a process rather than a destination, it makes more sense and is more congruent with situational realities.

In terms of a modern, global war on terror, that means the more prosaic work of filling in the names and hierarchy of al Qaeda organizational charts, determining who knows who else in order to establish bona fides, and tracing the support and operational lines of the movement.

High-level intelligence officials readily admit that we were woefully short of skilled linguists, cultural interpreters, and professional interrogators and had none of the infrastructure necessary to house, feed, medicate, protect, or care for captured enemy combatants in 2002. Consequently, we have no idea what intelligence we missed in those early days. We know that many were able to slip through our grasp because we didn't have the capability of vetting them properly. Testimony from released detainees shows that many were able to float a cover story and sell it to an untrained interrogator. We have seen that many who escaped our grasp later were responsible for several attacks in Europe and Central Asia that could have been prevented.[1]

The Continuing Threat

One of the consistent myths about Guantánamo is that the detainees are mostly ignorant opium farmers, Taliban conscripts who know nothing of importance and pose little future threat to America. In fact, some of these people are amazingly intelligent and well-educated. Mahvish Khan refers to an Afghani detainee named Taj, who so effectively concealed his actual level of education that he was naïvely considered "a goat herder genius."[2]

Confined behind Guantánamo wire are at least one physician and two pharmacists (all of whom practiced in America), several pilots (Embry-Riddle graduates), more than one electrical engineer (one received an MS from Purdue), financial experts (two with advanced degrees from the London School of Economics), and a large number of graduates from European, Egyptian, Saudi, and other universities. Many more have technical degrees in electronic and mechanical specialties and in administrative disciplines such as accounting and supply control.

Inside Gitmo are recruiters, paymasters, financial whizzes (one set up retirement and life insurance programs for terrorists), experts at laundering and moving large sums of money, public relations men who excel at al Qaeda propaganda in print, video, and Internet media, and a wide variety of other specialists. Of course, the muscle is there too, but even they have more than basic education.

Many Americans are surprised to learn that rather than prospect among the "poverty-stricken, ignorant, despondent masses," al Qaeda tries to recruit college graduates, or at least those with college or trade school experience. While some of them have made amazingly dumb mistakes—the kind of thing that good espionage "tradecraft" would correct—it is not because they are stupid, but are poorly trained. With better training, Qahtani would have skated through Immigration at Orlando International and with additional muscle on board, the hijackers on Flight 93 might have been able to suppress the passenger revolt and destroy the U.S. Capitol.

What about the question of who ought to be incarcerated at Guantánamo? While opponents deplore anyone being kept there at all, a good argument could be made for expanding the operation rather than shutting it down. While some high-value detainees were brought from "secret" CIA camps in August 2006, there is ample room for more. Certainly any captured al Qaeda terrorist leader of significance or who poses a special threat ought to be confined in Guantánamo. The infamous Bali Bomber would not have escaped from Guantánamo, as he was able to do from Bagram.

Some enemy combatants continue to be brought to Guantánamo, but at this point they are only a trickle. During 2007 at least three al Qaeda terrorists were transferred to Gitmo. They included Abdul Malik, who was involved in terrorist attacks in East Africa; Haroon al-Afghani, senior commander of al Qaeda in Afghanistan and an IED expert; and Abdullah Sudi Arale, an al Qaeda courier who made the

East Africa–Pakistan run regularly. The Department of Defense has announced that all will be subject to the standard CSRT processing.[3]

It would be an interesting experiment to transfer all those convicted of terrorism in U.S. courts to Guantánamo. There they could serve their allotted prison time, but more important, they could continue to be interrogated. Of what use is it, other than as retribution for criminal acts, to keep John Walker Lindh, Zacarias Moussaoui, Sami al Arian, José Padilla, and scores of others in U.S. penitentiaries? Under the criminal justice system, once a culprit is sentenced, questioning ceases—actually long before he is even brought to trial.

Yet the value of what these terrorists hold in their heads far outweighs any imagined advantage to keeping them in U.S. prisons merely doing time. Walker Lindh is reported to now be a highly esteemed imam in a medium-security prison in Victorville, California, and calls himself "Hamza" after Mohammad's uncle.[4] "He is an extremely well-liked, respected inmate," reports the New York *Daily News*.[5] Is this what we want to hear from terrorists engaged in operations against America? It would be far more useful to see Padilla, Moussaoui, Arian, and the rest talking to trained interrogators in Gitmo rather than watching cable TV, proselytizing radical Islam, and lifting weights in an American jail.

Hospital and Medical Issues

Hospital and medical issues were universally considered by Guantánamo personnel to be most vulnerable to detainee exploitation. By December 2006, the hospital commander had come to this realization independently and had already begun to institute corrective action.

Many of the issues involved with detainees being transported to the hospital for imaginary or feigned illnesses have been mitigated by Colonel Dennis's consolidation plan that moved them into Camps V and VI, with in-house dispensary and triage capability. This will not only reduce the hospital load and free the medical facilities for genuine health problems but will minimize opportunities for detainee communications and disturbances. This has been a positive implementation that ought to continue.

Much of the weakness on the medical side rests with personnel issues and the too-rapid rotation of medics. Six months is barely enough time to be well grounded in this kind of duty before shipping out. Not only that, but the detainees have learned well how to prey on the newcomers' good nature and vulnerabilities. "We're they're entertainment," one medic sighed. That needs to cease. If short-term rotations are necessary, then it would make sense to train the new group as thoroughly as possible prior to deployment. This could be done with a combination of prior-serving medics, perhaps along with a consultative team from U.S. military or federal prisons. Navy guards are trained at Fort Lewis, Washington prior to deployment, and it might be wise to institute a brief course for the medics there as well.

Public Relations and Media

It would also be useful to adopt a more proactive approach to public relations. Although a shocking lack of public communications about key issues has been a constant criticism of the Bush administration in virtually all of its programs, the failure to respond effectively to the concerted international propaganda campaign against Gitmo has been among its most damaging lapses. Needless to say, the government could be a lot more forthright in explaining exactly why Guantánamo is needed and what useful things are derived there. It may also be necessary to arm-twist the intelligence people into releasing more information on successes and not simply to apply platitudes and generalities.

Have Americans and the world been hearing the truth about Guantánamo? Mike Nicolucci thinks that "the mission has been politically misinterpreted for the purpose of discrediting America's efforts in Iraq and Afghanistan." These people were not "capriciously" picked off the battlefield. He adds, "They are being treated better than common criminals in American prisons." The kind of misreporting that characterizes what media and lawyers and human rights organizations say about Guantánamo "gets people killed on the streets of Pakistan."

Others are equally blunt. "They want to close this place," Paul Rester said. "They did it before when the Haitians were here and they want to do it again." Where do they want to put the detainees? What do they want done with them? "They don't want to talk about the practical side," he said. "They just want to holler about how their 'rights' are being violated."

What about the lurid stories that came out of Guantánamo about torture, abuse, and maltreatment? The duct-taping, extreme temperatures, lap dances, barking dogs, short-shackling, sleep deprivation, waterboarding, stress positions, and so on? Unfortunately, abuses by poorly trained, immature interrogation staff did take place in isolated circumstances, especially in the fall of 2002. These incidents were thoroughly investigated, and corrective measures have been taken.

There is also a constant rumor mill, grinding out stories, many of which originate with Guantánamo personnel. In one instance some Navy sailors were trying to impress a visiting female Marine JAG administrator, Sergeant Heather Cerveny, by "tough guy" stories of routine abuse they afflicted on detainees. As in every other case, this story was investigated and proved to be unfounded. It turned out, as one officer crudely described it, to be a "big dick" story designed to impress a gullible female, who was tougher in the end than the immature sailors.[6]

"Many people who served at Guantánamo," said Steve Rodriguez, former head of interrogation, "don't have to actually deal with detainees. They do other jobs in support or something. So they hear rumors, they hear stories, they want to be cool or macho, so they add twists, exaggerate, embellish. After this happens a few times then suddenly there is a horrendous story out there."[7]

In July 2006, the Afghan Ministry of Interior sent an inspection team to Guantánamo. After a thorough inspection including interviews with 96 Afghani prisoners, the team reported "only one or two complaints," and concluded, "Conditions of the jail was [sic] humane. There were rumors in this country about that. It was wrong. What we have seen was OK."[8]

There have of course been valid concerns about possible abuse, as well as administrative confusion, miscommunications, and interagency squabbling. Critics complained that there were no defined standards; in response, new manuals were issued. Courts made rulings and the Defense and Justice departments responded to these as well. Legislation has been passed on military tribunal procedures. Guantánamo is a work in progress, and more improvements and capabilities will be codified and implemented as time and experience warrant.

The Guantánamo operation as it now stands is the most transparent, visible detention system in the world, and virtually the only one with an interrogation mission. It was built in response to a critical need, and unfortunately, whether or not Guantánamo exists, that need will continue for the foreseeable future. It seems preferable to improve and upgrade the existing facility rather than abandon it in haste and regret this at leisure.

What Future for Guantánamo?

If we are going to have a rational discussion about the future of Guantánamo Bay as an interrogation/detention facility, two key questions must be addressed:

> *If not at Guantánamo, where? And if not Guantánamo, what?*

In other words, if we don't hold these detainees and possibly other terrorists at Guantánamo, then where do we propose to hold them? It is fatuous to argue, as some propose, that we should simply let them go.[9] To propose that the United States release them because they fail to meet criminal justice standards applied to private citizens in an American court is irresponsible. We simply invite renewed attacks upon the United States with such a proposal.

But if we are not in fact going to have an interrogation/detention facility like Guantánamo, then what alternative course shall we pursue?

If we seriously expect to be required for national security to pursue the war against the terrorists, then we must assume that in time more will be captured. These men—and possibly women—will need to be confined so that they cannot cause additional harm, and they will have to be questioned about present, past, and future terrorist activities.

Where in the world, and what other facility, would offer an option preferable to Guantánamo?

This is not a frivolous question. In November 2005, the *Washington Post* published a story on "secret CIA prisons" in Europe and the Middle East.[10] The alacrity with which other media ran the story and the political damage it did—regardless of factual accuracy—to allies in those areas points out the inadvisability of attempting to keep terrorist confinement facilities secret. Better to let the world know where they are and deal with their existence openly and aboveboard.

A study by the Center for Strategic and International Studies titled "Closing Guantánamo: From Bumper Sticker to Blueprint" outlines a policy that appears sensible and practical: Appoint a blue-ribbon commission to review all cases, recommend some for trial, and release the remainder. The former would then process through the judicial system. If found guilty, imprison them; if acquitted, release them. Then close Gitmo.[11]

While this seems to be a clean, logical solution, issues still arise. Of the 250 or so detainees remaining at the detention facility, approximately 80 are now on the list for trial before Military Commissions.

The Military Commission process has been highly controversial, requiring multiple judicial rulings and congressional legislation to resolve. It is a safe bet that its judgments will meet a firestorm of criticism and a string of appeals for judicial review. Nevertheless, progress has been made. Australian David Hicks pled guilty to multiple counts of supporting terrorism and was returned to his home country. Osama bin Laden's driver, Salim Hamdan, a Yemeni, was found guilty and sentenced to six years in prison, receiving time served for five and a half years in Guantánamo.

The list of those in the prosecutorial queue includes 9/11 architect Khalid Sheikh Muhammad and his lieutenant, Ramzi bin al-Shibh. Evidence gathered includes testimony of witnesses, circumstances, and individual confessions. Although defense attorneys have consistently challenged many of the confessions as derived through torture, some have been given voluntarily. KSM continues to stand by his statements proudly and expresses a desire for martyrdom.

Where will the guilty serve out their sentences? Some released detainees have been refused reentry by their home countries. Transferring others to certain countries could expose them to torture or arbitrary execution.

One proposed solution has been to shift detainees into the military or federal prison systems. As one commentator opined, "A wing of one of the military's larger prisons possibly at Ft. Leavenworth, Kan., or the Charleston Naval Base in South Carolina could work."[12] This could be a very dangerous option. Mixing hardened terrorists into a criminal population could result in the radicalization of other inmates, and would also present a target for terrorist attacks. Witness suicide attacks on prisons in Afghanistan and Yemen.

The practical issues of staffing a movement order, arranging transportation, and actual relocation can actually be resolved rather easily, according to former deputy assistant secretary of defense for Detainee Affairs Cully Stimson. "If they want to do it in a prudent manner they will have to go through a logical national-security-based analysis that can be completed in a matter of weeks," Stimson said. "The president gets sworn in January 2009; you could have them, easily, in a facility in the spring."[13] In other words, if the Pentagon is ordered to move Guantánamo detainees it will be able to do so. The big question remains: where?

Senator Tom Harkin (D-IA), who introduced a bill for relocation, and Senator Dianne Feinstein (D-CA), who introduced a similar, competing bill, advocate moving detainees to the Army's disciplinary barracks at Fort Leavenworth, Kansas, or to military prisons in South Carolina or Virginia.[14] Representative Jim Moran (D-VA) said, "United States military barracks have the capability to provide for the secure detainment of foreign nationals while ensuring the safety of communities within their proximate geographic location."[15]

These proposals met immediate bipartisan opposition from Kansas legislators, including Senator Sam Brownback (R-KS) and his Democratic colleague in the House, Nancy Boyda. Brownback argues that Leavenworth facilities "do not provide the level of security found at Guantánamo Bay." He cites the fact that currently, "80% of its inmates have some freedom of movement through the prison." Further, Brownback notes, hospital facilities are not available for detainees, and because the town of Leavenworth is so close to the current facility it is "impossible to build a separate detainee facility that is sufficiently separated from the general public." Brownback adds that overcrowding, segregation from the existing criminal population, and safety of the detainees themselves rule against Leavenworth as a viable alternative.[16]

Fort Leavenworth spokeswoman Janet Wray also pointed out in 2007 that the military prison there can hold 500 prisoners and already had 450 inmates.[17]

Meanwhile, one resident of Leavenworth, Kansas, expressed an attitude sure to be shared by a majority of her neighbors. "These people are not simple criminals," she protested to a *Chicago Tribune* reporter. "We don't want hundreds of terrorists here."[18]

Similar arguments are likely to emerge concerning any other location in the continental United States. While the Naval Brig in North Charleston has the physical capacity to house these detainees, the Pentagon has stated that "to do so would require significant security enhancements." Representative Henry Brown (R-SC) said, "To close Guantánamo and relocate hundreds of prisoners in the war on terror to the backyards of Charleston would be unconscionable."[19] Moreover, it is not as secure as Leavenworth, which is the only maximum-security military prison in the country.

An even more volatile set of issues will arise over the Gordian knot of legal arguments certain to face legislators and the federal courts if such a move is made. For example, there are currently approximately 135 detainees who the government lacks sufficient evidence to bring to trial, yet who have been judged by ARB procedures too dangerous to release. The prospect of confining such men indefinitely on American soil, while being constantly assailed by legal challenges, is daunting to say the least.

Considering the endless legal maneuvering by advocates for Guantánamo detainees, it is a given that activist organizations like the ACLU, CCR, and National Lawyers Guild and privately contracted law firms will exponentially raise the level of attack once the detainees are moved to the continental United States. What's more, chances are good that they will eventually find a sympathetic judge who will order their clients' release. "Then you would have 100-plus future sleeper-cell members unleashed in Kansas," said an unnamed midlevel Pentagon official, quoted by the *Los Angeles Times*. "That is what the government is trying to prevent."[20]

In early October 2008, federal judge Ricardo Urbina ruled on a case contesting continued confinement of 17 Uighurs held at Guantánamo. Judge Urbina's decision called for the men to be released into the United States—two probable locations were Washington, DC, and Tallahassee, Florida. The 17 had been removed to Guantánamo since capture in combat near the Tora Bora area. Previously four other Uighurs had been transferred to Albania, but that country and other possible venues, under pressure from the People's Republic of China, refused to accept any more.

"Because the Constitution prohibits indefinite detention without cause, the government's continued detention of petitioners is unlawful," Urbina said in his ruling. The White House appealed the decision and was granted an extension of compliance to Urbina's order to produce the Uighurs in his court within five days. Following the ruling, government lawyers issued a statement of "deep concern," noting that it has "the right to hold enemy combatants for the duration of the war on terror." The Department of Justice said following the ruling that "the government does not believe that it is appropriate to have these foreign nationals removed from government custody and released into the United States."[21]

Unlike the previous four, these 17 Uighurs had been designated as enemy combatants in their Combatant Status Review Tribunals. It was only in September 2007 that they were judged by an ARB to no longer constitute a threat to the United States. Once ARB members accepted the Uighur claim that their argument was not with the United States, but rather with the Chinese government, they became eligible for transfer or release.[22] During the ensuing months, the State Department had tried unsuccessfully to find a nation willing to accept them.[23]

Amnesty International USA executive director Larry Cox responded to the ruling by stating, "How many times does the Bush administration need to be told that detainees are entitled to essential rights? All the remaining detainees in Guantánamo Bay must be either charged and tried or released immediately." Other advocacy groups, such as the Center for Constitutional Rights, applauded the ruling and called for immediate release of Guantánamo detainees. If the precedent is set in Judge Urbina's ruling to release known terrorists into this country, then Americans must expect a flood of petitions from attorneys representing the other detainees to follow.

Uighur community spokespersons in the Washington and Tallahassee areas, supported by some church groups, have agreed to "temporarily" house the 17 Uighurs, but then what? These men are still committed to their cause, and are alleged members of the East Turkestan Islamic Movement, named on the U.S. list of terrorist organizations. Given the extraordinarily high recidivism rate of released Guantánamo detainees, there are compelling reasons to believe that they will continue the fight—from within the United States.

A ruling such as Judge Urbina's sets an extraordinarily dangerous precedent for release of hardened Islamist fighters into America's cities.

Defense Secretary Robert Gates is aware of these contingencies. Though he favors closing the prison, he has proposed enabling legislation prior to actually moving the detainees, saying, "What is needed is a law allowing indefinite detention of anyone who is a former enemy combatant." Such legislation would probably be extraordinarily difficult to pass and would face both a probable presidential veto and, if passed, an inevitable court challenge.[24]

Resolution of these issues still does not address a critical point. These men were brought to Guantánamo originally not to prosecute them for crimes but to remove them from the battlefield. They were deemed sufficiently dangerous to pose a continuing threat to America. They cannot be released or transferred to countries that might arbitrarily release them back into the field.

This is not a whimsical concern. Of the more than several hundred detainees released or transferred through the Annual Review Board process, many have returned to the battlefield. As previously discussed, Pentagon sources show that more than three dozen—an alarming recidivism rate—have gone back to the fight as bombers, kidnappers, promoters, or recruiters. Some former detainees have resumed or achieved top leadership positions.

What of those whom the Annual Review Boards have determined still pose a credible threat? At this time approximately 135 Guantánamo detainees fit that profile. Because of lack of hard evidentiary requirements—remarkably difficult, and sometimes impossible, to gather in a combat situation—the government has elected not to place them before Military Commission hearings. Yet these men, many by their proud admission, are committed jihadists who have pledged to resume attacks if released.[25]

It would be extraordinarily foolish and irresponsible to release these men simply because their cases do not meet the exacting standards of U.S. courts, designed for American citizens arrested by domestic law enforcement officers rather than soldiers working under entirely different (and equally complex) rules of war. Under all international conventions, principals are permitted to detain enemy combatants for the duration of hostilities. The fact that some detainees are being tried for war crimes does not obviate the need to continue to hold unlawful enemy combatants who will return to the fight.

The prospect of Congress passing enabling legislation, as Gates has suggested, that would allow them to be held indefinitely on U.S. soil without judicial proceedings is impossible to imagine. Such legislation, quite properly, would be viewed as a genuine weakening of Americans' constitutional rights, and would inevitably be challenged in higher courts. Even if it were passed, this kind of law would be inimical to long-term U.S. interests.

Continued Issues and Outcomes

One of the most telling errors in Guantánamo is not a unique characteristic of the facility but rather reflects institutional problems at the national agency level. That is the continuing, albeit diminished, interagency feuding and turf battles that inhibit development of necessary cross-agency communications and exchanges. It is a "September 10th" mentality that spills down the food chain from the Beltway appointees to the career bureaucrats in the trenches. Intelligence processing at Guantánamo is a microcosm of the greater community and is probably more collegial than in Washington, a fact that ought not to give great comfort.

Nevertheless, it is still possible, in the greater scheme of things related to the security of the United States and our allies, that Guantánamo will be recognized for what it has in fact become: the single greatest repository of human intelligence (HUMINT) in the war on terror, the single greatest accumulation of terrorism-related information, and the world's best, most humane, and most efficient interrogation facility. It ought to be, in keeping with the spirit of boundaryless institutions noted above, a place where terrorist-related criminals (out of the U.S. court system) and internationally apprehended terrorists (such as those nabbed in London, Madrid, and Germany) could be held and interrogated.

Ideally, we would see a civil, thoroughgoing debate on the subject that would lead to a well-conceived solution in the best interests of all concerned. I am not optimistic about that prospect. Ultimately long-term disposition of the Guantánamo detainees is going to be highly contentious and bitter, with jockeying on all sides for political, special-interest, and media advantage. Even a *New York Times* article reporting the Bush administration's decision to leave the issue for the next administration to resolve noted the many difficulties in the path of a swift resolution.

Meanwhile, Gitmo continues to function, and performs a vital mission in the daily defense of this country.

JTF GTMO commander Rear Admiral Mark H. Buzby, who replaced Admiral Harris, notes that the soldiers, sailors, airmen, marines, and coast guardsmen of the command ensure "safe and humane" detention. They also support the intelligence mission. "We are going to continue to do that as effectively and efficiently as we can without anyone getting hurt."[26]

Perhaps Gitmo should be closed, if for no other reason than that it requires too much effort to keep it open in the face of unremitting international hostility. Gitmo has become a public relations nightmare for the United States and in the end, shutting it down may be the path of least resistance. However, prior to any final decision it is imperative that a rational debate be held (if such a thing is possible) that examines all aspects of the problem and considers the full spectrum of options, along with the implications of selecting any particular one.

Meanwhile, for national security purposes, continuing to hold the terrorist detainees at Guantánamo is the least bad option. With hundreds of millions already spent on building facilities there, it seems more practical to resolve specific problems and controversies than start from scratch elsewhere. No matter where the detainees are ultimately confined, more lawsuits and accusations will arise along with entirely new controversies. Shutting down Gitmo primarily because it has been labeled an "embarrassment" will not automatically improve America's image in the eyes of the world—as so many hope—when all current alternatives will surely generate new challenges and exacerbate existing ones.

America fights an enemy who drifts in and out of the shadows, who hides behind women and children, abuses the sanctity of mosques and holy places, hides his weapons, disguises his person, flouts civilized rules of war, and answers to no recognizable chain of command. This enemy does not have his own country but is amorphous, drifting, and parasitic, using first Sudan as a base, then Somalia, then moving on to Afghanistan and beyond.

Now we fight him in Iraq and hear from trustworthy sources that he is building strength in Iran. He is solidifying a base in Somalia and infiltrating Nigeria. Al Qaeda operatives in South America have been in contact with Central American criminal gangs such as MS-13. Stories have been verified of al Qaeda men learning to pass for Hispanic in Guatemala and Mexico prior to slipping across the American border. We face enemy leaders and fighters who change names more frequently than socks, who possess forged documents and identities, who claim nationality in first one country, then another. Our enemy is stateless, boundaryless, and adheres to no rules save those of his jihadist ideology. To diminish their threat by considering them as common criminals is a huge—and potentially fatal—error in judgment.

Is JTF GTMO accomplishing the mission intended for it? The answer to that question is an unequivocal yes. The Guantánamo facility continues to provide value to America in that it keeps dangerous people off the streets and learns what it can from them. But the facility itself is under constant attack, including by members of Congress.

Such careless threats demand an answer to a key question: Who should be blamed for failing to prevent the next terrorist attack? Would the American people demand hard answers from elected officials who destroyed the single best source of intelligence available? Meanwhile, opponents continue to vilify the troops who serve quietly there. Columnist Jed Babbin, among others, rises to their defense. Whoever will be blamed for future intelligence failures, it will not be "the guys and gals of Gitmo who are working tirelessly, under awful conditions and politically correct restraints to get information from hard-core terrorists."[27]

For now, my recommendation is this: Rather than be ashamed of the soldiers, sailors, airmen, and marines who serve at Guantánamo Bay, we can and should be proud of them. And grateful for their service.

What does a practical, unemotional evaluation say? Is there an alternative to Guantánamo, either geographically or institutionally? Or even philosophically? When confronted at Guantánamo by an angry sergeant from his home state, Senator Ted Kennedy was asked where he wanted to keep "people like that who want to kill you and your family." He was unable to do more than shrug and walk away.

But Guantánamo is far too serious an issue to be shrugged off.

Glossary of Military Terms

- *AFB*–air force base.
- *ARB*–annual review board. A military board that reviews each detainee's case annually to determine whether the detainee 1) poses a threat to the U.S. and its allies, 2) possesses intelligence information, or 3) may be recommended for release or transfer.
- *CENTCOM*–U.S. Central Command, headquartered at MacDill AFB, located in Tampa, Florida. Headed by a four-star general or admiral, it has as its area of geographic responsibility the Middle East through South Asia.
- *CIA*–Central Intelligence Agency.
- *CSRT*–Combatant Status Review Tribunal. Meets once for each detainee to determine whether that person is in fact an enemy combatant or not. Can recommend continued detention, transfer, or release.
- *DIA*–Defense Intelligence Agency, a subordinate organization to DOD.
- *DOD*–Department of Defense.
- *DOS*–Department of State.
- *FBI*–Federal Bureau of Investigation.
- *JDG*–Joint Detention Group. Headed by an Army military police colonel, it has responsibility for all confinement activities at Guantánamo other than the Navy brig, which is handled by the U.S. Navy captain who commands Guantánamo as a Navy installation.
- *JIG*–Joint Interrogation Group. Headed by a Department of Defense civilian, it is responsible for all interrogation operations occurring at Guantánamo.
- *Joint Task Force (JTF)*–a task force formed to perform a specific mission, often for a limited time. The term "joint" means that members from two or more uniformed services participate in the task force.

- *JTF GTMO*–Joint Task Force Guantánamo, the agency that is responsible for control of detainee and interrogation operations in Guantánamo Base. Its commander is a flag-level officer (Army, Air Force, and Marines, a general; Navy, an admiral).
- *OARDEC*–Organization for the Administrative Review of Detained Enemy Combatants. Supervises and conducts CSRTs and ARBs.
- *Military Commission*–a process similar to a criminal trial or a military court martial under which detainees charged with war crimes may be tried.
- *NCO*–noncommissioned officer. A sergeant in the Army, Air Force, or Marine Corps; a chief petty officer in the Navy.
- *SOP*–Standard Operational Procedures, a detailed outline issued by the commander of procedures that must be followed in a particular circumstance, such as moving detainees, preparation of an interrogation plan, or actions in event of medical emergency.
- *SOCOM*–U.S. Special Operations Command, headquartered at Mac-Dill AFB, Tampa, Florida. Headed by a four-star general or admiral, it has functional responsibility for all special operations forces.
- *SOUTHCOM*–U.S. Southern Command, headquartered at Homestead AFB, Florida, south of Miami. A major geographical command headed by a four-star admiral or general, it has responsibility for Southern Hemisphere activities.
- *Tiger Teams*–Ad hoc combined agency teams (for example, DOD, CIA, and FBI) instituted in Guantánamo in 2002 in order to reduce friction and confusion in the interrogation process.
- *Zulu*–Phonetic alphabet for Greenwich Mean Time.

ACKNOWLEDGMENTS

———————

Thus was a challenging project from the start. Exploring the intricacies of Guantánamo was not the direction that I had intended to pursue following publication of my first book, on North and South Korea. But a fortuitous visit raised my awareness of the facility. Information learned on that visit turned into an article for a major print magazine. Reader response to that piece alerted me that others, too, are interested in the truth of what many—supporters and detractors alike—view as America's biggest international image problem. So I took on the project of writing this book.

Naïvely, I calculated a six-month research effort capped by a couple of months of writing. Now, more than three years later, with five visits to the detention facility, hundreds of interview hours, and thousands of research and writing hours under my belt, the book is ready for you to read. It was a bumpy road to publication. Controversies—tiresome, expensive, and distracting, but unnecessary to recount here—blocked the path. Eventually, thanks in large part to the dedication, patience, and commitment of my indefatigable editor, Adam Bellow, it reached completion. Now it is in your hands.

Not to say that this is a comprehensive work on Guantánamo. That exhaustive project I leave to future historians, for a time when tempers have cooled and Guantánamo's place in history may be viewed from a distance removed from distorting lenses of political agenda and preconceived notion. That time will be, in my opinion, long in coming, for human emotions are always the last to die.

For the contemporary historian—perhaps an oxymoronic concept in itself—access to personnel and information is always a challenge. That I was granted an unprecedented degree of access—to serving and former military and government officials, to documents, and to the facility itself—is testimony to a culture of openness and transparency that is a unique value in our American system. It is inconceivable that any other country would pull back the curtain of official protection to the extent that the United States has done with a facility such as Guantánamo even in peacetime, much less when involved in an ongoing war.

Consequently, prominent among those many to whom I owe thanks for support of this effort are the military and civilian members who make up the ever-changing staff at the Guantánamo detention facility. Without their patient cooperation and willingness to answer blunt questions with unfailing courtesy and honesty—even if the truth was unpleasant—I would not have been able to learn as much as I did.

The cooperation of serving and former government officials, members of nongovernmental organizations, senior military officers and noncommissioned officers, and most of all the soldiers, sailors, coast guardsmen, airmen, marines, and civilians who stand the watch and walk the blocks at Joint Task Force Guantánamo on a daily basis, was outstanding. On every one of my visits they took extra steps to share their experiences and knowledge. This superb hospitality was demonstrated by their infinite patience in answering repetitive questions, and by their response to constant requests to tour new areas, see all facilities, and talk to anyone and everyone possible.

In more than four decades of dealing with military institutions and personnel I can say unequivocally that the personnel at JTF Guantánamo are the most transparent, cooperative, and eager to share of any with whom I have had the pleasure to work. For this I thank them. They are all great patriots serving in a thankless, difficult posting. We as a country owe them a huge debt. They do a job the vast majority of us would refuse.

Commanders at all levels, including General Jay Hood and Admiral Harry Harris, both commanders of JTF GTMO, lent personal support to the completion of this book. And they did so without prior restrictions or constraints. Along with colonels Michael Bumgarner and Wade Dennis and their amazingly capable staffs, they made certain that all doors were open to me and that I was able to go where I needed to go and see all I needed to see in order to make this book a reality. On the interrogation side, Paul Rester, a brilliantly talented individual, was always available to field queries, arrange for briefings, and permit me to observe proceedings. His overworked staff, led by Navy Captain Mike Reynolds, always responded to my requests with a smile and made things happen.

Special thanks are in order to the JTF Guantánamo public affairs section, especially Lieutenant Colonel Jeremy Martin and later Colonel Lora Tucker and her workaholic staff. They took care of my every need regardless of how trivial and answered all requests regardless of how inane. Their "care and feeding" skills, matched by tireless cooperation, made each of my several visits not only informative but enjoyable.

Many of the service members in Guantánamo are reservists and National Guard personnel sent to augment the regular forces and serve their country. They bear a special burden, because on return to civilian life they are accused of heinous crimes and reprehensive behavior by those ignorant of the true circumstances. To the contrary, they are as fine a group of Americans as you will find anywhere, and they serve with a patience and dedication that would both baffle and astound their civilian counterparts. I thank them for their service, along with their regular component colleagues.

Other than my initial visit to Guantánamo, which was done as part of a government-sponsored media outreach program, all expenses associated with my long research and travels were paid out of my own pocket. There was never official sponsorship of this project, nor was I granted special favors. I was never influenced to support an official line or policy. No one laid requirements on me to report in a particular manner. My work was never subject to official oversight or review. The observations and conclusion I drew are my own.

While this book relies heavily on primary sources—personal

observations, interviews, and direct communications with participants—much of the foundation and factual support was accomplished by thorough research. For this I relied heavily on the tireless efforts of the enormously capable team of Avery Johnson and Chuck Martin. With their incredible sourcing and data management skills they found documents and reports I thought unobtainable, raised issues that might otherwise have been ignored, and suggested roads for exploration that might have been bypassed. For their dedication, friendship, and solid support, I thank them.

On several trips to Guantánamo my traveling companion was the irrepressible former Air Force dentist Lieutenant Colonel, ret., John "Rudy" Rudisill. Like the great friend he is, Rudy refused to let me get tired, distracted, or out of sorts. His unique background of both medical and prison experience made him a most valuable member of the team and a font of knowledge. Rudy saw things that I missed and asked questions that I would not have thought to raise. Much of what you read here concerning the medical operations on Guantánamo is because of Rudy's presence, and our endless dialogue that continued long after we returned from exploring Guantánamo.

No author embarks on such a journey without family support. I thank my wife, Ranyee Lee, for her patience in this long endeavor, and also my mother, Elizabeth Louise Cucullu. Both saw this as a worthy endeavor. Unfortunately, Mom passed away before this book saw print. Their consistent, cheerful confidence that it would eventually get written was both a prop and an incentive to make it happen.

Naturally, I wish to thank the great management and staff at HarperCollins for their courage and commitment to this book. They recognized the need for the story to be told and had the courage to stay with it, knowing that Guantánamo is a highly controversial subject and that they would endure criticism as a result of publication.

I have done my best to bring you as factual, detailed, complete, and unapologetic a picture of Guantánamo as I can recount it. I hope you find it useful and informative. There are certain to be errors in this work. They are mine. I accept full responsibility for them.

NOTES

Preface

1. Remarks of Senator Barack Obama: "The War We Need to Win," Washington, DC, delivered August 1, 2007.
2. Mark Appuzo and Laura Jakes Jordan, "Obama Planning US Trials for Guantánamo Detainees," Associated Press, November 10, 2008.
3. Ibid.
4. Ibid.

Introduction

1. Details of this incident are compiled by extensive author observations and interviews with personnel involved: guards, commanders, and medical, escort, and civilian support.
2. In "War Inside the Wire: You Can Handle the Truth about Guantánamo Bay" (*Wall Street Journal*, September 16, 2006), James Taranto reported that guards found stockpiled prescription drugs hidden "around the toilet area" and "inside the bindings of the Holy Quran."
3. A Joint Task Force Guantánamo memorandum titled "Camp Delta Interim SOP Modification: Inspecting/Handling Detainee Korans Standard Operating Procedure (SOP)" was issued January 19, 2003, detailing rules for handling Korans. Also see Department of Defense, "Guantánamo Procedures on Handling Koran / Inspecting/Handling Detainee Korans Standard Operating Procedure (SOP)," May 11, 2005, available on the Internet at http://tirana.usembassy.gov/press20050523.html.
4. More than 440 incidents between guards and prisoners from December 2002 through summer 2005 alone were reported in response to a 2006 Freedom of Information Act request filed by the Landmark Legal Foundation. The reports confirm that "Male guards are frequently derided as

'donkeys' while female guards are routinely called 'bitches' or harassed by references to their breasts or genitalia . . . In all, nearly a quarter of incidents involved female guards, the reports show" (quoted from John Solomon, "Gitmo Guards Often Attacked by Detainees," Associated Press, July 31, 2006).

5. This is a pseudonym. The actual Navy ensign requested that his name not be used. "I don't care if they come after me," he said, "but I want to protect my family from these bastards." Such is a common, shared concern among those who work inside the wire. Standard operational procedure is for name tags to be covered with black tape or to read the job position. Santos's name tag read "OIC, Camp IV."

6. For additional descriptions of the various camps, facilities, and detainee living conditions within Guantánamo Bay, please see "Detainee Living Conditions" section of the Joint Task Force Guantánamo "Mission" webpage, available on the Internet at http://www.jtfgtmo.southcom.mil/mission.html.

7. Deroy Murdock, "Terror Camp," *National Review*, August 8, 2006.

8. *Wall Street Journal* reporter James Taranto noted that the detainees who quietly retreated to their bunks during the riot later became the sole residents of Camp 4 (from "War Inside the Wire: You can handle the truth about Guantánamo Bay," September 16, 2006).

9. National Criminal Justice Reference Service, "Impact of Oleoresin Capsicum Spray on Respiratory Functions in Human Subjects in the Sitting and Prone Maximal Restraint Positions," May 12, 2000.

10. Author interview with Colonel Michael Bumgarner, May 2006.

11. Author interview with SFC Allen Rich, January 2006.

12. Details of this historical occurrence may be found at "The Battle of Badr," an unattributed article on Islam.com.

13. Author interviews with Colonel Michael Bumgarner. See also Tim Golden, "The Battle for Guantánamo," *The Times Magazine, New York Times*, September 17, 2006.

14. Press release, Amnesty International, May 25, 2005.

15. *Der Spiegel*, interview with Jimmy Carter, August 15, 2006, "The US and Israel Stand Alone."

16. For an example of such reports, refer to Dan Eggen and R. Jeffrey Smith, "FBI Agents Allege Abuse of Detainees at Guantánamo Bay" *Washington Post*, December 21, 2004. For a more comprehensive and detailed accounting, one can also review the 438-page *Review of the FBI's Involvement in and Observations of Detainee Interrogations in Guantánamo Bay, Afghanistan, and Iraq* by the U.S. Department of Justice Office of the Inspector General, May 2008.

17. Dan Eggen, "FBI Reports Duct-Taping, 'Baptizing' at Guantánamo," *Washington Post*, January 3, 2007.

18. Schmidt-Furlow Report, Department of Defense.
19. Ibid.
20. Ibid.; also Church Report, Department of Defense.
21. Neil A. Lewis, "Fresh Details Emerge on Harsh Methods at Guantánamo," *New York Times,* January 1, 2005.
22. Editorial, "Getting Guantánamo: Teddy Kennedy Is Embarrassed," *Manchester Union Leader,* July 19, 2005.
23. Shailagh Murray, "Durbin Apologizes for Remarks on Abuse," *Washington Post,* June 22, 2005.
24. "Republican Urges Closing Guantánamo Facility," Associated Press, June 11, 2005.
25. Quoted in *UN: Gitmo Violates World Torture Ban,* CNN, May 19, 2006.
26. Colum Lynch, "Military Prison's Closure Is Urged," *Washington Post,* May 20, 2006.
27. "US 'Must End Secret Detentions,'" *BBC News,* May 19, 2006.
28. Sam Cage, "U.N. Urges U.S. to Shut Guantánamo Prison," Associated Press, May 19, 2006.
29. *New York Times,* May 30, 2005.

Chapter 1
1. "A historical look at Guantánamo Bay and the Northeast Gate," undated webpage at http://www.jtfgtmo.southcom.mil/negatehistory.html.
2. J. A. Sierra, "History of Cuba," History of Cuba.com.
3. Kathleen T. Rhem, "From Mayberry to Metropolis: Guantánamo Bay Changes," American Forces Press Service, March 3, 2005.
4. "Bosnia Admits US Terrorist Renditions Violated Human Rights Law," *Serbo Journal,* June 18, 2006.
5. Robin Moore, *The Hunt for Bin Laden: Task Force Dagger.* New York: Random House, 2003. Also, Gary Berntsen and Ralph Perillo, *Jawbreaker: The Attack on bin Laden and al Qaeda.* New York: Crown, 2005; and Anonymous, *Hunting al Qaeda.* St. Paul, MN: Zenith Press, 2005.
6. Department of Defense "Guantánamo Detainees" fact sheet, February 13, 2004 (available on the Internet as an Acrobat PDF file at http://www.defenselink.mil/news/Apr2004/d20040406gua.pdf).
7. February 13, 2004 U.S. Department of Defense *Briefing on Detainee Operations at Guantanamo Bay* with Paul Butler, principal deputy assistant secretary of defense for special operations and low-intensity conflict, and Army Maj. Gen. Geoffrey D. Miller, commander, Joint Task Force Guantánamo.
8. Author interview with Brigadier General Vincent Brooks, Pentagon, Washington, DC, December 2005.
9. Supreme Court of the United States, *Johnson, Secretary of Defense, et al.*

v. Eisentrager, alias Ehrhardt, et al., No. 306, argued April 17, 1950, decided June 5, 1950.

10. Author interview with Brigadier General Thomas Hemingway, Pentagon, Washington, DC, December 2005.

11. Matthew Waxman,"The Smart Way to Shut Gitmo Down," *Washington Post*, October 28, 2007.

12. Author interview with Douglas Feith, December 2005.

13. James Taranto, "War Behind the Wire," *Wall Street Journal*, September 16, 2006.

14. Department of Defense, "Guantánamo Detainees" fact sheet, February 13, 2004 (Acrobat PDF file available on the Internet at http://www.defenselink.mil/news/Apr2004/d20040406gua.pdf).

15. "Box Cutters Found on Other September 11 Flights," CNN, September 24, 2001.

16. Centers for Disease Control report, "Investigation of Bioterrorism-Related Anthrax," December 7, 2001.

17. Donald Knox and Alfred Coppel, *The Korean War: Volume 2: Uncertain Victory: An Oral History*. Fort Washington, PA: Harvest/HJB Books, 2002.

18. Author interview with Brigadier General Vincent Brooks, December 2005.

19. Author interview with DASD Matthew Waxman, Pentagon, Washington, DC, December 2005.

Chapter 2

1. Quoted by David Kaspar, *Davids Medienkritik*, January 2006.

2. There are many articles and reports documenting the use of child soldiers—some as young as just six years old—in Afghanistan and Iraq. Some selections covering this problem during the early days of the war in Afghanistan include Hannah Beech Farkhar, "The Child Soldiers," *Time*, November 4, 2001; Rachel Stohl, "Children on the Front Line: Child Soldiers in Afghanistan," Center for Defense Information, October 15, 2001; and David Rohde, "12 Year Olds Take Up Arms Against Taliban," *New York Times*, October 2, 2001. More recent articles of interest on this subject include Monte Morin, "Taliban Recruiting Afghan Children for Suicide Bombings," *Stars and Stripes*, June 27, 2007; Marc Perelman, "A New, Younger Jihadi Threat Emerges," *Christian Science Monitor*, December 28, 2007; Nick Owens, "Child Soldiers Trained by the Taliban to Kill British Soldiers," Mirror.co.uk, February 8, 2008; and "Juvenile Detainees Gain Second Chance through Dar Al-Hikmah" from the Operation Iraqi Freedom Official Website of the Multi-National Force Iraq, August 17, 2007. Videos of child soldiers, including six-year-old Juma Gul, who had been tricked by the Taliban into wearing a sui-

cide vest and instructed to throw himself at U.S. soldiers, can be found by typing "child soldiers Taliban" into the search box at YouTube.com.

3. Charge sheet as filed in the case against Khalid Sheikh Muhammad, Walid Muhammad Salih Mubarak Bin 'Attash, Ramzi bin al-Shibh, Ali Abdul Aziz Ali, Mustafa Ahmed Adam al Hawsawi, and Muhammad al Qahtani, dated February 11, 2008.

4. Documentation of Atta's presence in the Orlando airport parking garage includes *The 9/11 Commission Report*, p. 248; charge sheet as filed in the case against Khalid Sheikh Muhammad, Walid Muhammad Salih Mubarak Bin 'Attash, Ramzi bin al-Shibh, Ali Abdul Aziz Ali, Mustafa Ahmed Adam al Hawsawi, and Muhammad al Qahtani, dated February 11, 2008; Adam Zagorin and Michael Duffy, "Inside the Interrogation of Detainee 063," *Time*, June 12, 2005.

5. "Statement of José E. Melendez-Perez to the National Commission on Terrorist Attacks Upon the United States," January 26, 2004.

6. As discussed in the documents cited above.

7. Ibid.

8. Charge sheet as filed in the case against Khalid Sheikh Muhammad, Walid Muhammad Salih Mubarak Bin 'Attash, Ramzi bin al-Shibh, Ali Abdul Aziz Ali, Mustafa Ahmed Adam al Hawsawi, and Muhammad al Qahtani, dated February 11, 2008.

9. *Unclassified Summary of Evidence for the Department of Defense Administrative Review Board, Muhammad Mani Ahmed al Shal Lan al Qahtani,* October 31, 2005.

10. "Substitution for the Testimony of Khalid Sheikh Muhammad" provided by the Reporters Committee for Freedom of the Press, undated Acrobat PDF file at http://www.rcfp.org/moussaoui/pdf/DX-0941.pdf.

11. Tim McGirk with Ghulam Hasnain, reporting from Waziristan, "In These Remote Hills, a Resurgent al-Qaeda," *Time*, September 15, 2003; Rahimullah Yusufzai, "Waziristan: Bin Laden's Hiding Place?" BBC, March 3, 2004; Karen DeYoung, "Letter Gives Glimpse of Al-Qaeda's Leadership," *Washington Post*, October 2, 2006; and Declan and Allegra Stratton, "Waziristan: The Hub of al-Qaida Operations," guardian.co.uk, January 7, 2008.

12. Craig Whitlock, "Al Qaeda Detainee's Mysterious Release: Moroccan Spoke of Aiding Bin Laden During 2001 Escape," *Washington Post*, January 30, 2006.

13. *Unclassified Summary of Evidence for the Department of Defense Administrative Review Board, Muhammad Mani Ahmed al Shal Lan al Qahtani,* October 31, 2005.

14. Interview with Paul Rester, June 2006.

15. *A Review of the FBI's Involvement in and Observations of Detainee Interrogations in Guantánamo Bay, Afghanistan, and Iraq,* U.S. Department of

Justice Office of the Inspector General, May 2008. Also see Adam Zagorin and Michael Duffy, "Inside the Interrogation of Detainee 063," *Time*, June 12, 2005.

16. Steven Schwartz, *The Two Faces of Islam: The House of Saud from Tradition to Terror*. New York: Doubleday, 2002.

17. *Summary of Administrative Review Board Proceedings for ISN 063*, Department of Defense.

18. *The 9/11 Commission Report*, National Commission on Terrorist Attacks Upon the United States, p. 226.

19. Transliterations into English are always confused. Can also be found as "al Farouq." See Global Security, "Terrorist Training Camps," for background into al Qaeda's Afghanistan camps.

20. Judith Miller, "Pentagon Says Bombs Destroy Terror Camps," *New York Times*, October 10, 2001.

21. *United States v. David Hicks—First Report of the Law Independent Legal Observer for the Law Council of Australia*, September 2004. This report notes that Hicks attended an eight-week training course at the al Farouk training camp starting in January or February 2001, and then began a seven-week al Qaeda training course in April 2001 at an unspecified camp.

22. FBI Special Agent Anne E. Asbury, *United States v. John Philip Walker Lindh*, "*Affidavit in Support of a Criminal Complaint and an Arrest Warrant*," January 15, 2002.

23. Ibid.

24. Phil Hirschkorn, "Four Embassy Bombers Get Life," CNN, October 21, 2001.

25. Jayna Davis, *The Third Terrorist*. Nashville, TN: Thomas Nelson, 2004.

26. Louis Freed, *My F.B.I.* New York: St. Martin's Press, 2005.

27. Author interview with Paul Rester, Chief of the Detention and Interrogation Group, Guantánamo Bay, June 2006.

28. Schwartz, *The Two Faces of Islam*.

29. Charge sheet as filed in the case against Khalid Sheikh Muhammad, Walid Muhammad Salih Mubarak Bin 'Attash, Ramzi bin al-Shibh, Ali Abdul Aziz Ali, Mustafa Ahmed Adam al Hawsawi, and Muhammad al Qahtani, dated February 11, 2008.

30. *Unclassified Summary of Evidence for the Department of Defense Administrative Review Board, Muhammad Mani Ahmed al Shal Lan al Qahtani*, October 31, 2005.

31. *Summary of Administrative Review Board Proceedings for ISN 063*, October 2006.

32. Ibid.

33. "Substitution for the Testimony of Khalid Sheikh Muhammad" provided by the Reporters Committee for Freedom of the Press, undated Acrobat PDF file at http://www.rcfp.org/moussaoui/pdf/DX-0941.pdf.

34. Charge sheet as filed in the case against Khalid Sheikh Muhammad, Walid Muhammad Salih Mubarak Bin 'Attash, Ramzi bin al-Shibh, Ali Abdul Aziz Ali, Mustafa Ahmed Adam al Hawsawi, and Muhammad al Qahtani dated February 11, 2008. This charge sheet is available on the Department of Defense website at www.defenselink.mil/news/Feb2008/d20080211chargesheet.pdf.

35. Ibid.

36. *Statement of José E. Melendez-Perez to the National Commission on Terrorist Attacks,* January 26, 2004.

37. Ibid.

38. "Guantánamo Provides Valuable Intelligence Information," Department of Defense press release, June 12, 2005; "Interrogation Log Detainee 063" covering the period of November 23, 2002 to January 11, 2003; Richard A. Serrano, "In Court, Two 20th Hijackers Stand Up," *Los Angeles Times,* April 3, 2006.

39. *Statement of José E. Melendez-Perez to the National Commission on Terrorist Attacks,* January 26, 2004.

40. Ibid. Additional documentation of Qahtani's behavior and other specifics detailing his attempted entry into the United States are also available through numerous newspaper articles as well as the charge sheet as filed in the case against Khalid Sheikh Muhammad, Walid Muhammad Salih Mubarak Bin 'Attash, Ramzi bin al-Shibh, Ali Abdul Aziz Ali, Mustafa Ahmed Adam al Hawsawi, and Muhammad al Qahtani dated February 11, 2008.

41. "Substitution for the Testimony of Khalid Sheikh Muhammad" provided by the Reporters Committee for Freedom of the Press, undated Acrobat PDF file at http://www.rcfp.org/moussaoui/pdf/DX-0941.pdf.

42. *The 9/11 Commission Report,* p. 236. This training method is also mentioned in Scott Shane and Neil A. Lewis, "At Sept. 11 Trial, Tale of Missteps and Management," *New York Times,* March 31, 2006, which attributes KSM as a source of this information.

43. *The 9/11 Commission Report,* p. 235.

44. Ibid., p. 236.

45. *United States v. Zacarias Moussaoui.* Also see Rochelle Steinhaus, "Zacarias Moussaoui: The '20th Hijacker'?," Court TV, June 24, 2002.

46. "Substitution for the Testimony of Khalid Sheikh Muhammad" provided by the Reporters Committee for Freedom of the Press, undated Acrobat PDF file at http://www.rcfp.org/moussaoui/pdf/DX-0941.pdf.

47. KSM recalled that Qahtani in fact realized that a suicide attack would take place and that he was to take part. However, not all al Qaeda operatives are aware of the nature of their deadly assignments: Post–9/11 videos of Osama bin Laden entertaining a visiting Saudi sheikh show him smiling faintly while relating that some of his jihadists "were not aware that this was intended to be a martyrdom operation."

48.   Presidential Address to the Congress, September 12, 2001.

49.   There are many good accounts of the battle for Qala-i-Jangi, including Robin Moore's *Hunt for Bin Laden*, and contemporary news accounts such as Alex Perry, "Inside the Battle at Qala-I-Jangi," *Time*, December 1, 2001. Some information for these accounts is derived from author interviews with U.S. Army Special Forces Captain Erick Roitsch, who was a participant in the battle.

50.   Alex Perry, "Inside the Battle at Qala-I-Jangi," *Time*, December 1, 2001.

51.   Moore, *Hunt for bin Laden*.

52.   Author interview with JIG director Paul Rester, January 2006.

Chapter 3

1.   Author interview, December 2005.

2.   Author interview at the Pentagon with General Vincent Brooks, December 2005.

3.   "Detainees treated humanely, officials say," CNN, January 21, 2002; "Gitmo's 'gourmet fare,'" *Washington Times*, June 29, 2005; Petty Officer 3rd Class John R. Guardino, "Rumsfeld Discusses Guantánamo Bay Detainee Issues," USN American Forces Press Service, June 26, 2005.

4.   *Hearing of the House Armed Services Committee; Subject: detainee operations at Guantánamo Bay*, June 29, 2005.

5.   *The Wire,* Joint Task Force Guantánamo newsletter, January 10, 2003.

6.   *AR-15-6 Report FBI Allegations of Abuse* (Schmidt-Furlow Report), June 9, 2005, p. 4.

7.   The Manchester Manual, discovered in a counterterrorist police raid in Manchester, England, revealed specific instructions for captured operatives to make extravagant claims of torture. In the chapter entitled "Prisons and Detention Centers," the al Qaeda "brothers" are instructed to "prove that torture was inflicted on them" and to "complain of mistreatment while in prison." Al Qaeda operatives are told to memorize the names of guards and to "mention those names to the judge." If brought to a trial, the terrorists need to make certain to "notify [the court] of any mistreatment." While in confinement they are encouraged to establish clandestine communications links with each other and to "master the art of hiding messages." Most important, the Manual stresses, is for the jihadists to "create an Islamic program for themselves inside the prison," and to "shout Islamic slogans out loud" if exposed to the public. These enemy combatants were thoroughly prepared to resist interrogation, defy convention, upset the court processes, and play to the interests of anti-American, pro-Islamic organizations to sow dissension and further their cause. The full text of the Manual can be found in translation at www .usdoj.gov/ag/manual.

8.   Andrew Buncombein, "Washington condemns first suicides by Guan-

tánamo inmates as 'a PR exercise,'" *The [London] Independent,* June 12, 2006.

9.   *A Review of the FBI's Involvement in and Observations of Detainee Interrogations in Guantánamo Bay, Afghanistan, and Iraq,* U.S. Department of Justice Office of the Inspector General, May 2008, p. 78. Note that al Qaeda has a history of operating falcon camps; for more information, see pages 137–39 of the 9/11 Commission report and the Save the Falcons website located on the Internet at http://savethefalcons.org.

10. Ibid.

11. Ibid., p. 80.

12. Ibid., p. 82.

13. Author interview with Paul Rester, June 2006.

14. *A Review of the FBI's Involvement,* p. 83.

15. Ibid., p. 84.

16. "Gitmo Called Death Camp," *Washington Times,* June 16, 2005.

17. *A Review of the FBI's Involvement,* p. 84.

18. *AR-15-6 Report: FBI Allegations of Abuse* (Schmidt-Furlow Report), June 9, 2005.

19. *A Review of the FBI's Involvement,* p. 85.

20. Ibid.

21. Ibid., p. 86.

22. Ibid., p. 87.

23. Ibid., pp. 87–88.

24. Ibid., p. 89.

25. Ibid., p. 58.

26. Ibid., p. 102.

27. Ibid., p. 83.

28. The U.S. Army Southern Command ordered an investigation into allegations about military interrogations and FBI concerns regarding possible detainee abuse. Lieutenant General Randall M. Schmidt and Brigadier General John T. Furlow were appointed as the chief investigators and published the *AR-15-6 Report FBI Allegations of Abuse* on June 9, 2005. The report found that three violations had occurred out of 24,000 interrogations conducted at Guantánamo Bay. It also concluded that one detainee had been the subject of degrading and abusive treatment that nonetheless did not rise to the level of inhumane treatment.

29. In May 2004, Defense Secretary Rumsfeld directed the naval inspector general to conduct a detailed review of DOD interrogation operations in military zones worldwide. The resulting 373-page report, referred to as "The Church Report," was published on March 7, 2005. A scanned copy of the partially redacted unclassified version is available through the ACLU website at http://www.aclu.org/torturefoia/legaldocuments/july_docs/(L)%20Church%20Report.pdf.

30. Ibid., pp. 102–103.
31. Adam Zagorin and Michael Duffy, "Inside the Interrogation of Detainee 063," *Time*, June 12, 2005. A copy of the log is available through the *Time* website at www.time.com/time/2006/log/log.pdf.
32. Author interview with interrogator at Guantánamo Bay, June 2006.
33. *A Review of the FBI's Involvement in and Observations of Detainee Interrogations in Guantánamo Bay, Afghanistan, and Iraq*, U.S. Department of Justice Office of the Inspector General, May 2008, p. 101.
34. Department of Defense press release, "Guantánamo Provides Valuable Intelligence Information," June 12, 2005.
35. Ibid.
36. Center for Constitutional Rights webpage entitled *al Qahtani v. Bush, al Qahtani v. Gates*, located at http://ccrjustice.org/ourcases/current-cases/al-qahtani-v.-bush,-al-qahtani-v.-gates.
37. Author interview with Paul Butler, December 2005. As a federal prosecutor, Butler handled the case against al Qaeda for the African Embassy bombings. His cousin was a New York City firefighter captain who died on September 11 at the World Trade Center.
38. Author interview with Paul Rester, January 2006.
39. Numerous author interviews with JIG director Paul Rester, 2005–2006.
40. FM 34–52. Headquarters Department of the Army, Washington, DC, May 8, 1987, "Field Manual for Intelligence Interrogation."
41. Author interview with Paul Rester, January 2006.
42. Comments by Senator Richard Durbin, D-IL, Congressional Record.
43. Bill Dedman, *Battle over Tactics Raged at Gitmo*, MSNBC, January 2, 2007.
44. Author interview with Paul Rester.
45. Dedman, *Battle over Tactics*.
46. Ibid.
47. Author interview with Admiral Harry Harris, December 2006.

Chapter 4
1. Thomas A. Fogarty, "Companies Bid on Rebuilding Iraq," *USA Today*, March 26, 2003.
2. Carol J. Williams, "Guantánamo Prepares for Renovations," *Los Angeles Times*, January 19, 2005.
3. Author interview with Steve Rodriguez, December 2005.
4. Josh White, "Abu Ghraib Tactics Were First Used at Guantánamo," *Washington Post*, July 14, 2005.
5. Guy Taylor, "Terror War, South Front: Interrogators Glean 'Golden Threads,'" *Washington Times*, December 21, 2003.
6. Mark Benjamin and Michael Scherer, "A Miller Whitewash," *Salon*, April 25, 2006.

7. Maj. Gen. Antonio Taguba, "Executive summary of Article 15-6 investigation of the 800th Military Police Brigade," as posted on the MSNBC website on May 4, 2004.

8. Seymour M. Hersh, "The Gray Zone," *The New Yorker*, May 24, 2005.

9. Author interview with Paul Rester, January 2006.

10. R. Jeffrey Smith, "General Is Said to Have Urged Use of Dogs," *Washington Post*, May 26, 2004.

11. Author interview with Paul Rester, January 18, 2006.

12. Josh White, "General Asserts Right on Self-Incrimination in Iraq Abuse Cases," *Washington Post*, January 12, 2006.

13. Author interview with Army Brigadier General Vincent Brooks, December 2005.

14. Josh White, "General Who Ran Guantánamo Bay Retires," *Washington Post*, August 1, 2006.

15. J. D. Leipold, "Maj. Gen. Geoffrey D. Miller Retires after 34 Years," Army News Service, August 1, 2006.

16. Jackie Northam, "Guantánamo Commander Prepares to Leave Post," *All Things Considered*, NPR, March 14, 2006.

17. Author interview with Steve Rodriguez, 2005.

18. Author interview with Paul Rester, January 18, 2006.

19. "Sex Scandal at Guantánamo," CBS News, March 11, 2005.

20. Alexandra Olsen (AP), "Guantánamo Officers Leave Without Appeal," *Newsday*, March 26, 2005.

21. Author interview with Colonel Michael Bumgarner, January 2006.

22. Ibid.

23. Author interview with Colonel Wade Dennis, JDG commander, December 2006.

24. It is all too common to hear military people conducting operations involving non-Americans say things like, "He's really smart. He speaks good English," and "You can depend on him, he knows English."

25. Bumgarner interviews, June 2005 and January 2006.

26. Author electronic mail exchange with Colonel Michael Bumgarner, February 14, 2007.

27. Interview with Guantánamo interrogator who requested anonymity, December 2006.

28. Tim Golden, "The Battle for Guantánamo," *New York Times*, September 17, 2006.

29. Bumgarner interviews, June 2005 and January 2006.

Chapter 5

1. Matthew Waxman, "Beyond Guantánamo," *Washington Post*, August 20, 2005.

2. Ibid.

3.   Author interview with Brigadier General Vincent Brooks, December 2005.

4.   See the Manchester Manual, *The Al Qaeda Training Manual*, previously cited, for details on how terrorists are trained to react when captured.

5.   Author interview with Paul Rester, January 2006.

6.   *The 2005 USG Periodic Report to the UN Committee on the Convention Against Torture*, Department of Defense, Office of Detainee Affairs, 2005.

7.   Jeff Babbin, "The Gitmo Varsity," *American Spectator*, July 18, 2005.

8.   "Danish Detainee 'to Join Rebels,' " *BBC News*, September 30, 2004.

9.   Walter Pincus, "Ex-Guantanamo Prisoner ID'd as Iraq Bomber," *CBS News*, May 7, 2008; Walter Pincus, "With Other Nations Refusing Detainees' Return, 'We Are Stuck' with Guantanamo, Gates Says," *Washington Post*, May 26, 2008.

10.   Michael Melia, "U.S. Says 6 Ex-Guantanamo Prisoners 'Rejoined Fight' in Afghanistan," Associated Press, May 15, 2007.

11.   David Morgan, "US Divulges New Details on Released Gitmo Inmates," Reuters, May 14, 2007.

12.   "Fact Sheet: Former GTMO Detainee Terrorism Trends," Defense Intelligence Agency, June 13, 2008.

13.   Ibid. Also see Nabi Abdullaev, "From Russia to Guantánamo, via Afghanistan," *St. Petersburg Times* (Russia), December 24, 2002.

14.   Elisabeth Bumiller, "Cheney Calls Guantánamo Prison Essential," *New York Times*, June 14, 2005; John Mintz, "Released Detainees Rejoining The Fight," *Washington Post*, October 22, 2004.

15.   "Taliban Commander 'Kills Himself,' " aljazeera.net, July 25, 2007.

16.   John Mintz, *"Released Detainees Rejoining the Fight," Washington Post*, October 22, 2004.

17.   Laura King and Josh Meyer, "Baitullah Mahsud Is Blamed for Bhutto's Assassination, but His Power May Be Greatly Exaggerated," *Los Angeles Times*, February 12, 2008.

18.   "Taliban Commander: Abdullah Mahsud Killed in Pakistan," *Pakistan Times*, July 25, 2007.

19.   Mark Simkin, "Democrats Demand 'Torture Tapes' Probe," *ABC News* (Australia), December 8, 2007.

20.   Cog Coglin, "Begg 'Told FBI He Trained with al Qaeda,' " *UK Telegraph*, March 9, 2006.

21.   Tim Golden, "Jihadist or Victim: Ex-detainee Makes A Case," *New York Times*, June 15, 2006.

22.   Coglin, "Begg 'Told FBI.' "

23.   "Why Did Moazzam Begg Travel to Afghanistan?" *UK Telegraph*, March 2, 2006.

24.   For more information, see the website Cageprisoners mission statement at http://www.cageprisoners.com/page.php?id=2.

25. Coglin, "Begg 'Told FBI.'"
26. Golden, "Jihadist or Victim?"
27. Author interview with Paul Rester, June 2006.
28. "Guantánamo Britons may stand in election," Vikram Dodd, *The Guardian*, January 22, 2005.
29. Mark Bowden, *Black Hawk Down*. New York: Grove/Atlantic, 1999.
30. Charge sheet, *The United States of America v. Ibrahim Ahmed Mahmoud al Qosi*, available on the Internet at news.findlaw.com/hdocs/docs/dod/alqosi22404chrg.pdf. Although undated, the file name indicates February 24, 2004. Further note that charges were reinstated against Qosi in 2008 in a document that did not include all of the information found in this initial charge sheet.
31. Ibid., Item 19(b).
32. Ibid., Items 19(c) and (d).
33. "Summary of Evidence for Combatant Status Review Tribunal—Al Qosi, Ibrahim Ahmed Mahmoud," United States Department of Defense, Office for the Administrative Review of the Detention of Enemy Combatants, September 14, 2004, Item 3(a)(1). The Qosi summary can be found on pages 65 and 66 of the 98-page file located on the Internet at http://www.dod.mil/pubs/foi/detainees/csrt_arb/000001-000100.pdf #65.
34. Ibid., Item 3(a)(2).
35. Ibid., Item 3(a)(3).
36. Charge sheet, *The United States of America v. Ibrahim Ahmed Mahmoud al Qosi,* Item 19(e), located at news.findlaw.com/hdocs/docs/dod/alqosi-22404chrg.pdf (see endnote above).
37. Ibid., emphasis added by author.
38. See Alan Parrot's excellent work on his website www.savethefalcons.org for more details of the mysterious money camps.
39. Charge sheet, *The United States of America v. Ibrahim Ahmed Mahmoud al Qosi*, Item 19(f).
40. Ibid., Item 19(k).
41. Anne Gearan, "US Orders Trial of Two Prisoners at Guantánamo," Associated Press, February 25, 2004.
42. William Glaberson, "US Detainee Says He'll Boycott His Trial," *New York Times*, April 11, 2008.
43. "Alleged al-Qaida Accountant Praises bin Laden, Refuses Lawyer at Guantánamo," Associated Press, April 11, 2008.
44. Charge sheet, *United States of America v. David Matthew Hicks*, May 1, 2007, available on the Internet at http://www.defenselink.mil/news/d20070301hicks.pdf.
45. Steve Larkin, "The Journey of David Hicks," *Gold Coast Bulletin*, goldcoast.com, December 28, 2007.

46. Emma Alberici, "Hicks' Kids Eager to Reunite with Dad," *ABC World News*, Australia, May 28, 2007.

47. Charge sheet, *United States of America v. David Matthew Hicks*, May 1, 2007, Item 5.

48. Larkin,"The Journey of David Hicks."

49. Julia Gorin, "Remember Srebrenica," *Jewish World Review*, July 11, 2005.

50. Charge sheet, *United States of America v. David Matthew Hicks*.

51. Charge sheet, *United States of America vs. David Matthew Hicks*, Item 6. Also note that Lashkar-e-Tayyiba has also been translated as "Army of the Righteous" or "Laskar-e-Toiba," *Global Security*.

52. "Hafiz Muhammad Saeed: Pakistan's heart of terror," *Kashmir Herald*, July 2002.

53. Charge sheet, *United States of America v. David Matthew Hicks*, May 1, 2007, Item 6(b).

54. "Profile: Lashkar-e-Tobia," BBC report, March 17, 2006.

55. Steve Larkin, "David Hicks Must Renounce Terrorism, Says Human Rights Lawyer," AAP, December 30, 2007.

56. Charge sheet, *United States of America v. David Matthew Hicks*, May 1, 2007, items 7 and 8.

57. Item 19(a), *United States of America v. David Matthew Hicks,* 2004. This initial charge sheet, which contains additional information not provided in the charges filed in 2007, is available on the Internet at http://www.globalsecurity.org/security/library/news/2004/06/d20040610cs.pdf.

58. Eric Schmidt with Erik Eckholm, "US Takes Custody of a Qaeda Trainer Seized by Pakistan," *New York Times*, January 6, 2002.

59. Dana Priest, "Al Qaeda-Iraq Link Recanted," *Washington Post*, August 1, 2004. Also see Michael Isikoff and Mark Hosenball, "Al-Libi's Tall Tales," *Newsweek* web exclusive, November 10, 2005.

60. *United States of America v. Zacarias Moussaoui*, available on the Internet at http://www.usdoj.gov/ag/moussaouiindictment.htm.

61. CNN Producer Phil Hirschkorn,"Training camp links millennium, embassy bombers," July 5, 2001.

62. "Pakistan Hands Over Senior Al-Qaeda Leader," Associated Press, April 1, 2002.

63. Dana Priest, "Al Qaeda-Iraq Link Recanted," *Washington Post*, August 1, 2004.

64. Charge sheet, *United States of America v. David Matthew Hicks*, May 1, 2007, Item 9.

65. Ibid., Item 20(a).

66. Ibid., Item 24(b).

67. Suzanne Goldenberg, "Seven Year Sentence Likely to Mean Hicks Can

Go Home," *UK Guardian*, March 31, 2007. Also see Sergeant Sara Wood, "Judge Accepts Australian Detainee's Guilty Plea," American Forces Press Service, March 30, 2007.

68. Charge sheet, *United States of America v. David Matthew Hicks*, May 1, 2007, Item 24(c).

69. Ibid., Item 24(d).

70. Ibid., Item 24(e).

71. Charge sheet, *United States of America v. David Matthew Hicks*, 2004, Item 20(d).

72. Sergeant Sara Wood, "Judge Accepts Australian Detainee's Guilty Plea," American Forces Press Service, March 30, 2007.

73. Charge sheet, *United States of America v. David Matthew Hicks*, May 1, 2007, Item 24(f).

74. Ibid., Item 24(g).

75. "David Hicks Must Renounce Terrorism, Says Human Rights Lawyer," Steve Larkin, AAP, December 30, 2007.

76. Charge sheet, *United States of America v. David Matthew Hicks*, May 1, 2007, Item 24(h).

77. Ibid., Item 24(i).

78. Wood, "Judge Accepts Australian Detainee's Guilty Plea." Also see Goldenberg, "Seven Year Sentence."

79. Charge sheet, *United States of America v. David Matthew Hicks*, May 1, 2007, Item 24(j).

80. Wood, "Judge Accepts Australian Detainee's Guilty Plea."

81. Charge sheet, *United States of America v. David Matthew Hicks*, May 1, 2007, Item 24(k (e.g., "The special demands of guarding a facility like Guantánamo call for a concerted effort among several branches of the military . . .").

82. Ibid., Item 24(l).

83. Ibid., Item 24(m).

84. Ibid., Item 24(m).

85. Ibid., Item 24(n).

86. Ibid., Item 24(o).

87. Ibid., Item 24(p).

88. Ibid., Item 24(q).

89. Ibid., Item 24(r).

90. Ibid., Item 24(s).

91. Wood, "Judge Accepts Australian Detainee's Guilty Plea."

92. Charge sheet, *United States of America v. David Matthew Hicks*, May 1, 2007, Item 24(t).

93. Ibid., Item 24(v).

94. Ibid., Item 24(w).

95. Wood, "Judge Accepts Australian Detainee's Guilty Plea."

96. Charge sheet, *United States of America v. David Matthew Hicks*, May 1, 2007, Item 24(x).

97. Various books and articles have identified John Walker Lindh as ISN 001 or Detainee 001, for example, "Prisoner of political fortune set free," *Sydney Morning Herald*, December 29, 2007, and Philippe Sands, "The Green Light," *Vanity Fair*, May 2008. The author was also told by interrogators at Guantánamo Bay that ISN 001 was indeed Walker Lindh.

98. Based on a series of author interviews with a U.S. Army Special Forces officer present at the Battle of Qala-i-Jangi who requests anonymity for security purposes, 2004–2005.

99. The complete "Transcript of Debbie Whitmont's investigation 'The Case of David Hicks,'" dated October 31, 2005, is available on the Australian Broadcasting Corporation's website at http://www.abc.net.au/4corners/content/2005/s1494795.htm.

100. Ibid.

101. Author interview with interrogator (protected identity) who worked with Hicks, December 2006. Also see Mark Dunn, "Hicks Drops Islamic Faith," *Herald Sun*, February 28, 2007, which further elaborates, "A former Guantánamo inmate has claimed Hicks was denounced by Muslim prisoners for his change of faith."

102. Author interview with Guantánamo interrogator (protected identity) who worked with Hicks, December 2006.

103. "Australian Gitmo Detainee Gets 9 Months," *Boston Globe*, March 30, 2007.

104. Khalid Sheikh Muhammad confession transcript, Department of Defense, http://www.defenselink.mil.

105. Timothy J. Burger and Adam Zagorin, "Fingering Danny Pearl's Killer, *Time*, October 12, 2006.

106. "Key 9/11 figure 'beheaded Pearl,'" *BBC News*, March 15, 2007.

107. "Al-Qaida No. 3 says he planned 9/11, other plots," MSNBC, March 15, 2007.

108. "US judge orders CIA to turn over 'torture' memo—ACLU," Reuters, May 8, 2008.

109. "Khalid Sheikh Muhammad's own words provide glimpse into the mind of a terrorist," Associated Press, March 15, 2007.

110. "Khalid Sheikh Muhammad's own words provide glimpse into the mind of a terrorist," *International Herald Tribune*, March 15, 2007.

111. James Gordon Meek, "Alleged 9/11 mastermind, Khalid Sheikh Muhammad, asks judge for death," *New York Daily News*, June 5, 2008.

112. Dan Slater, "Khalid Sheik Muhammad on Same-Sex Marriage, Value of Counsel," *Wall Street Journal*, June 6, 2008.

113. Ibid.

114. Bob Simon, "The Mastermind," *CBS News*, March 5, 2003.

115. "Al-Jazeera reporter speaks on terrorist plans," *LATELINE*, Australian Broadcasting Company, September 30, 2002.
116. "Guantanamo Sees 'Extraordinary Day'," Jonathan Beale, BBC News, December 9, 2008.
117. Charge sheet, *United States of America v. Binyam Ahmed Muhammad*.
118. "Al Qaeda Reportedly Appoints Commanders for Afghanistan," *PakTribune*, November 11, 2005.
119. Yoram Schweitzer, "The Arrest of Abu Zubaydah: An Important Achievement with More to Come," *ICT Researcher*, April 9, 2002.
120. Gordon Cucullu, "Electronic Jihad," *TechCentralStation*, March 8, 2006.
121. Plutonium is the world's most poisonous known substance. Webelements .com.
122. *Fact Sheet on Dirty Bombs*, U.S. Nuclear Regulatory Commission, March 2003.
123. Charge sheet, *United States of America v. Binyam Ahmed Muhammad*.
124. Sergeant Sarah Wood, "U.S. Military Commissions to Resume This Week at Guantánamo," American Forces Press Service, April 3, 2006.
125. Moore, *The Hunt for Bin Laden*, p. 298.
126. "Khadr Was the 'Grenade Man' US Soldier Maintains," CBC News, February 6, 2008.
127. Glenn Kessler, "File the Bin Laden Phone Leak under 'Urban Myths,'" *Washington Post*, December 22, 2005.
128. Charge sheet, *United States of America versus Salim Ahmed Hamdan*.
129. Exact identity of the bomb specialists currently held in Guantánamo remains classified. In order not to disclose useful information to the enemy, we use pseudonyms when referring to them.
130. Charge sheet, *United States of America v. Muhammad al Khazan*.
131. Dr. Rachel Ehrenfeld, "Europe's Last Chance, *FrontPageMag*, February 16, 2006.
132. Ivian C. Smith, "Inside: A Top G-Man Exposes Spies, Lies, and Bureaucratic Bungling Inside the FBI," *Nelson Current*, 2004, p. 6.
133. Ben Fox, "Casio Watch Is Terror 'Evidence' at Guantánamo," Associated Press, *Seattle Post-Intelligencer*, March 10, 2006.
134. Christopher Wren, "US Jury Convicts 3 in a Conspiracy to Bomb Airlines," *New York Times*, September 6, 1996.
135. Fox, "Casio Watch Is Terror 'Evidence' at Guantánamo."
136. Author interview with Guantánamo JDG operations officer who requested anonymity, May 27, 2006.
137. Captured Iraqi documents of Saddam Hussein's internal meetings, translated by Bill Tierney, 2006.
138. *JTF GTMO Information on Detainees*, JTF GTMO, March 4, 2005.
139. Charge sheet, *United States of America v. Ghassan Abdullah al Sharbi*.

140. Charge sheet, *United States of America v. Ali Hamza Ahmad Sulayman al Bahlul.*

141. Ibid.

Chapter 6

1. Gordon Cucullu, "Gitmo Jive," *The American Enterprise Magazine*, September 2005.

2. Ibid.

3. Ibid.

4. Author interview with officer who requested anonymity, February 2007.

5. O'Reilly interview, *The O'Reilly Factor*, Segment Summaries, June 7, 2005. See chapter 7, "Compliance Rewarded: Inside the Camp IV Wire," for a detailed explanation of this categorization and how it was applied.

6. Extensive interviews with Colonel Michael Bumgarner, June 2005–April 2008.

7. Tim Golden, "The Battle for Guantánamo," *New York Times Magazine*, September 17, 2006; also author interviews with Colonel Michael Bumgarner and anonymous staff/guard force members, 2005–2006.

8. Mike Mount, "Hunger Strike at Guantánamo Grows," CNN, September 13, 2005.

9. Golden, "The Battle for Guantánamo."

10. Michael Gordon, "Guards Tighten Security to Prevent More Deaths: Human rights groups, lawyers call for investigation of 3 men's suicides in military prison," Michael Gordon, *Charlotte Observer*, June 13, 2006.

11. Golden, *The Battle for Guantánamo.*

12. "Guantánamo Inmates Commit Suicide," Al Jazeera, June 15, 2006.

13. Josh White, "Three Detainees Commit Suicide at Guantánamo," *Washington Post*, June 11, 2006.

14. Adan Zagorin and Richard Corliss, "Death in Guantánamo," *Time*, June 11, 2006.

15. Sarah Baxter, "Three Die in Guantanamo Suicide Pact," Sarah Baxter, *London Times, The Sunday Times*, June 11, 2006.

16. "Guantánamo Suicides 'an Act of Warfare,' Says Camp Commander," *The Telegraph*, June 12, 2006.

17. White, "Three Detainees Commit Suicide at Guantánamo."

18. Golden, *The Battle of Guantánamo.*

19. David Rose, "How US Hid the Suicide Secrets of Guantánamo," *The Observer*, June 18, 2006.

20. Brian Brady, "Three Dead in Guantánamo Suicide Pact," *The Scotsman*, June 11, 2006.

21. "Saudis Allege Torture in Guantánamo Deaths," *Seattle Post-Intelligencer*, June 11, 2006.

22. Mahvish Rukhsana Khan, *My Guantánamo Diary: The Detainees and the Stories They Told Me*. New York: Public Affairs, 2008.
23. "NCIS Statement on Guantánamo Suicides," *Miami Herald*, August 22, 2008.
24. "Guantánamo Bay Suicide Prisoners 'Showed No Sign of Being Depressed,'" *The Independent*, June 28, 2006.
25. Michael Gordon, "Career Crisis Hovers over Guantánamo Commander: COL Mike Bumgarner: The Hardest Job He Ever Loved," *Charlotte Observer*, June 18, 2006.

Chapter 7
1. Author interview with Lieutenant Colonel Nicolucci, June 2006.
2. Author interview with U.S. Navy guard at Camp IV.
3. Author conversation with chief petty officer in charge of Camp IV, September 2005.
4. Author interview with Lieutenant Colonel Nicolucci, June 2006.
5. Author interview with Lieutenant Colonel Baptiste, January 2007.
6. Author interview with Brigadier General Leacock, January 2007.
7. Author interview with Lieutenant Colonel Nicolucci, June 2006.

Chapter 8
1. Author interview, January 2006.
2. Author interview, February 2007.
3. In a bit of unintended irony, released Guantánamo detainee Moazzam Begg denied that the detainees use semen. "That would be un-Islamic," he said.
4. Author interviews with SFC Allen Rich, JTF GTMO, May 23, 2006.
5. "Guantánamo Better than Belgian Prisons—OSCE Expert," Reuters, March 6, 2006.
6. James Taranto, "Nice Place to Visit," *Opinion Journal, Wall Street Journal*, March 7, 2006.
7. JTF GTMO, May 23, 2006.
8. Al Pessin, "Dead Taliban Leader was Guantánamo Detainee," *Global Security*, July 25, 2007.
9. Author interview with Sergeant Philip Smell, JTF GTMO, May 23, 2006.
10. Omar Rezak, "Regret and Resentment at Guantánamo," *BBC News*, October 18, 2006.
11. Author interview with Admiral Harry Harris, December 2006.
12. Author interview with Colonel Wade Dennis, December 2006.
13. Author interview with Camp VI NCOIC who requested anonymity to protect his family, December 2006.

14. William Glaberson and Margot Williams, "Pentagon Files Offer Details on Detainee in Suicide," *New York Times*, June 1, 2007.
15. Author interview with Colonel Dennis, January 2007.

Chapter 9
1. "GWOT Detainee Policy Briefing," Department of Defense unclassified handout, July 6, 2005, p. 5.
2. Fact sheets, November 2005, Office of the Secretary of Defense.
3. Author interview with DASD Matthew Waxman, December 6, 2005.
4. Ibid.
5. Ibid.
6. Author interview with Sandy Chen, China expert, February 2006.
7. Adrienne Lauzon, "The War Against Terror and China's Treatment of the Uigher Ethnic Minority," Marquette University paper.
8. Author interview, January 2006.
9. R. Jeffrey Smith and Julie Tate, "Uighurs' Detention Conditions Condemned; Lawyers' Complaint Part of Effort to Get Expedited Review," *Washington Post*, Tuesday, January 30, 2007, p. A4.
10. Author interview with Brigadier General John Gong, Deputy Commander JTF GTMO, January 2006.
11. "Libyan Prisoner at Guantánamo Fears Torture if Repatriated," *Free Republic*, June 16, 2007.
12. Golden, *The Battle for Guantánamo*.
13. Interview with Army National Guardsman who asked to remain anonymous, March 29, 2006.
14. Kathy Gannon, "Al Qaeda Fighter Commits Suicide During Escape Attempt," Associated Press, January 9, 2002.
15. "Taliban Prisoners Escape in South Afghanistan's Kandahar," *Xinua*, People's Daily Online, October 12, 2003.
16. "Four Escape U.S. Bagram Base," Associated Press, July 11, 2005.
17. "Seven Taliban Rebels Escape from Afghanistan's Main High-Security Prison," Associated Press, January 24, 2006.
18. "Key Asia Militant 'Escaped Jail,'" *BBC News*, November 2, 2005. Like Reuters, the BBC apparently does not know a terrorist when it sees one, describing them as "militants."
19. Ibid.
20. "Seven Taliban Rebels Escape from Afghanistan's Main High-Security Prison," Associated Press, January 24, 2006.
21. Micha Halpern, "Yemen: Al-Qaeda's Escape Hatch," *Front Page Magazine*, February 7, 2006.
22. Neil Graves, "Cole Fiend Bolts," *New York Post*, February 6, 2006.

Chapter 10

1. Author conversation with head Medical Officer, JTF Guantánamo, who asked to stay anonymous, June 2005.
2. Author interview with CSM Menendez, JTF GTMO, Joint Detention Operations Group, June 2005.
3. Author interview with USN Lieutenant David Sym, January 2006.
4. The term *halal* refers to a special handling, processing, and slaughtering technique compatible with strict Koranic precepts. It is very similar to kosher food processing.
5. Author interviews June and September 2005, January and March 2006.
6. "General Says Guantánamo Vital for Gathering Terror Intelligence: Detention Center Provides Humane Treatment, Facilitates Religious Worship," Merle D. Kellerhals, Jr., Washington File Staff Writer, State Department Press Release, March 29, 2005.
7. Susan Okie, MD, "Glimpses of Guantánamo—Medical Ethics and the War on Terror," *The New England Journal of Medicine*, Vol. 355:2529-2534, No. 24, December 15, 2005.
8. Ibid.
9. Carol J. Williams, "Kicked Out of Gitmo," *Los Angeles Times,* June 18, 2006.
10. Author interview with hospital commander who wished to remain anonymous, May 2006.
11. Author interview with hospital personnel, May 2006.
12. Conversation with Lieutenant Colonel (Ret.) John Rudisill, May 2006.
13. Author interview with hospital commander, December 2006.
14. Ibid.
15. Dennis interview, January 2007.
16. Group interview with medical personnel, May 2006.

Chapter 11

1. Author interviews, January 2006.
2. Author interview with Guantánamo Base security personnel, July 2005.
3. Much of the material for this section was extracted from Gordon Cucullu, "Gitmo Jive," *American Enterprise Magazine*, September 2005.
4. Author interview with former JDG officer who requested anonymity, February 2006.
5. Donna Baptiste, series of author interviews via e-mail, 2008.
6. United Nations, Commission on Human Rights, *Report of the Chairperson of the Working Group on Arbitrary Detention*, February 15, 2006.

Chapter 12

1. David Beresford, "The Deaths That Gave New Life to an IRA Legend,"
    [London] *Guardian*, October 5, 1981; David Mckittrick, "Remembering
    Bobby Sands," *The Independent*, May 5, 2006; Melanie McFadyean,
    "The Legacy of the Hunger Strikes," [London] *Guardian*, March 4,
    2006.

2. See the "Chronology of the Conflict" summaries covering 1980 and
    1981 as provided by the Conflict Archive on the Internet (CAIN) web-
    site, http://cain.ulst.ac.uk.

3. Peter Taylor, "Provos: The IRA & Sinn Féin." London: Bloomsbury Pub-
    lishing, 1997.

4. Michael Ratner, "How We Closed the Guantanamo HIV Camp: The
    Intersection of Politics and Litigation," *Harvard Human Rights Journal*,
    Vol. 11, Spring 1998.

5. David Horowitz, "Unholy Alliance: Radical Islam and the American
    Left." Washington, DC: Regnery, 2004, pp. 179ff.

6. Reuters, "Serious Turn to Guantánamo Protest," October 7, 2005.

7. Carol Rosenberg, "Guantánamo Inmate Says Guards Forced Feeding
    Tubes Up His Nose," *San Luis Obispo Tribune*, October 25, 2005.

8. Nat Hentoff, "Is This *Your* America?," *The Village Voice*, November 15,
    2005.

9. Adam Zagorin, "At Guantánamo, Dying Is Not Permitted," *Time*, June
    30, 2006.

10. Alasdair Palmer, "This Is al Qaeda Rule 18: 'You Must Claim You Were
    Tortured," *The Telegraph*, January 30, 2005.

11. Neil A. Lewis, "Guantánamo Detainees Deliver Intelligence Gains,"
    New York Times, March 20, 2004.

12. Julia Preston, "Lawyer Is Guilty of Aiding Terror," *New York Times*, Feb-
    ruary 11, 2005.

13. Interview with Julia Tarver, "Lawyer: Guantánamo Detainees on Hun-
    ger Strike Tortured and Violently Force-Fed by Guards, Medical Staff,"
    Democracy Now, November 21, 2005.

14. Suzanne Goldenberg, "UN Report Calls for Closure of Guantánamo,"
    The Guardian, February 14, 2006.

15. Cog Coughlin, "UN Inquiry Demands Immediate Closure of Guan-
    tánamo," *The Telegraph*, February 13, 2006.

16. Manchester Manual, lesson 18.

17. Author interview with Lieutenant Colonel Jeremy Martin, PAO JTF
    GTMO, January 2006.

18. Tim Golden, "U.S. Steps up Force-Feeding at Guantánamo Bay," *New
    York Times*, February 9, 2006.

19. Author interview with Navy Captain Stephen Edmonson, July 2005.

20. Shakir Ami, ISN 239, told Bumgarner that his attorney, Clive Stafford

Smith, was "using" him and that he was in turn "using Clive." Bumgarner interview, June 2006.

21. Author interview with anonymous Navy hospital corpsman, May 2006.

22. Author interview with Navy nurse who requested anonymity, May 2006.

23. Camps I through IV are open air, without air conditioning.

24. Tim Golden, "Tough U.S. Steps in Hunger Strike at Camp in Cuba," *New York Times*, February 6, 2006.

25. Author interviews with Major General Jay Hood, Commander JTF GTMO, January 2006, and with Admiral Harry Harris, June and December 2006.

26. Author interview with Navy captain hospital commander, June 2006.

27. Author interviews with Admiral Harris and Navy captain detainee hospital commander, December 2006.

28. Department of Justice, *Lead Petitioners' Counsel in Guantánamo Habeas Cases*, FOIA release, January 2007. Full list of counsels are available in Appendix.

29. "*Hamdan v. Rumsfeld*, Supreme Court Syllabus," October 2005.

30. Anna Palmer, "Attack on Guantánamo Firms Cements Bond with Clients," *New York Lawyer Legal Times*, January 24, 2007.

31. The directory is located on the Internet at http://law.shu.edu/guantanamoteachin/page8.htm.

32. See the list on the Internet at http://law.shu.edu/guantanamoteachin/page1.htm.

33. Interview with Joshua Colangelo-Bryan, *cageprisoners*, October 19, 2005.

34. Khan, *My Guantánamo Diary*.

35. Alan Mittelstaedt, "Stephen Yagman Can Only Blame Himself," *LA City Beat*, November 29, 2007.

36. Judge Stephen Wilson, who sentenced him, said, "I was shocked by [Yagman's false testimony]. To me, it was so transparently untrue in so many areas. So I came away with the view that he compounded the lies by concocting documents that weren't true. He testified so falsely and produced such false documents. I must impose a serious sentence." "Famous, High-Living Lawyer Convicted of Tax Evasion, Fraud," Associated Press, June 26, 2007.

37. Jackie Northam, *Guantánamo Commander Prepares to Leave Post*, NPR, March 14, 2006.

38. Author interview with Commander Patrick McCarthy, June 2006.

39. Ibid.

40. USAF Brigadier General Thomas Hemingway, legal adviser to the Appointing Authority Office of the Military Commissions, is an OSD–level attorney who came back on active duty from private practice to assist with Guantánamo detainee issues.

41. "Jimmy Carter: Guantánamo Is a "Disgrace to the USA," Al Jazeera, July 30, 2005.
42. Two cases before the SCOUS were *Handan v. Rumsfeld* and *Rasul v. Bush.*
43. United States District Court for the District of Columbia, *Amended Protective Order and Procedures for Counsel Access to Detainees at the United States Naval Base in Guantánamo, Cuba*, signed by Judge Joyce Hens Green, November 8, 2004. Exhibit A: *Revised Procedures for Counsel Access to Detainees at the U.S. Naval Base in Guantánamo, Cuba*; Exhibit B: *Memorandum of Understanding Regarding Access to Classified National Security Information*; Exhibit C: *Acknowledgement.* Note: Exhibits B and C must be signed by counsel.
44. Ibid., Exhibit C.
45. Ibid., Exhibit B.
46. Andrew McCarthy, "Sentencing Day Arrives for Lynne Stewart," *National Review*, October 16, 2006. See also Michael Tremoglie, "Who Is Behind Lynne Stewart?" *FrontPageMag*, September 25, 2002.
47. United States District Court for the District of Columbia, Exhibit A.
48. Author conversation with Colonel Michael Bumgarner, January 2006.
49. Author conversation with Lieutenant Colonial Michael Nicolucci, December 16, 2006.
50. Author conversation with Admiral Harry Harris, December 17, 2006.
51. Neil A. Lewis, "Official Attacks Top Law Firms Over Detainees," *New York Times*, January 13, 2007.
52. Anna Palmer, "Attack on Guantánamo Firms Cements Bond with Clients," *Legal Times, New York Lawyer*, January 24, 2007.
53. Vesselin Mitez, "NY Lawyer Disbarred for Terror Conviction Stirs Up Furor with Campus Appearance," *New York Law Journal*, October 9, 2007.
54. Jim McElhatton, "Kuwait Helps Pay Detainees' Legal Bills," *Washington Times*, July 25, 2008. Ref: http://www.washingtontimes.com/news/2008/jul/25/kuwait-helps-pay-detainees-legal-bills/.
55. Interview with Guantánamo attorney Clive Stafford Smith and Mohammad al Shafey, *Algeria Watch*, November 19, 2005.
56. "Stop Funding America's Enemies," *Defense Tech*, May 25, 2006.

Chapter 13
1. "Torture and the Constitution," *Washington Post*, December 11, 2005.
2. Jed Babbin, "No Thumbscrews for Terrorists: An Alternative to Torture," *National Review Online*, March 17, 2003.
3. Author interview with Wayne Simmons, December 10, 2005.
4. Babbin, "No Thumbscrews for Terrorists."
5. Author interview with Navy Captain (Ret.) Chuck Nash, December 10, 2005.

6.   Suzanne Goldenberg, "UN report calls for closure of Guantánamo," [London] *Guardian*, February 14, 2006.

7.   James Yee, "For God and Country: Faith and Patriotism Under Fire," *Public Affairs*, 2005.

8.   Clive Stafford Smith, "Gitmo's Hunger Strikers," *The Nation*, October 17, 2005.

9.   Khan, *My Guantánamo Diary*, p. 255.

10. Stafford Smith, "Gitmo's Hunger Strikers."

11. Brigitte Gabriel, "What the Arab World Thinks," FamilySecurityMatters .com, November 22, 2005.

12. James Taranto, "War Inside the Wire," *Wall Street Journal*, September 16, 2006.

13. Author interview with Paul Rester, January 2006.

14. Author interview with Colonel Lora Tucker, JTF GTMO, PAO, December 2006.

15. Tim Golden and Don Van Natta, Jr., "U.S. Said to Overstate Value of Guantánamo Detainees," *New York Times*, June 21, 2004.

16. Neil Lewis, "Guantánamo Detainees Deliver Intelligence Gains," *New York Times*, March 20, 2004.

17. Author interview with Paul Rester, May 2006.

18. Charlie Savage, "Guantánamo Tip Tied to Arrests of 22 in Germany," *Boston Globe*, January 24, 2005.

19. Ansar al-Islam had extensive training facilities in Iraq prior to the 2003 war. Jonathan Schanzer, "Ansar Al-Islam: Iraq's Al-Qaeda Connection," The Washington Institute for Near East Policy, January 17, 2003.

20. Savage, "Guantánamo Tip."

21. Author interview with Steve Rodriguez, Pentagon, Washington, DC, December 2005.

22. Robert Spencer, "US-educated Saudi Is 'Proud' He Fought Against the US," *Jihad Watch*, April 28, 2006.

23. Bumgarner interview, June 2006.

24. *The 9/11 Commission Report*, pp. 521 and 225.

25. Roya Aziz and Monica Lam, "Chasing the Sleeper Cell," *Frontline*, PBS, October 16, 2003.

26. "Three Men Charged with Conspiring to Commit Terrorist Acts Overseas," FBI Cleveland Department of Justice press release, February 21, 2006.

27. Michael Powell, "No Choice But Guilty," *Washington Post*, July 29, 2003.

28. Butler interview, December 2005.

29. Compartmentalization or need-to-know specific information means that even though an agency may contribute a piece to a large intelligence

puzzle, they may never get to see the finished product because the result does not concern their mission. Hence interrogators and analysts may not learn what field operatives accomplish with the information they provided and the latter may never know the real source of the actionable intelligence that sent them on their mission.

30. Numerous author interviews with Paul Rester and staff.

Chapter 14

1. For a summary of some shocking intelligence failures, see Congressman Curt Weldon, *Countdown to Terror: The Top Secret Information That Could Prevent the Next Terrorist Attack on America . . . and How the CIA Has Ignored It.* Washington, DC: Regnery, 2005.
2. Khan, *My Guantánamo Diary,* p. 65.
3. News releases, U.S. Department of Defense, March–June 2007.
4. Tom Junod, "Innocent," *Esquire,* Vol. 146, Issue 1, July 2006.
5. Adam Lisberg, "An Exclusive Look at Lindh's Life Behind Bars," *New York Daily News,* April 2, 2006.
6. "Exclusive: Marine Sergeant Comes Forward to Report Abuse at Guantánamo Bay," ABC News, October 12, 2006.
7. Rodriguez interview, December 2005.
8. "Afghans Declare Guantánamo Bay Jail Conditions 'Humane,'" *Fox News,* July 14, 2006.
9. Nat Hentoff, "Gitmo's Innocent Victims," *Washington Times,* March 6, 2006.
10. Dana Priest, "CIA Holds Terror Suspects in Secret Prisons," *Washington Post,* November 2, 2005, p. A01.
11. Sarah E. Mendelson, "Closing Guantánamo: From Bumper Sticker to Blueprint: A report of the CSIS Human Rights and Security Initiative and the Working Group on Guantánamo and Detention Policy," Center for Strategic and International Studies, September 2008.
12. Julian E. Barnes, "Guantánamo Closure Not an Easy Prospect," *Los Angeles Times,* April 14, 2008, http://articles.latimes.com/2008/apr/14/nation/na-gitmo14.
13. Ibid.
14. Martha T. Moore, "Guantánamo Bay Puzzles Candidates," *USA Today,* June 18, 2007.
15. Tom Curry, "What Are the Alternatives to Guantánamo?" MSNBC, December 1, 2007.
16. Senator Sam Brownback, "Don't Put Detainees at Ft. Leavenworth," *Los Angeles Times,* April 18, 2008.
17. Moore, "Guantánamo Bay Puzzles Candidates."
18. Thom Shanker and David Sanger, "New to Job, Gates Argued for Closing Guantánamo," *New York Times,* March 23, 2007.

19. Curry, "What Are the Alternatives?"

20. Barnes, "Guantánamo Closure."

21. Ariane de Vogue, "'Ironic' Task: Resettling Gitmo Detainees Refugee Group Prepares to Help Uighur Detainees from Guantánamo Bay Settle in the U.S.; Justice Department Prepares Appeal of Court Ruling," *ABC News*, October 7, 2008. http://www.abcnews.go.com/TheLaw/Story?id=5977907&page=2.

22. "China: Attacks Possibly Linked to Terror Groups," *USA Today*, August 13, 2008. http://www.usatoday.com/news/world/2008-08-13-china-terror_N.htm.

23. Hope Yen, "Judge: Let Chinese Muslims from Guantanamo into US," Associated Press, October 7, 2008. http://news.yahoo.com/s/ap/20081007/ap_on_go_ca_st_pe/guantanamo_chinese_detainee;_ylt=ArurTzmsA_UncDg4mfEN4dIDW7oF.

24. Ibid.

25. Barnes, "Guantánamo Closure."

26. Jim Garamone, "Commander Discusses Perceptions of Guantánamo," American Forces Press Service, June 27, 2007.

27. Jeff Babbin, "The Gitmo Varsity."